KIDNAPPED
in Haiti

ISBN: 978-1-63813-124-3

Cover and text layout design: Kristi Yoder

Printed in the USA

Published by:

TGS International
P.O. Box 355
Berlin, Ohio 44610 USA
Phone: 330.893.4828
Fax: 330-893-4893
www.tgsinternational.com

THE AMAZING STORY OF SEVENTEEN MISSIONARIES

KIDNAPPED
in Haiti

KATRINA HOOVER LEE

ACKNOWLEDGMENTS

- I wish to express my thanks to all the people who fasted and prayed for the hostages during their time of captivity, and to all those who assisted behind the scenes in this fascinating story of God's work.

- Thank you to Alina Miller and Alma Yoder from TGS for their help with cataloguing the many prayers that came in to enable us to select a few for the book.

- Many thanks to educator Sharon Martin, private editor Rick Steele, and best-selling author Dean Merrill (co-author of *In the Presence of My Enemies*) for their excellent advice and help with my questions about this book.

- Thank you so much to the editorial team at TGS, especially lead editor Dennis Kline, for his detailed and skillful work. I don't even want to think about what this book would look like without his corrections and refinement.

- I also want to thank Bobby Miller for his tireless encouragement and direction. There were a few times I wasn't sure if I could handle the intensity of the project. With his encouragement and coordination with other departments, I was able to continue with my role.

- The book would not exist without the willing cooperation of the former hostages. My deepest thanks to Cheryl (and her husband Ray), Kay, Ryan and Melodi, Matt and Rachel, Sam, Austin, Cherilyn, Dale, Wes, Courtney, Brandyn, Kasondra, Shelden, Andre, and Laura. Each of you had a slightly different perspective. Together, these viewpoints create a story more amazing because of its diversity. Thank you especially to those of you who read the manuscript for errors and provided feedback. My deepest hope is that you will be happy with the finished product.

- Thank you to Stephanie Leinbach and her eight daughters for helping watch our daughter Anina during my times of intense concentration on this project.

- This book truly would not have made it through to completion without the support of my husband Marnell. Marnell encouraged me to take on the project and changed his plans for the sudden trip to the press conference on December 20, 2021. He picked up carry-out food, helped with laundry and cleaning, and spent extra time with Anina, all while working a full-time job himself. Whenever I was perplexed by how to handle the story line, he provided excellent feedback and advice.

- Ultimately, I feel privileged that God allowed me to help share this great story of His work in the lives of the hostages and the many people involved. I thank God for the ways He prepared me for this task by taking me through projects in the past, including ones that didn't seem valuable at the time. I am amazed at God's ability to take broken and random pieces to bring glory to Himself. May He receive all the honor and praise.

CONTENTS

FOREWORD

"*A* group of our staff in Haiti has been kidnapped!"

I know exactly where I was going with the lawnmower when my wife handed me the phone and I heard those shocking words! The beautiful, calm Saturday afternoon suddenly changed into something altogether different.

Even though CAM works in many needy places around the world, many of them on the U.S. State Department's "do not travel" list, this was the first time in our forty-year history that any of our people had been kidnapped.

How are they doing? Are they safe? How are the women and children being treated? Will they be free before dark, or by tomorrow, or surely the day after? These and many other questions swirled through our minds as we prayed and pleaded and grappled with what this meant. There were lots of questions, but few answers.

The kidnapping quickly became a top news item in the United States and abroad. Sam Stoltzfus's "We are being kidnapped" message, which he managed to send off as they were being taken, quickly found its way into the headlines of major news outlets everywhere.

Over the next two months, CAM's board and Haiti Hostage Crisis Team grappled with what to do. There were many tense moments and differences of opinion; consensus wasn't always arrived at easily, if at all. After all, *seventeen lives* were at stake, including women and children. And possibly the lives of the kidnappers themselves, depending on how things went.

It was everyone's hope and prayer that no lives would be lost and that the emotional trauma to follow would be minimal. We never doubted that God was in control and that He is all-powerful. We knew He was able to bring everyone home safely. But was that His will? The waiting was long and agonizing for everyone, especially for the families of the hostages, who were very patient and trusting. The days were full, the nights short—always with a phone nearby.

Although the ordeal was difficult, it provided many opportunities to share the Good News of Christ, as well as the Biblical teachings on nonresistance and loving one's enemies that the Anabaptist people hold so dear.

Thousands of people from around the world assured us of their prayers, and many joined us in days of fasting. They sent beautiful notes, prayers, songs, and poems to comfort the families of the hostages. A few of these are inserted throughout the story. None meant more than those from our Haitian brothers and sisters who daily face nearly insurmountable odds to simply exist in the country where God has placed them.

The kidnapping of seventeen CAM missionaries in Haiti caught the attention of the world. It will now once again capture yours as you read Katrina Hoover Lee's masterful portrayal of the story. The hostages' harrowing experiences will tug at your hearts, and their faith and trust in God will strengthen yours.

Throughout the entire hostage experience, all involved did the best they knew to help gain the hostages' release. In the end, I believe God used everyone and everything, but He did it HIS way. To GOD be the glory!

"If the Son therefore shall make you free, ye shall be free indeed" (John 8:36).

David N. Troyer
General Director, CAM

Chapter one

HIJACKED

Saturday, October 16, 2021

1 p.m., Eastern Haiti

Screee-e-e-ech!

Bristling with gun barrels, the white pickup truck careened across the road and skidded to a stop, sliding sideways in front of the white Toyota bus. The driver of the bus, a young man from Ontario named Dale, slammed on the brakes. The vehicle shook from the sudden deceleration, then quivered to a halt, narrowly avoiding a collision.

Making quick stops was nothing new for Dale. In his twenty-four years, he had done it many times. He could bring a vehicle safely to a halt whether or not he had sixteen passengers, as he did today.

But having gun barrels pointing at him was a different story. He gazed in shock as three or four men in the bed of the pickup turned their assault rifles toward the bus. Dale wondered how he should react. He had no prior experience for situations like this.

In the front passenger seat, 23-year-old Wes also sat frozen in shock. Although he had been in Haiti for over a year and had faced earlier roadblocks, this one seemed much more serious.

Other men with guns leaped from the front of the truck and ran toward the bus, screaming and yelling in Haitian Creole, a language Dale had not yet mastered. Bandanas and ski masks covered their faces. One gangster wore a close-fitting hat over his entire face, with only slits for his eyes. Some wore bulletproof vests, and all had black bracelets circling their wrists. As their fingers twitched close to the triggers, the eyes of the gangsters darted and rolled.

Dale fought the urge to panic. He knew that any rash movements or a failure to act could cause the gangsters to open fire. He raised his hands into the air, still looking down the barrels of the guns. *Be calm,* he told himself. *Make it clear that I want to cooperate. They probably just want our money and valuables, then they'll let us go.*

Before Dale had much time to think, a gangster in a mask came up to the window and stuck his head inside, only inches from Dale's face. The man was obviously in his element, riding with his comrades on a fast truck, cutting off an unsuspecting traveler, and waving a gun in the frightened driver's face. This was his normal routine, the way he earned his living and his identity.

But what the gangster saw in the bus beyond Dale's shoulder was not what he expected. His eyes widened as he saw all the people on the bus.

Beside the driver, a young boy sat between the two front seats, fear on his face. Another young man about the same age as the driver sat in the passenger seat.

Immediately behind the driver, a woman with a dark blue dress and a black veil stared back at him. Beside her sat two other young ladies with matching blue and white floral dresses and white veils. The one by the door had her eyes closed.

The gangster was speechless as he peered back through the bus. There were rows and rows of people—women wearing head coverings and men with shirts and long pants. There were also children. Even a baby.

Roadways in eastern Haiti did not usually come with scenery like this. The gangster, eyes wide, stepped away from the window.

Dale had arrived in Haiti only a few months before. Unlike some of his fellow missionaries, he had no reassuring memories of how he had survived earlier gang interactions.

Sitting directly behind Dale, Kay stared at the guns too. Kay had lived in Haiti longer than any of the others and had seen plenty of riots and roadblocks and rising smoke. She had heard gunshots and shouting. But this was scary. She had never before had guns pointed at her at such close range. She expected the gangsters to fire at any moment.

Melodi, holding baby Laura, sat in the seat behind Kay. She had a comforting memory of how her husband Ryan had been down this road with the field director Barry Grant recently. Although they had seen gang activity, everything had turned out fine. Melodi thought of her family and friends and how their eyes would widen at her description of gangsters at close range. *This is going to make a great story!* she thought. She memorized the details for her email update: *Bandanas. Ski masks. Bulletproof vests.*

In the fourth row, Matt, sitting beside his wife Rachel, stared at the gangsters with concern. He remembered how he and another staff member had been robbed a few months earlier while driving in Port-au-Prince. While stuck in traffic, a well-dressed man had pointed a gun at them as five or six other men had surrounded them, pounding on the windows and demanding their money. To their relief, everything had turned out okay.

Now, as Matt peered out the window, he could see that the situation was much worse this time. This truck full of pointed gun barrels was scary. *We're in big trouble,* he realized.

In the very last row of seats, Sam's life flashed before his eyes as he looked down the gun barrels. From multiple years in Haiti, he understood more of the shouted Creole than anyone else on the bus. Like Kay, his years in Haiti had exposed him to much political turmoil. But he had never been held up. This was something new. His heart pounded as he called out to God.

Beside Sam sat a short-term missionary named Austin who had been in Haiti less than twenty-four hours. He was totally unprepared for all the shouted words and the pointed guns. He had seen the pickup coming from behind, bristling with guns and had questioned what he should do. Should he duck? Working as a construction worker in Oregon had provided no training for something like this.

Behind him and beside him, Dale heard his fellow missionaries imploring God for protection. In front of him, gun barrels glinted in the sunlight. All around the bus, gangsters shouted and yelled.

With wild gestures, they motioned to Dale to turn the vehicle around. Dale quickly complied, turning back toward Port-au-Prince. At least they were going in the right direction again. They were heading toward home. Back toward the mission base at Titanyen.

For a moment the missionaries thought maybe the drama was over. Perhaps the gangsters had been looking for someone else and were ready to let the bus go on its way. At the very least, it was nice to have the gun barrels pointed away from them.

The feeling of relief evaporated as Dale was forced to a halt again, right in front of a blockade of vehicles swarming with armed men. A gangster waved the bus to the right, onto a narrow side road bounded by stone walls.

Kay, however, felt hopeful. It wasn't just because she had nerves of steel, as her fellow missionaries later reported. Rather, she remembered a time a few years earlier when a gangster had hijacked the vehicle of a fellow missionary. After driving around a roadblock through back alleys, the missionary was allowed to go on his way. Apparently the gangster had just needed a ride. She hoped this would be the same.

In the back seat, Sam felt his heart sink. He was pretty sure they were not going home.

Sam Stoltzfus, twenty-seven years old, was in Haiti for a second term of missionary service. Since his arrival, he had noticed an increase in the unrest in the country compared to his first term. At that time, the United Nations had been present. Though there had been plenty of political drama, including gang activity and roadway blockades, it seemed worse this time.

Gangs now controlled much of Haiti, including parts of the capital city and the roadways leading to it. These gangs often created roadblocks to stop traffic so they could steal, terrorize, or kidnap. The smaller gangs, like the ones close to Titanyen, drove motorbikes, while the larger ones had vehicles and lots of guns.

The gangs operated on a simple principle: instead of creating a product or service and offering it for sale, they disrupted or stole either people or things, then demanded money to restore them to their rightful owners. The gangs around Titanyen had even threatened the mission base, including Barry, the director.

Barry found that many of the gangsters threatened and bluffed to get attention and to manipulate others so they could get their next fix of drugs or alcohol. He remembered his own bondage to these things and knew what the gang members really needed was Jesus Christ. So every other Friday night the men from the CAM base held a preaching service for the gangs. Several times during the services, the missionaries had seen tears streaming down the face of one of the gang leaders.

Barry knew that many of the men joined the gangs for a sense of identity; they belonged nowhere else and lacked any meaningful work.

To help them, Barry and the team involved the gangs in a Work-for-Wages program, paying them a fair wage to complete honest work, such as building streets and repairing riverbanks. They had even hired some of them to help build a new wall around the mission compound, replacing the old chain link fence.

In early October, Barry and the other Haiti missionaries had received an email from the Ohio office of Christian Aid Ministries asking for updated information about a CAM-supported orphanage southeast of Port-au-Prince.

CAM did not have a huge orphanage program in Haiti. Unlike the school program, which sponsored 7,000 Haitian students, this was the only orphanage in Haiti the organization worked with. Many of the country's orphanages were run by unprincipled people, but this one had proven its integrity, and CAM Ohio wanted an update. Today, October 16, was the day they had chosen to make a trip to the orphanage.

The director and his family had decided to stay at the Titanyen base instead of going along. Barry's children had begged to go, but Barry had decided against it. With seventeen people aboard, the bus was full.

When so many people showed interest in going, Barry had wondered momentarily if it was a good idea to fill the vehicle so full. But he had pushed aside his concerns, glad everyone could go. Some of them had not been able to get out recently, and he knew it would be good for them to interact with the children at the orphanage.

Barry had no illusions about the safety of Haitian roadways. He was no stranger to roadblocks and gang activity. But overall, Barry didn't find the atmosphere in Haiti a lot different than it had been when he first arrived in 2016. They had faced occasional roadblocks ever since he was there.

"Haiti is Haiti," he would tell people. "It is known for its unrest."

Although the gangs often kidnapped people for ransom, this was not something Barry worried about for his staff. As far as he knew, the gangs did not kidnap white Americans. Perhaps it wasn't fair, but that was just the way it was. They kidnapped people all the time, sometimes Haitians, sometimes Haitian Americans, and sometimes people from other countries.

But to Barry's knowledge, they never kidnapped white Americans.

———

Dale eased the bus onto the side road between the stone walls as gangsters surrounded them, screaming and yelling.

"Guns!" they shouted in Creole. "Give us all your guns!"

"They're gonna shoot us! They're gonna shoot us!" cried Shelden, ducking as low as he could between the two front seats. Shelden was the six-year-old son of Ray and Cheryl Noecker, who were serving short-term in Haiti. Shelden had been in Haiti only two weeks and had family members in each row of the bus behind him. His sisters Courtney and Cherilyn sat in the second row, with Cherilyn doing what she always did in times of stress—closing her eyes. Shelden's mother Cheryl was farther back in the bus, along with his sister Kasondra and brother Brandyn.

"Guns! Give us your guns!"

"They're gonna shoot us!" Shelden sobbed.

The gunmen opened the side door to the bus. From the back seat, Sam, the most fluent in Creole, explained that they didn't have any guns. This seemed to calm the gangsters a bit, and they backed off.

Dale attempted to calm the terrified boy beside him. Robberies were common in Haiti, so Dale was hoping the gangsters had pulled them off the road just to rob them more thoroughly. "I think they only want our money," Dale reassured Shelden in his calm Canadian accent. "After they have our money, they will probably let us go."

When it became obvious that there were no guns, the gangsters asked for their money and phones. The missionaries decided not to respond, since the gangsters didn't seem focused on their demands. Instead, they seemed nervous, first staring at the group inside the bus, as if sizing them up, and then glancing back over their shoulders at the highway. While no gangsters were looking, Dale hid his phone and credit card between the seats. When a gangster asked for his phone, Dale showed him his wallet. The man took a ten-dollar bill.

In the middle seat, Melodi and her husband Ryan hid their phone inside the baby's diaper cover. From the seat behind them, Rachel slid a flat package to Melodi containing driver's licenses and credit cards wrapped in a small amount of cash. Melodi added this to the diaper cover as well.

Melodi had a black and red striped diaper bag that included changes of clothes for her two children, along with a writing tablet and a pen.

The clothes Melodi had brought were just in case the children had accidents. She had not brought a change of clothes for herself. Neither had anyone else. Everyone planned to be back at the mission base in Titanyen for the night.

After about ten minutes, the procession got underway again, with Dale following a box truck in front of him. When the road turned left, Dale could see the vehicles ahead. A white Toyota Prado led the way, followed by two box trucks. A Haitian ambulance and the white pickup came behind.

As they moved on, Dale's heart sank. This did not look like a quick robbery. They were heading deeper and deeper into what looked like gang territory.

In the back of the bus, Sam began sending messages to his family and youth group asking them to pray. He still didn't know if they were really being kidnapped, but the thought now crossed his mind. Since he did not think kidnappings happened to white Americans in Haiti, he hadn't been worried, but this was looking serious.

As the road widened, the box truck in front of Dale sped ahead.

Behind them, horns began honking. Dale increased his speed slightly, but with the road full of potholes, he continued to navigate cautiously around the ruts.

Suddenly the white pickup blazed past him again, blasting through the shrubs at the side of the road. Once again it lurched to a stop in front of the bus. The white Prado and the box truck ahead of them kept going.

As the bus screeched to a stop, several gangsters ran to the driver's door. Dale unbuckled his seat belt, sensing that he was about to be removed. The men yanked open the driver's door and pulled Dale out. As if in a strange nightmare, Dale saw a raised hand coming toward his face. The blow hit him squarely, so hard it knocked him off balance, but strangely, he felt no pain. Screaming and yelling, the men dragged Dale past the windows of the bus where his friends sat. They took him to the back of the ambulance and shoved him inside.

"Lord, save Dale!" the other missionaries prayed aloud.

Kay revised her level of concern. She still wasn't sure what was happening, but it was beginning to look bad.

One of the gangsters leaped into the driver's seat, slammed the door, and stepped on the gas. As the bus shot up the road, rocketing in and out of potholes and careening through washouts, the passengers bounced up and down in their seats. Heads hit the ceiling, and bodies crashed against each other.

"We were on the wildest ride of our lives," Sam remembered later.

Someone started singing and everyone joined in. This seemed to make the driver angry. "Tell them to stop singing!" he ordered Wes, sitting in the front passenger seat.

"I can't really do that," Wes replied.

The driver reached back and slammed his hand against the ceiling of the bus. "Stop singing!" he yelled. Although they didn't want to stop, the missionaries feared for the girls sitting right behind the driver. Was there any point in further angering him? For the moment, they let the song die out.

Sam cradled his phone, debating. He was part of a social media group designed for reporting roadblocks, gas shortages, or other problems in the country of Haiti. Should he share their circumstances? He composed a brief message and hit *send.* Sam watched the phone trying to send, and realized they were in an area with poor service. Sam prayed that if the Lord did not want his message to go out, He would keep it from going through.

Up in the passenger seat, beside the gangster, the thoughts churning through Wes's mind were as frightening as the course of the bus on the bumpy road. *They took Dale. They're going to keep him. They'll rob the rest of us and tell us to go empty our bank accounts to get Dale back.*

For the first time, he too began to consider the possibility that this was a kidnapping.

Had he known how long it would be before he got back to the mission base, he might have despaired. But he didn't know. He was as unprepared as everyone else. No one had considered the durability of the clothes they were wearing, nor how well they protected against mosquitoes and fire ants.

They all knew how important it was to read God's Word, but no one had packed a Bible. Why do that when they would be back that afternoon?

Matt, who took daily medication, had not bothered to bring his pills along. Nor had anyone brought extra food.

All they knew as they careened wildly down the road was that they were at the mercy of the gangsters, and their future was in God's hands.

Chapter two

THE TEAM

The Missionaries

The seventeen missionaries kidnapped on October 16, 2021, by a Haitian gang were young, energetic, and devoted to the Lord. Their average age was twenty-two. They came from their family homes in Pennsylvania, Ohio, Tennessee, Wisconsin, Ontario, Oregon, and Michigan. All came from large families, each having at least four siblings.

Although they represented eight different churches, they were all Anabaptist. They had grown up attending Christian schools where each day's agenda included Bible memorization, prayer, and Christian songs.

There were two married couples and one married woman whose husband was not along. Five of the seventeen were minors. In general, they were in good health and accustomed to activity. All except three had arrived in Haiti within the last five months.

Their passports, which they did not have with them that day, contained diverse stamps. Collectively, they had been to twenty-seven countries. Many of them were at least partially fluent in a language other than English. These included Pennsylvania German, Polish, Swahili, Belizean Creole, Spanish, Russian, and, of course, Haitian Creole.

They knew how to work with their hands. The group included an electrician, a baker, two stay-at-home moms, a mechanic, a construction worker, a waitress, a cabinet maker, and a garage door technician. One had started a Christian library, and several liked to write.

Although they liked to travel, most also loved to read and sing and spend time alone. There were more introverts than extroverts in the group, although they all had opinions and the confidence to voice them—even Laura, who was only eight months old.

Although all these missionaries were working for Christian Aid Ministries at their base in Titanyen, the seventeen had never been together in a vehicle before that day. On October 16, 2021, they entered a new relationship, as enduring as it was unexpected.

They became fellow hostages in a gangster camp.

Titanyen CAM Base

The country of Haiti occupies the western part of an island in the Caribbean Sea called Hispaniola. The eastern side of the island is the Dominican Republic, a Spanish-speaking country with a culture distinct from Haiti. On a map, Haiti appears to have an open mouth, with the capital of Port-au-Prince at the throat. The top jaw of the mouth reaches northwest toward Cuba, less than fifty miles away. The bottom jaw stretches west toward Jamaica, about one hundred miles away. Like part of a tongue, La Gonâve Island is in the open water between the northern and southern parts, less than twenty miles across the bay from Port-au-Prince.

The Christian Aid Ministries base at Titanyen, established in the mid-1990s, sits on the edge of Port-au-Prince Bay, just north of the capital. From the top of the tallest building in the CAM compound, missionaries can watch the sun setting over the water.

From the air, the Christian Aid Ministries compound has the shape of a dented tin can. A gate at the northern end of this dented rectangle allows visitors into the compound. Coming through the gate, visitors pass a large warehouse on the right and a mechanic shop on the left. Single-family homes and a large, three-story dorm house rise among the trees on either side. At the southern end of the compound, a cluster of buildings provide the setting for the pastor-training program. There is a chapel, dorms, classrooms, and a kitchen. A nearby house is for visiting pastors and their families who teach classes for the Haitian pastors.

Off to the side, a basketball court provides a safe place for the children to play. On Wednesday evenings, the staff often meets at the court for a family game of Knock Out. Everyone plays, from grandpa to preschooler. After the game, people sit and talk, sometimes having deep conversations as light fades into night.

Barry & Julia

In August 2020, Barry Grant arrived at the CAM base in Titanyen with his wife Julia and five small children. Since February 2016, the Grants had lived in Haiti except for furloughs and visits home. Barry had preached all over the country, encountering demon possession, gang violence, and roadblocks. He had also planted a church north of Titanyen.

Neither Barry nor Julia grew up in an Anabaptist home. In high school, Barry made a mark for himself as a rebel. After graduating, he joined the Marine Corps in an effort to become a better person and improve his unhandy reputation. Although he was with the Marines for two and a half years, he continued to struggle with addictions and rebellion. Finally dismissed from the Marine Corps, Barry cycled in and out of jail. The local police knew him well. While incarcerated, he always intended to reform, but once free, he returned to the drug and alcohol addictions that drove him.

Barry's lawyers usually extricated him from his difficulties. Finally, however, he crossed a line. On his eighth count of driving while intoxicated, Barry's lawyer informed him that there was nothing more he could do. Barry would likely face multiple years of prison time, along with an indefinite suspension of his license.

As Barry sat on the floor of his jail cell, contemplating his gloomy future, he heard his cellmate complain about his circumstances. "This isn't me," the rough-looking young man said over and over. "I don't belong here."

Unlike Barry, the cellmate looked like a gangster. Frustrated, Barry finally let him have it. "You do belong here," he told the man. "But I don't."

At that moment, God opened Barry's eyes, and for the first time he saw things as they really were. He saw all the damage he had done to himself and others. He saw all the people he had hurt. His sins flashed before his consciousness like a horrible news story.

Right there on the floor of his cell, Barry told God he wanted to be different. He hated who he was, but he didn't know the solution. He knew going to church wouldn't make a difference; he had tried that.

"God," Barry cried, not knowing what to ask, "you need to change my heart!" He promised God that if this happened—if his heart truly changed—he would serve Him with everything he had.

Barry continued to struggle over the next weeks, but he was a changed man. He accepted the prospect of years in prison and the loss of his license as the reaping he must endure for his wrongdoing.

On the day of his sentencing, he waited with his lawyer for the judge to show up. Finally someone else arrived in blue jeans and took the judge's seat. The man explained that the judge was not able to be present, so court was being canceled for the day. "However," he said, "we'll hear one case—the first one on the docket." He called Barry's lawyer to the front, along with the prosecuting lawyer.

Perhaps the prosecuting lawyer was thinking of what he would do with his unexpected day off. For whatever reason, the sentence was decided within minutes. There would be no prison time, only probation, and Barry's license would be reinstated immediately.

Thus began Barry's second chance with God. He never again struggled with drug addiction or alcoholism.

Barry soon found a church and started meeting other members for Bible study. One of the people in the Bible study group was a girl named Julia, the daughter of a Baptist pastor. Barry and Julia both felt that God was calling them together. After a three-month relationship, they were married.

As they studied the Bible with friends, Barry and Julia debated joining an Anabaptist church. They weren't sure about the women's head veiling, although they could see that it made sense based on the 1 Corinthians 11 passage. It just seemed so strange. However, after fasting, they decided it was the right thing to do. This decision made it much easier for them to join an Anabaptist church, a step they soon took.

Within a few years, Barry was preaching the Gospel in Haiti. After the church he had planted began thriving, Barry and Julia weren't sure if they were needed there anymore. Should they go somewhere else? At this point, a death in the family brought them back to Ohio. It was a time of much soul-searching. What did God have for them?

At a meeting with church brothers, Barry shared a thought that had occurred to him. "What if I would go back to Haiti but would work with CAM? I recently filled out an application."

The Christian Aid Ministries base at Titanyen was not far from the area where they had been before. This would enable him to keep in touch with the brothers and sisters in Christ at his former church.

His church brothers at the meeting agreed that this might be a good idea.

On the way home from the meeting, Barry called one of the men he had talked to. He explained that CAM had never asked him to work with them. In fact, they focused more on humanitarian aid than on preaching, Barry's passion. It was just an idea.

"Trust the Lord. He will show you what to do," the man replied.

The next morning, Barry received a phone call. It was Phil Mast from Christian Aid Ministries. He was calling in response to Barry's application. "We need a director at our base in Titanyen," Phil began. "You have experience in working with the Haitian people, so I think you would be the man for the job. Would you consider this?"

Phil & Grace

Phil and Grace Mast gained their missionary experience not in Haiti but in Liberia. When they returned to their home in Ohio after five years in the West African country, Phil served on the CAM board of directors for six years. In September 2019, he joined CAM full-time as the country supervisor of the mission in Haiti.

Earlier that same year, Phil had been devastated to learn that a staff member had been molesting young Haitian boys. Even after the child molester went to prison, navigating through the nightmare was difficult. Some people thought the ministry should shut down. The local Haitian community, however, disagreed. They were terrified that their CAM friends would leave.

Painful meetings stretched on for months and were ongoing when Phil assumed leadership of the Haiti mission in September 2019.

Soon after becoming country supervisor, Phil took a trip to Haiti. On this first trip, he received a phone call from his wife Grace back in Ohio. Their thirteen-year-old son had passed away in his sleep.

Despite this deep grief, Phil continued his work. He often made trips to Haiti, sometimes with family members. He interviewed potential staff and acted as a liaison between the missionaries and the administration back in Ohio.

Shortly after calling Barry Grant about the director position in Titanyen, Phil received an application from a mechanic named Wes from Tennessee.

Wes

Westley Yoder grew up on a Tennessee plateau. He and his twin brother Weston roamed the area around their home with their BB guns, even teaching their younger sisters to shoot.

Westley also developed a love for reading, especially adventure stories such as prisoners escaping from captivity. When Westley grew older, he enjoyed deer hunting.

If Wes had followed in his father's footsteps, he would have become an electrician. But while Wes found outlets and electric boxes somewhat interesting, he preferred things that could roar and smoke. So he became a small-engine mechanic.

After a short-term hurricane clean-up project with Christian Aid Ministries in the Bahamas, Westley signed up for long-term service. He offered to go wherever the mission needed him. He soon got a call from Phil Mast, wondering if he would be interested in serving as a mechanic on the CAM compound just northwest of Port-au-Prince, Haiti.

Wes arrived in Haiti's capital in September 2020. With the eye of a woodsman, he noticed with sadness the landscape of cement and the lack of trees. He was relieved to find some trees at the CAM compound.

The previous mechanic stayed for another week to show Westley the diesel trucks, generators, and cisterns he would manage. Westley had no experience in working with diesel vehicles, but he discovered that the vehicles on the Titanyen base contained very basic engines. The International box trucks occasionally gave him some grief, but overall the job was manageable.

Wes was pleased to discover that Haiti produced one of his favorite foods—peanut butter. The only trouble with the local version was that it was just smashed peanuts and nothing else. It was good but so thick it stuck to the roof of your mouth. With a little trouble-shooting, Wes found a solution. He plopped a healthy scoop of Haitian peanut butter into a bowl, dug a well in the center, filled it with pancake syrup, and stirred. Not only was it delicious, but it went down with perfect ease.

Kay

Kay Yoder was new to the Titanyen base when she arrived in December 2020, but she was not new to the Barry Grant family. Kay had first come to Haiti to help Julia Grant with her small children.

Now, at the CAM base, Kay worked with the cooks in the kitchen, planning menus for the Haitian employees and other staff from the United States and Canada. Kay had grown up in Ohio, where Mennonite and Amish cooking and cookbooks abounded. She had worked at a bakery, making granola. But by now she had come to thoroughly enjoy Haitian food.

Every week one of the Haitian employees at the Titanyen base drove Kay and the head cook to the local market, where people assembled under tarp roofs to hawk their produce. As vendors yelled out their bargains, with customers and chickens and dogs milling around them, Kay and the cook picked out the food they needed for the week. To transport their purchases back to the vehicle, they hired one or more of the wheelbarrow men standing by in the market. They heaped the wheelbarrows full with rice, plantains, bananas, and Haitian vegetables.

Kay had lived in Haiti through a recent presidential election that turned the country on its head. When many Americans returned home, Kay and the Grants stayed, sometimes listening to gunshots and watching rising smoke as people demonstrated about the latest political development. As gangs moved closer to their village, they heard threats from people who said they would burn down the whole country. Sometimes Kay thought she would never see her family again. Still, she didn't normally find herself living in fear.

To Kay, faith in God seemed bigger in Haiti than it had in America. In Ohio, where resources abounded, people didn't seem to need God as much. Kay's faith in God was simple in this riotous land. She needed Him each day, and she trusted Him with her future.

Sam

Sam Stoltzfus was not new to Haiti. After serving there for two and a half years, he had returned to his home in Lancaster, Pennsylvania. For the next two years, Sam enjoyed being back with his family and driving a truck for a ministry called Blessings of Hope.

To help him remember his time in Haiti, he had mounted several pieces of Haitian decor on his bedroom wall. Haitian craftsmen created word art in a place called Tin Village, where tourists stopped to hear the "ting-ting-ting" as their implements beat out the words. Sam had purchased three pieces. One piece of tin decor simply said "Haiti." He mounted this over a shelf of other Haitian souvenirs and flags. Another piece of tin had the words "Peace is not the absence of trouble, but the presence of Christ." The third said *Avek Jezi tout bagay byen,* which is translated "With Jesus everything is well."

Sam thanked God for his time in Haiti and thought perhaps he would someday return to the country he had come to love. Growing up, Sam had been taught to pray for God's direction, so he believed God would lead him if the time were ever right to go back.

One day as Sam drove his truck up the grades and down into the valleys of the Pocono Mountains in northeastern Pennsylvania, he replayed the rises and falls of his life in recent weeks. He had felt that God was leading him in one direction, only to discover this was not the case. Sam knew that God did not always lay out His plans in black and white, but today he prayed desperately for direction.

"What is your will for my life?" he cried out to God. "What is your plan?"

Besides working for Blessings of Hope, Sam was involved in another ministry. He and his family provided a Christian library for the community in Lancaster. Starting with 1,600 titles, Sam had begun the project before he went to Haiti the first time. Now there were around 4,000 volumes in the library. Despite being involved in these ministries, Sam wondered if God was calling him to something else.

Then, as his hands gripped the steering wheel, Sam felt God speaking to him with perfect clarity. "Sam, there's something I want you to do. There's somewhere I want you to go."

Shock and relief diffused through Sam, replacing discouragement with overflowing hope. God was with him! God had heard. And God did have a plan. Tears rose to his eyes.

"Lord, I'm willing to go. I'll go wherever you want me to go. I'm ready." Peace flooded his soul, even though God had not given him specific instructions.

More than five years earlier Sam had written in his journal, "If I ever die as a missionary of the Gospel of Christ, or as a martyr for Christ's sake, I would count that the ultimate way to die." His opinion had not changed. He didn't know what God was asking him to do, but he was serious about being willing to go.

Three hours later Sam found a message on his phone from Phil Mast of Christian Aid Ministries in Ohio. "Sam, would you consider going back to Haiti?"

That evening when Sam walked into his parents' home, he had a surprise announcement: "Mom, I'm going back to Haiti!"

When Sam arrived back at Titanyen in February 2021, he was already fluent in Haitian Creole. He joined Wes in the third-floor single men's dorm. The first time he saw Wes stirring peanut butter and pancake syrup in a bowl, he questioned the sanity of his new friend. Was this how they did things in Tennessee? Then he tried it for himself and decided Wes wasn't so crazy after all.

Matt & Rachel

Matt Miller first met his wife Rachel at a wedding where Rachel's sister married one of Matt's good friends. At the time, Rachel lived in Lancaster, Pennsylvania, and Matt was volunteering as a nurse's assistant at Mountain View Nursing Home in Virginia. When he returned home to Ohio from the nursing home, Matt worked in the Berlin office of Christian Aid Ministries in the PR department.

In May of 2019, Matt and Rachel celebrated their own wedding, decorated in shades of blue. They served chipotle to the guests, along with three kinds of whoopie pies for dessert.

Matt and Rachel decided to live close to their church, which took them too far from CAM to justify a daily commute. Matt took a job at a cabinet shop, designing kitchens. Rachel worked at a cafe and bakery, a ministry of their church, serving breakfast platters, running the cash register, and baking pastries.

Although Matt had been around the world and had spent many hours helping others, he battled his own physical challenges. Born with a rare genetic condition, Matt's immune system worked excessively. This kept him from getting sick easily, but he endured other health problems.

Sometimes he experienced extreme exhaustion, and inflammation often attacked his joints. This caused severe pain, especially in his hands.

"I don't like to be called handicapped because I don't really believe that's what I am," Matt said. "But I am hindered in doing some things."

With his doctor's direction, Matt discovered that he did better when he took immunosuppressants. These medications normally make people prone to sickness, but because Matt's immune system was so active, he still did not get sick easily. Matt took these medications by mouth every day and gave himself a shot every two weeks.

Matt and Rachel arrived in Port-au-Prince in May 2021. Both had previously traveled to other countries and were not expecting much culture shock. However, Matt found himself astounded at the craziness of the traffic in Haiti. Rachel was shocked in another way. She found it hard to believe that many people, even women, took care of their bodily functions at the side of the road instead of finding a restroom.

Matt and Rachel settled into the first floor of the only three-story building at the CAM base. Sam and Westley lived on the top floor of this building, and the middle floor housed guests. Matt had been able to bring his medication along to Haiti, so there was no reason to be concerned about his health condition. A few weeks later, another young couple joined them.

Ryan & Melodi, Andre, and Laura

Melodi grew up in the mountain-ringed Grande Ronde Valley in eastern Oregon, a land of spectacular clouds, majestic evergreens, and rustic wooden fences. When overnight guests visited, Melodi's family often took them to the Oregon Trail Interpretative Center, a museum on the Oregon Trail with its own covered wagon and wax figurines of pioneers. Melodi's mother inspired her to love writing.

However, Melodi's family did not stay home if God called them to serve. From the time she was five until she was nine, Melodi's family lived in Washington, where her father taught at a Christian school for Russian immigrants. Melodi attended this school too. Then, in her teenage years, her family moved to Belize as missionaries. In addition to these cross-cultural experiences, Melodi's family adopted two new members—Danny, a four-year-old from Russia, and Conrad, fourteen months old, from Belize.

Shortly after returning from Belize, Melodi, at age seventeen, went with her grandparents to help cook for CAM volunteer workers at a hurricane rebuilding project in New Orleans. While there, Melodi met a tall young man from Wisconsin named Ryan Korver, just a year older than she was. No romantic conversations occurred, but Melodi and Ryan did not forget each other. Both returned home and spent time teaching in Christian schools during the next few years.

Around Christmas 2015, Ryan sent Melodi a letter asking if she would like to pursue a relationship with him. In June 2017 they were married. With Melodi's parents now serving as missionaries in Romania, the newly married couple lived in their house for one year. They then moved to Ryan's homeland of Wisconsin and bought a forty-acre hobby farm to fix up while Ryan worked with his dad installing garage doors. They cleaned and remodeled the old farmhouse and raised beef cattle in the grassy fields surrounding it.

On a beautiful day in September 2018, when yellow leaves stood out against a bright blue sky, Andre joined the Korver family.

When Andre was eighteen months old, Ryan and Melodi went to Texas to help with another service project through CAM. While they were there, Phil Mast visited. After returning home from Texas, Ryan and Melodi received a call from Phil, asking if they would consider applying for a position in Haiti to help with the school program.

By the time they completed the application and the resulting interview, Melodi was pregnant with a second child. On the day of little Laura's birth, the thermometer showed a reading of −25°F.

Andre had been a good baby, but Laura was almost perfect. She slept and ate and smiled. She sat in her baby seat and watched the world around her, as content as a porcelain doll. On two occasions, people asked Melodi if the baby was all right. When Laura began crawling, however, she began to bulldoze around her world with energy and determination.

On June 1, 2021, the Korver family arrived in Haiti. Reminiscent of Melodi's homeland, the name Haiti meant "the land of high mountains." But the similarities ended there.

Ryan and Melodi had been exposed to other cultures and assumed those experiences had prepared them for Haiti. Still, the poverty and chaos of the country shocked them.

They had been in the country only about five weeks when the president of Haiti was assassinated.

July 7, 2021, Titanyen Base

Early on the morning of Wednesday, July 7, Titanyen staff received the news that Haiti's president had been assassinated at his home. His body was found with broken bones, a gouged eye, and twelve bullet holes. His wife received three bullet wounds but survived. The president had been in office for about four and a half years, with his term nearly up.

Because riots were expected, the airport and embassies were closed, and the Haitian government declared a fifteen-day period of mourning.

At the base, director Barry Grant asked all the Haitian staff to stay home from work for their own safety. Haiti had been violent ever since Barry had arrived some years before, and he himself had been threatened and robbed. Described by one of his staff as someone who is not afraid of anything, Barry still exercised caution.

The next day armed men showed up at the Titanyen base, demanding money from the white missionaries. "If you don't pay us $150,000 by morning," the gang leader threatened, "we will close down the compound." This same gangster had earlier worked for Barry through the Work-for-Wages program.

"But we don't have $150,000 to give to you," Barry replied.

"If I don't have the money by morning, I'll kill everyone on this base!" the gang leader warned. "I'll burn everything to the ground!" In a huff, he put a chain around the gate and left.

By the next morning, the chain had disappeared from the gate. The leader soon called Barry and apologized for his threats. He asked Barry to come visit him.

Barry took Westley, Matt, and Ryan with him. Under a thorn tree, they preached to the gang leader and his cousin who sat beside him.

"This life of killing is not worth living!" Barry told them. "We see pictures of people full of bullet holes lying in the street every day. That is what is going to happen to you! You are going to die and go to hell unless you change."

"I know. I know," the gang leader said, looking at the ground.

This was a new response. Earlier this same man had said that if he ever met Jesus Christ, he would cut off his head. Today, however, he was subdued.

Barry took his chance. "Would you give permission for me to come and hold a Bible study on Friday?"

"Yeah, that'd be great," the gangster agreed. "There would be a lot of people who would come."

"Do you have a place where we could meet?"

"I'll find one."

Barry went back to the base and called Phil Mast. With excitement, he told Phil that the gang leader who had threatened their lives had agreed to host a Bible study.

He was still talking on the phone when Ryan came charging into the room, his face white.

"What's going on?" Barry asked.

"Those two men we were talking to have just been shot! They are lying in the street—dead!"

A flurry of discussion occurred among the staff. Should they go back to the scene? Murder scenes often deteriorated rapidly into violent riots. However, they decided it would be better to go back immediately rather than wait for the violence to start.

Wes and Matt stayed at the base while Barry and Ryan and another worker drove back to the site. Wes, like the deer hunter he was, grabbed a pair of binoculars and went to the roof of the dorm to watch the scene. From there he could see Ryan's blue shirt, allowing him to reassure Melodi that her husband was all right. He saw Barry leap up on a wall to speak to the people. To everyone's relief, the police soon arrived and the crowd remained quiet.

A few weeks later Barry got another phone call from a gang. These too threatened to attack the compound that night. Barry and Julia were hosting the other staff members for a meal, including a new worker who had just arrived the day before.

Dale

The last permanent staff member to arrive in 2021 hailed from Canada. Dale Wideman grew up on a hobby farm in southern Ontario. Along with caring for the family's chickens and goats and his mother's large garden, Dale cultivated a love for books and adventure. As he read missionary stories about David Livingstone and others, Dale imagined what it would be like to be a missionary someday. In their free time, Dale and his siblings climbed trees, hunted raccoons, and played in the river on their thirty-acre farm. They built a log cabin in the woods and spent nights camping in it. Dale loved nature, especially a quiet walk alone in the outdoors.

Dale took a job as an electrician, holding it for six years. After he gave his life to the Lord at age eighteen, he felt a deep desire to share the Gospel. When a friend spoke of going to Liberia to serve as a medicine program director for Christian Aid Ministries, Dale listened and offered encouragement. When Dale's friend was unable to take the post, Dale reached out to see if CAM still needed someone there. "No," they replied, "the Liberia position is no longer open. But would you consider going to Haiti as director of the warehouse and the medicine program there?"

Dale considered this. He knew of many others who had served in Haiti, including some of his siblings, so it didn't seem as adventuresome as a country in Africa. Still, Dale wanted to serve God, and his heart wasn't set on any particular place.

On July 24, 2021, he landed on the runway in Port-au-Prince. He felt peaceful about submitting to God's call to this country. He felt he had made the right decision.

But on one point he was wrong: his time in Haiti would not lack adventure!

On the second night after his arrival, Dale was invited to Barry and Julia Grant's house for supper with the rest of the team. During the meal, Barry received a threatening phone call. "We will be coming by later tonight to raid the compound," the caller warned. Although nothing came of the threat, Dale considered himself duly welcomed and warned.

The high regard for peanut butter in the third-floor dorm was a more pleasant welcome. Dale loved peanut butter too. Sometimes he had a piece of toast in the morning with peanut butter and honey. And sometimes he ate it with applesauce. Or, at the end of the day, he would enjoy a big spoonful before going to bed. Wes showed him his peanut butter/pancake syrup recipe, and Dale tried it with high appreciation.

Dale soon realized that travel in Haiti meant passing through gang-controlled areas. If the traffic was moving, a driver could assume the street was safe. If no one was around, the best thing to do was to turn around and go back the other way. Several times as they drove Haiti's roads, Dale saw gangsters with guns close by.

As Dale adjusted to life in Titanyen, he really appreciated his fellow workers at the base. He started to enjoy his work in the warehouse. Barry's enthusiasm for spreading the Gospel infected him and the others on the team. They grew closer together as they struggled with and preached to the gangs. A shared vision for their little corner of Haiti excited them all.

Mid-August 2021, Titanyen Base

Barry was at the kitchen sink on a Saturday morning when the whole house started to shake. He turned around and saw both recliners rocking.

"Earthquake!" he yelled. He had never been in one before, but there weren't many other options to explain this phenomenon. As the children came running, the shaking stopped. It was over.

Barry reported to Christian Aid Ministries that he didn't think the earthquake had caused much damage. Later he found out that the area around the epicenter in southern Haiti had been devastated.

CAM began to look for construction workers to help rebuild in the worst areas.

Early October 2021, Titanyen Base

Every Thursday afternoon at 4:00, the men on the base gathered for a meeting. Often one of the ladies sent iced coffee or popcorn to the meeting, and the men had an enjoyable time as they talked, prayed, snacked, and reviewed the programs they led. They took turns sharing. Sam and Ryan talked about the school programs, Dale reported on the warehouse and the medicine program, Matt discussed any concerns in the accounting department, and Wes gave updates from the mechanic shop. Often the meeting lasted for three or four hours.

Barry felt confidence in each of his staff. One had even told him, "Barry, I'm ready to die." *This,* Barry thought, *is the true missionary spirit.*

At a meeting in early October, Barry asked for volunteers to take charge of the upcoming orphanage visit. When no one offered to do it, he assigned it to Dale. Since he was the newest member of the team, he didn't have as many responsibilities as some of the others.

"I'll let you take it from here," Barry told Dale.

Dale asked Sam to help with making phone calls, since Sam was more fluent in Creole.

Sam called the orphanage director and made plans to visit the orphanage on Thursday, October 14.

"We'll keep the children home from school that day," the director told him.

"Oh, we didn't think of that!" Sam replied. "Why don't we come on a Saturday? That way the children won't have to miss school."

They decided on Saturday, October 16.

Once the date was finalized, Dale sent out a message to everyone on the base to see who was interested in going along.

Dale would go, of course, along with Sam and Wes. Matt and Rachel wanted to go, as did Kay. Ryan and Melodi would go, with their children Andre and Laura. And Barry's children wanted to go.

Also eager to go was the mother and five children of a family who had recently come for a short-term stay.

The Noecker Family: Ray & Cheryl, Cherilyn, Courtney, Brandyn, Kasondra, and Shelden

Ray and Cheryl Noecker and their family lived on a bluff about ten miles from Lake Michigan. One day Phil Mast called to ask if Ray could assist Barry for two months with the pastor-training program in Haiti. "And if you like it there," Phil told them, "I'd like you to consider staying there long-term."

The Noecker family loved mission work. Twice they had lived in Kenya for a total of seven years. Ray had also taught in their local Christian school in Michigan.

Ray enjoyed working with his hands and had experience working in construction. He had also worked in a cabinet shop, where he lost a finger to the spinning blade of a table saw.

Cheryl loved babies, especially her own. She canned hundreds of quarts of fruits and vegetables for her seven daughters and two sons. When she ran out of space in the pantry, Ray constructed heavy wooden shelves in a family room off the kitchen. There, rows of jars containing peaches, green beans, and applesauce created a pleasing scene.

Their oldest daughter, Cherilyn, twenty-seven, especially loved mission work. Besides spending her childhood in Kenya, she had been to Thailand and Papua New Guinea. "When I was younger, I always said I would like to marry a Kenyan and live in a mud hut," she said. She loved the Kenyan lifestyle, where most of life happened outdoors, and people had time for relationships.

As the Noeckers discussed Haiti, they told CAM they would like to take their four youngest children along. Courtney (18), Brandyn (15), and Kasondra (13) were too young to remember much about living in Kenya. Shelden (6) had been born after the family moved back to Michigan.

The older children, all girls, discussed the trip. All of them wanted to go, but some felt they should stay at home to watch the house, finish the seasonal canning, and work at their jobs. Cherilyn, however, decided to go along.

At a camping trip with relatives in September, cousins plied the Noeckers with questions about their upcoming trip to Haiti. Courtney, the only child who had been born in Kenya, was asked several times what she planned to take along.

"Just a tote of candy and a tote of books," she finally replied.

When the others asked what she would wear, she seemed unconcerned. "I'll just take what I'm wearing!" she told them. When the others laughed, she insisted that one set of clothes would be enough.

Other people asked Cheryl about their trip to Haiti. "Is it safe to go there?" they asked with concern.

"If God is leading us there, He will take care of us," Cheryl replied.

Now, after having been in Haiti for two weeks, Ray didn't hesitate when asked about the orphanage trip. "I'm sure my girls would love to go along," he replied. "And probably my wife too. But I had better stay home to study." Ray had a week of pastor training ahead of him, and he wanted to be prepared. Also, the base was planning for Communion the next day, and Ray was scheduled to preach the sermon. In the end, Cheryl and all five of the children planned to go.

Austin

Austin Smucker was eating supper with his family in early September 2021 when his father mentioned an email he had received that day. Christian Aid Ministries was looking for two young men to go to Haiti to help with construction work following the latest disaster. A 7.2 magnitude earthquake had struck the southern part of the country. The quake had caused large-scale destruction of buildings, along with thousands of deaths and injuries.

Austin had spent ten of his growing-up years, from age seven to seventeen, living in Poland with his family as missionaries. Now, in Oregon, he worked on a construction crew, making him well qualified to assist with rebuilding efforts. He had been seeking God's direction for his life recently and wondered if God had been preparing him for this opportunity.

Austin's passport, however, had expired. He had sent in the renewal forms earlier in August, but the passport office predicted a wait time of twelve to fifteen weeks. This meant it could be November before Austin received his passport. The CAM team was asking for construction workers before that. Perhaps this was not the right time.

Austin contacted CAM and explained his situation. They suggested he keep them updated about his passport situation. Austin continued working with his construction crew. "God," he prayed, "I'd like to go to Haiti, but I can't if I don't have my passport. If you want me to go, make my passport come." There was nothing to do but wait and see what happened.

Thirty-one days after Austin sent off his paperwork, a shiny new passport arrived in the mail. It had taken about four and a half weeks. With this confirmation, Austin made plans to fly on October 15. The first stamp in his new passport would be the red oval from the airport in Port-au-Prince, Haiti.

Austin arrived in Haiti on October 15. He planned to be at the CAM base for a few days before going on south to help with earthquake rebuilding. A visit to a Haitian orphanage sounded like a great use of the extra time.

Chapter three

A BEAUTIFUL SUNNY DAY

8:30 a.m., Titanyen Base

On the morning of October 16, Dale headed early to the mechanic shop and filled the seventeen-passenger bus with fuel. Even though they called it a bus, the vehicle was really a Toyota van. The driver sat above the front axle, and the engine was hidden under the body.

By 8:30, the rest of the group arrived, walking over from the three-story house and various other houses scattered among the trees and lawns. It was a beautiful morning. As always, it was warm. Ray Noecker was there too, with his wife, three daughters, and two sons. Ray was glad his wife and children had the opportunity to go to the orphanage, even though he had to stay home and study. He prayed with the group before they climbed into the bus.

If things went well, they would arrive at the orphanage around 10 a.m. Even though it was only about twenty miles away, the clogged and clunky Haitian roads prevented efficient travel.

After the bus exited the gate of the CAM base with his wife and five children inside, Ray took a walk outside the compound to expand his view of the community. So far he hadn't seen much more than the base.

As he stood below the chapel, looking out over the ocean, he asked God a question: "God, what do you want us to do? Please show Cheryl and me what we are to do. Why did you bring us here to Haiti?"

After the walk, he began preparing his sermon for the Communion service the next day. Although everyone living on the base came from an Anabaptist background, there were six different church affiliations represented. All likely practiced Communion in slightly different ways, but Ray hoped to share something that would be meaningful to each one.

Barry also had his day planned. One thing on his agenda was a meeting with Ray after lunch. They had arranged to meet on the porch of the warehouse. He wanted to find out what Ray's plans were about coming back to Haiti to stay long-term.

10 a.m.–1 p.m., At the Orphanage

The trip to the orphanage was without incident except for the remnants of a roadblock about ten minutes before the group arrived at their destination. Carefully Dale navigated the bus past some smoldering tires. Obviously there had been gang activity earlier, but now the police were there and had pushed the tires off the road to clear the way for travelers.

The missionaries had a wonderful time at the orphanage. It was evident the staff at the orphanage truly cared for the children and prioritized cleanliness, education, and health.

Some of the visitors from Titanyen played a rousing game of soccer with the children in the courtyard, surrounded by trees and a block wall. Six-year-old Shelden played on the swings. Several times he felt small, inquisitive hands finger his straight hair, but he did not mind the attention.

Matt's hair also received a diligent assessment from the children, but for a different reason. They were amazed that white people could have curly hair. With their little fingers, they tried to twist his hair into small braids.

Dale, who was leading the visit, found himself in a different activity. Melodi noticed him sitting with a row of little girls playing church with their doll babies. On closer inspection, she noted that one of the larger doll babies was her daughter Laura, eight months old to the day. She snapped a photo on her phone.

Cheryl's oldest daughter, Cherilyn, who had come to Haiti because of her love for missions, wandered into the kitchen to help. The cooks put her to work cutting up potatoes for French fries and smashing fried plantains to prepare them for a second sizzle in the oil. The cooks tossed pieces of chicken, bananas, and plantains into a giant pot of stew.

The only disappointment about the orphanage was that there was only one baby. In Kenya, the Noecker family had loved to visit a baby orphanage that had enough babies for all seven sisters and their mother to each hold one. In fact, the Noecker family dreamed of starting a baby orphanage someday.

Here at the Haitian orphanage, however, there was only one baby, a little boy. Cheryl did her best to claim him, although she had to compete with her daughters. Cheryl had lost her second to last baby to a miscarriage at twenty-three weeks. They had named this daughter Caroline Maria.

The director of the orphanage saw Cheryl with the baby. "If you want him, he's yours!" he said. "You can take him along home."

"He was such a cutie," Cherilyn remembered weeks later. "He was so much fun."

The only drawback about the day was the heat. It was a typical Haitian day—hot. As the temperature continued to rise, sweat drenched the shirts of the soccer players.

When it was time to leave, Dale realized that the orphanage staff was preparing lunch for them. The women were bringing plates of French fries and chicken and setting them on a table, along with carbonated drinks.

"When women make food, you have to stay and eat it," the administrator of the orphanage chided. "You can't be running off."

Thus encouraged, the group gathered around the table and picked up pieces of food with their fingers. It was time for the orphanage children to eat lunch too, but they ate the stew from the large pot, not the special food offered to the guests.

"I felt a little bad about that," Ryan remembered later. "I'm sure they would have enjoyed what we had."

By 1 p.m., the group said goodbye and headed out. They agreed with the orphanage director that they would come more often after this, maybe every few months.

While at the orphanage, Sam had suggested they visit Tin Village, where he had purchased the wall art for his bedroom back in Pennsylvania. Unlike Sam, most of the current missionaries had never visited Tin Village. Since this tourist attraction was practically on the way home, they decided to stop.

Early Afternoon, Titanyen Base

As the bus left the orphanage, Barry and Ray were chatting on the warehouse porch back at the CAM base.

Barry explained the value of long-term staff and his hope that Ray and Cheryl and their family would take up the challenge to join them. The men discussed the vision for the Titanyen mission base.

Barry described the struggles with the gangs and the spiritual warfare. As the minutes ticked by, he recounted the difficulties of reorganizing and letting some of the employees go.

"We've been through a lot," Barry said. "You've come at a great time."

1 p.m., Leaving the Orphanage

In the bus, Dale was once again at the wheel. After turning right onto Highway 8, they headed toward Tin Village and home.

Behind Dale, Kay broke out some snacks. She shared them with Cherilyn and Courtney, then passed them around the bus. Maple sandwich cookies, Oreos, and a can of Pringles circulated among the rows of passengers. The group chatted and discussed their visit to the orphanage.

Melodi, with Laura in her lap, mulled over the email update she would write to friends and family back home. In previous weeks, she had written about the gangs threatening the CAM base. She had written about the assassination of Haiti's president and the shock of experiencing an earthquake. She had chronicled the sudden murder of the two gang members to whom Barry had shared the Gospel. What would she write about this time?

In the row behind Melodi, Matt helped himself to a maple sandwich cookie. The cookies, shaped like a maple leaf with frosting between the halves, finished lunch nicely.

In the very back seat, Sam pulled out a Christian Creole publication and began to read to strengthen his skills with the language. Beside him, Austin, who had been in the country less than twenty-four hours, and Brandyn, who had been in Haiti about two weeks, took in the unfamiliar scenery.

After about ten minutes, they approached the area where the burning tires had been. Wes, in the front passenger seat, noted that the roads seemed empty. Sometimes this was an ominous sign that trouble was ahead. However, the presence of the police that morning reassured him. When gangs roamed the countryside, the police were often too fearful to confront them. It had been a relief to see the police in charge of the road.

"Roadblock ahead!" The voice from the back of the bus startled everyone. The tone was urgent but not panicky. The reaction, however, was immediate. Slamming on the brakes, Dale brought the bus to a quick halt.

Sixteen pairs of eyes—everyone except eight-month-old Laura—peered down the stretch of Highway 8 ahead of them. Later, not one of the seventeen could remember who had shouted the two words that got their attention. Only a few remembered the announcement at all. Their attention was focused on the cluster of vehicles blocking the roadway ahead.

A box truck, a Haitian ambulance, and a white pickup similar to a Ford Ranger blocked the road home, the only main highway leading from southeastern Haiti to the capital. Men surrounded the vehicles. The sun glinted on the guns in their hands: shotguns, pistols, and huge assault rifles.

In the passenger seat, Wes conferred with Dale. They quickly decided to turn around and head back the way they had come. Between Dale and Wes, six-year-old Shelden stared through the windshield, his eyes wide. Wes sympathized with the boy, who had only been in Haiti with his family for the last two weeks. Although he felt his heart rate accelerating, Wes felt more inconvenienced than scared.

Roadblocks were a normal part of life in Haiti and had been for years. The gangs operated a brisk business by controlling roadways and stealing from people who drove on them. By some estimates, there were 150 gangs in Haiti, some small and some large. They consisted of restless men who banded together to give themselves the power and identity they could not have as individuals.

Around their mission base in Titanyen, the missionaries in the bus had shared the Gospel with the gangs. Barry, their field director, had shown them by example how to interact without fear. But Wes and Dale also knew how unpredictable the gang members could be, and they knew the best approach to volatile situations like this: avoid them, if possible. It wasn't worth getting robbed, especially not with a bus full of people, including children.

Dale whipped the bus around and headed back toward the orphanage they had just visited. He quickly accelerated to get out of the area.

Melodi, holding baby Laura, heard her husband groan and say, "Oh no," as they turned around. He sat beside her in the third seat, holding three-year-old Andre on his lap. Ryan had no concerns about being abducted; he was much more concerned about how much time this would take. He had been down this same road several times recently with Barry, their field director. He knew there were gangsters around, but they had never presented any great danger.

Oh dear, now we have to go back and go a different way, Melodi thought, looking over baby Laura's soft hair. She had no fears of being kidnapped either. *This is going to be inconvenient. We might get home really late today.*

In the front, Dale and Wes looked ahead, wondering what detour they could take to get back on track. Suddenly Dale saw a white Ford Ranger pickup, bristling with gun barrels, right outside his window, moving fast. Three or four men sat on the back of the truck holding guns, and others pushed guns out the windows of the cab. As the truck shot past the bus, Dale gave a sigh of relief. He was delighted to let the vehicle pass and continue on its way down the road. They would be able to plan their detour better if they didn't have to share the road with this heavily armed truck.

But the truck was not moving on. It was cutting in ahead of them. *Screee-e-e-ech!*

2:11 p.m., Titanyen Base

As Barry talked with Ray, telling him he had come to Titanyen at a great time, he felt his phone vibrating.

Barry's phone, though a valuable tool, was also a source of daily frustration. Whether he was speaking with his family, his brothers in Christ, or with gangsters, he tried to give his full attention to the person in front of him, not to the person trying to reach him through the phone.

In particular, the phone habits of some of the gangsters tried his patience. If they called and Barry didn't answer, they kept on calling, sometimes up to fifty times an hour.

On this warm afternoon under the shade of the porch, Barry ignored the phone as long as he could, engrossed in his conversation with Ray. Finally he pulled the culprit from his pocket and unlocked the screen. His eyes fell on a brief message: "Are your people okay?"

A missionary from southern Haiti had sent this ominous text. Barry tried to reassure himself. *Of course they are okay.*

But he was still uneasy. *Why is he asking this question?* It was an unsettling thought.

Barry swiped his thumb across the phone's face and saw another message. This one from a different person. "Do you have fifteen[1] people out?"

He looked up at Ray.

"We might have an emergency."

───────────

Back at the house, Barry's wife Julia had put the children into their beds for naps. She decided to lie down for a nap herself.

It was hot. Very hot. Julia knew that Barry and Ray were talking outside on the warehouse porch, and she was concerned; Barry had been

---

[1] Initially, the number of hostages was incorrectly reported as fifteen.

KIDNAPPED *in Haiti*

getting dehydrated lately. At 2:11, she sent him a text: "Are you drinking water? It's 100 degrees in the shade."

He didn't answer immediately. At 2:13, she got a call from him. "The whole group that went to the orphanage got kidnapped." Barry's voice broke as he shared the news.

Because it was Saturday, there were no employees on the compound. Julia quickly abandoned all thoughts of a nap and hurried through the eerie stillness to join the men. She thought of her oldest son Abram, taking his nap. He had wanted so badly to go along to the orphanage with his friends. For a brief moment, she and Barry had considered this.

She met the men at the office. On this normally bustling compound, they were now the only three adults.

Coshocton, Ohio

In the busyness of life in Coshocton County, Ohio, Phil Mast knew he had to be intentional to create pockets of family time. The afternoon was cool but beautiful when Phil's wife Grace and their daughters dropped Phil and his son off at a woodsy park. The men stepped onto the first cement pad of the park's disc golf course and threw the colored plastic discs toward the first basket. Phil enjoyed being out among the trees in the park, breathing the cool autumn air and hearing the rattle of the chains as the Frisbee-like discs hit their mark. But he especially enjoyed the quality time with his son. While the men practiced their aim, Phil's wife Grace and their two daughters ran an errand with the vehicle.

Like Barry, Phil struggled against the tyranny of his cell phone. However, he had it with him today, and when he saw a call coming through from Barry Grant in Haiti he answered it.

Phil was not a stranger to startling phone calls. Just two years before, he had been in Haiti when his wife called from Ohio with the devastating news that their son had passed away. Today the call came the other direction, from Haiti to Ohio. No one had died, but the news was not good. Phil heard Barry's voice shake as he shared the news: "Most of our staff have been kidnapped. Please get the word out to pray."

Since Barry's most urgent request was for prayer support, Phil began making phone calls as soon as he hung up with Barry. The disc-throwing competition suspended, Phil dialed several people who did not answer. Finally he reached someone who was able to compose an email to the entire Christian Aid Ministries team, spread across several states.

Phil's wife Grace returned to the park to find her husband on the phone, his game abandoned. She soon realized they might be making a trip to Haiti. She had invited guests for the noon meal after church the next day, and she debated un-inviting them. But she already had most of the meal prepared, and Phil assured her they would not fly to Haiti until Monday.

Besides, he hoped everyone would be safely at home by then.

2:22 p.m., Titanyen Base

After calling Phil, Barry sent a message to a friend from his home church in Indiana, across the state line from the Grants' Ohio home.

"Just about everyone here at CAM just got kidnapped—seventeen people. Could you get the church to pray? Thank you."

"Brother Barry, does that include your wife and children?"

"No, it does not. My family is still here."

2:31 p.m., Berlin, Ohio, CAM Headquarters

Email to "CAM Everyone"

"Prayer request: Fellow colleagues and prayer warriors. We've received word that about fifteen of our staff people in Haiti have been kidnapped on their way home from visiting an orphanage. We have the American Embassy and the field director working to see what can be done. Please pray that the staff members could return safely."

Mid-Afternoon, Cochranton, Pennsylvania

Sixteen years after returning from Haiti as a full-time missionary, Bobby Miller and his wife mingled in the reception hall at a friend's wedding. The ceremony and meal complete, people chatted with old friends and gathered their belongings and children. The Millers had made the three-hour drive from their home to help support and celebrate a young couple from church. Several other church friends were there, some of whom, like Bobby, worked at Christian Aid Ministries. Bobby noted Phil Troyer, a supervisor, approaching him, his phone open.

"Did you hear what happened?" Phil asked.

Bobby had not.

"Our missionaries in Haiti have been kidnapped."

3:35 p.m., Greeneville, Tennessee

Tommy Wagler, chairman of the Christian Aid Ministries board, was out sightseeing with two long-time friends, one who lived in the Tennessee neighborhood they were touring. All of them former missionaries in Kenya, the three men and their wives had planned the weekend to reconnect, relax, and reminisce about their years together in Africa. The men drove around to different local businesses that afternoon and talked about what they were doing with their lives. Tommy and his wife intended to go to church with their friends the next day before returning to their home in Ohio.

Tommy looked down at his phone and saw a text message from David Troyer, the general director of Christian Aid Ministries. He opened the message. The relaxing afternoon vanished like a mirage on the roadway as he read David's words: "Tommy, just want to make sure you're aware of the kidnappings in Haiti this afternoon of fifteen of our staff members and dependents."

Soon Tommy was scheduling a meeting for that night.

Chapter four

TEN MOTHERS ACROSS NORTH AMERICA

2 p.m., Lancaster, Pennsylvania

Why does my phone keep ringing? Sam's mom wondered. She was busy hosting a large group of her husband's family and had left her phone upstairs. Finally she went to get it.

She saw a message from Sam on their family's group chat and opened it.

"Urgent prayer request. We're being kidnapped right now! It's an armed gang ordeal!"

Sam's mom knew Sam would not lie. But for a second she could not believe that the message was true. She stood beside the phone, struck numb.

Sam was the fifth of her ten children. Perhaps because he was sandwiched between three older brothers and three younger brothers, he had always been an instigator, quick to speak his mind and irritate his siblings. About the only time she could remember him being docile was when he had chicken pox as a two-year-old. She knew though that this energy and fearlessness now enabled him to share the Gospel with boldness. With shock, she suddenly remembered something Sam had told her a few years earlier—that he had a feeling he might die at a young age.

She stood rooted to the floor, feeling as if her heart would stop.

She finally found the strength to go down and break the news to her husband and family. Quickly the news spread, and the planned family gathering became a somber time of prayer.

Morning, Grande Ronde Valley, Oregon

Melodi's mother had a busy day ahead of her. She had visions of cleaning the basement, raking pine needles, and tilling her strawberry patch. Since it was such a beautiful day, she decided to work outside instead of in the basement.

She was pleased to get a text from Melodi, her firstborn, about approaching Christmas plans. Melodi hoped her parents were still considering coming to Haiti for the holiday. Melodi's mom sent a reply, but did not receive any more messages. Her other daughter was waiting to give birth to her first child, and Melodi wanted to know the minute there was news. There was none yet.

Sometime later she saw a text come through from a friend: "Have you heard from Melodi?"

Something about the text sent a shock through her. After all, Melodi had not responded to her last text. She immediately called the number for the CAM base in Titanyen and asked for Melodi.

Ray Noecker, who picked up the phone, asked who was calling. When he heard who she was, he asked another question: "Is your husband with you?"

A chill spread through her. "No," she replied, "he's out in the mountains cutting firewood."

"Well, I'm sure they would want you to know," Ray went on. "There's been an abduction."

That afternoon, as the family supported each other, Melodi's sister began to show signs of going into labor. She had suspected it that morning and had thought of calling Melodi but had put it off. Now she was almost sure.

But calling Melodi was no longer an option.

Morning, Madras, Oregon

Austin's mom received the call from her husband while breathing in the aroma of homemade candles and soap she sold in her small boutique. It was still morning in Oregon.

"Austin may have been kidnapped," her husband said. "A group of people in Haiti were kidnapped after visiting an orphanage. The man who called me didn't know if Austin had gone along or not. Since he only arrived in Haiti yesterday, maybe he stayed at the base to rest."

But no, Austin's mom knew he did not sit around when there were places to go and things to see. The second of their five children, Austin had always been a livewire, one with boundless energy and a love for good conversation.

Would his upbeat attitude sustain him now?

Afternoon, Ladysmith, Wisconsin

Ryan's mom prepared to lie down for a nap. She was amazed that she and her husband were both an hour ahead of schedule for their last-minute trip to Iowa to help a sister church with an ordination. They had visited the same church in August, during which time her daughter-in-law Melodi had sent a message from Haiti, worrying that Ryan had been killed or injured. He had been traveling with Barry

Grant to southern Haiti to assess earthquake damage, and when Melodi couldn't reach him she had imagined him smashed inside an unstable building. In the end, everything had turned out all right. Ryan's mom often thought of that incident when she remembered their visit to the Iowa church. Now they were ready to go again. But first she needed a nap.

When she heard her phone ring and saw it was a friend, she answered.

"Are Ryan and Melodi okay?" the caller asked.

"I don't know. I guess. Why?"

"Well, we heard that Sam Stoltzfus was kidnapped."

Her nap forgotten, Ryan's mom dialed the Titanyen base.

No answer.

Next she went upstairs to spend time in prayer. When she felt peaceful again, she returned to the couch to try to rest. Soon she got an out-of-state text message: "Praying for your son and his family."

She stared at the phone, then replied, "What did you hear?"

This friend informed her that seventeen of CAM's missionaries had been kidnapped. There could be no question now. Ryan and Melodi must have been along.

Ryan was her second of nine children. In the early days, when they still lived in Kansas, Ryan had loved playing on the farm with his grandpa and his cousin Grant, nearly his own age. He had sustained an injury or two on these occasions. Once his left thumb had been smashed in a door, and another time he had put his fingers in an air compressor pulley, with similar results.

As he grew older, Ryan often shared witticisms at unexpected times. His slightly malformed thumb was an opportunity to reassure people that his injury was not a disadvantage. "It just helps me remember which is right and which is left."

Ryan was also one who could not stand being idle. He thrived on activity. "For him," his mother said, "sitting still is just about the worst punishment in the world."

The childhood scrapes on the farm had been painful at the time, but none of them were life-threatening. This time it was different. Ryan, Melodi, and their two small children were being held by armed gangsters. Would they survive?

2:45 p.m. CST, Monterey, Tennessee

"Is Wes okay?"

Wes's mom had just gotten up from her nap. She and her daughters ran a bakery in a separate building on their home property, supplying four stores with bread, cookies, and pies. They had begun this venture shortly before Wes moved to Haiti. The work started early in the morning, so Wes's mom usually took an afternoon nap. When she awakened, she often checked her phone first thing. With three children out of state and two out of the country, she needed to check her phone regularly.

This message from a church friend, however, sent a chill through her. Quickly she tried to call her son, but he didn't answer. She then sent a text, but there was no reply.

She and her husband had plans to attend the viewing of an elderly gentleman who had once been a missionary to Paraguay, where she had grown up. Much as she wanted to pay her respects and connect with other former missionaries who would surely be present at the viewing, she began to have second thoughts.

"I'm not going anywhere until I know what's going on," she told her husband. She then called the church friend who had sent her the message asking about Wes. The friend didn't know much, but she gave her the phone number for Phil Mast, the country supervisor of the Haiti mission.

Phil confirmed the rumor. Wes, along with sixteen others, had been kidnapped. As Wes's parents absorbed the shocking news, they abandoned all plans of going out in public.

"There's no way I can go out into a crowd of people," Wes's mom said. "I would make a scene."

3:10 p.m. CST, Pulaski, Tennessee

Matt's mom was cleaning a bathroom in her daughter-in-law's house when she heard a text come through on her phone. She saw it was from her sister and decided it could wait until she finished her task. Everyone in the family except Matt and Rachel had met for the weekend at the home of Matt's brother and his wife in Tennessee.

They were also missing their handicapped daughter, who had passed away two years before. She had been unable to talk or walk, but Matt had been her favorite sibling. Before she passed away, Matt was the one who could best comfort her. Between watching his sister struggle and battling his own genetic disease, Matt had developed a soft heart and a vision to reach out to others.

Matt had several close brushes with death as a child. Once, as a three-year-old, he had slipped away from his father and fallen into a trough of water. Thankfully, his father heard him choking and gasping and pulled him out just in time. Another time, in a race with his brother to their outside phone booth, he had broken the glass in the door of the booth, cutting one of the main arteries in his arm. By the time they reached the hospital, he was turning blue.

Later, Matt's mom had worried for a time that he would spend his life pursuing hunting trophies and professional bull riding rather than the things of the Lord. But Matt had grown in his walk of faith, and now, even though she wished he and Rachel could be at the family gathering, she was glad to know he was serving the Lord.

When the bathroom finally glistened and the cleaning supplies were put away, Matt's mom checked her phone.

A sense of dread crept through her, though she didn't know why because the text was not bad news. It was just a question: "In what part of Haiti is Matt?"

Like the other moms, Matt's mom realized instantly that her sister wouldn't be asking this question without a reason. She called her sister, who explained that she had seen a prayer request coming from a CAM worker in Haiti. Matt's mom felt her fears coming to life as her sister read her the chilling message:

"Please pray for us. We just got kidnapped."

Afternoon, Chester County, Pennsylvania

Like Ryan's mom, Rachel's mom was just settling down on the couch for a nap. She liked to arrange her schedule to allow Saturday to be a light day. Just a little cleaning and arranging, with time for relaxation.

She saw that someone was trying to reach her. It was one of her daughters, and she decided to let the call go unanswered until after her nap. But her daughter did not want to wait, so she called her father, who was outside working.

"Have you heard what is going on in Haiti? There's been a kidnapping."

Rachel's parents scarcely had time to discuss the news before a message came through from Rachel's husband, Matt. "We are being taken. We don't know where they're taking us. Pray, pray, pray."

Rachel, the sixth of nine children, had been an easygoing baby with a large amount of long, dark hair. She had been a reserved child, often struggling with an upset stomach until she realized around the age of twenty that she was sensitive to gluten. Once gluten was cut out of her diet, she finally attained better health.

But what will happen to her now? her mom wondered. *Maybe good food is the least of her worries.*

4 p.m., Fremont, Michigan

Kay's mom was getting to the end of a long day of preparation. She and her family planned to host church services at their house the next day—a congregation of about fifteen families. They cleaned the house and prepared food.

Around 4:00 that afternoon, the phone rang and she answered. It was her son Reuben from Ohio.

"Hey, Mom. You all need to pray. Kay is with a group in Haiti that has been kidnapped by a group of gangsters."

Later Kay's mom described her feelings at that moment. "It was such a shock. Such numbness. Such helplessness."

The family got together to pray and called others in their family and church to join them in prayer. Kay's mom found she could barely go on with preparations for the next day. Kay, her third child of eight, had always been an unselfish person. She loved to sew and had shown interest in this skill at an early age. Kay's mom knew this came in handy in Haiti, where she was able to provide clothing for anyone who needed it. On her furloughs home, Kay shopped at thrift stores to supplement her supply of dry goods to take back to Haiti with her.

Perhaps Kay had learned lessons in unselfishness from her parents, who went ahead with their plans and hosted the fifteen families the next day.

"Everything was ready," Kay's mom said. "But it was a difficult time."

5:30 p.m., Moorefield, Ontario

Dale's mom, like Rachel's mom, was enjoying a relaxing Saturday afternoon when her phone rang at 5:30 p.m. It was Phil Mast from Ohio. "I'm sorry to tell you," he said, "but Dale has been kidnapped in Haiti along with sixteen others."

Dale's mom found the news hard to absorb. When her husband walked into the kitchen where she was sitting at the table, she shared the bad news with him.

Dale was the fifth of six children, all of whom loved to read and could get lost in books. Perhaps because of this, they had great imaginations and could create their own adventures if nothing exciting was happening. Although Dale had been a quiet boy, he made his words count. And he had a signature laugh that often came at the end of one of his pithy statements.

Would they ever hear his laugh again?

Evening, Chambersburg, Pennsylvania

Cheryl's mom enjoyed quiet Saturday evenings with her husband. Sometimes they played a few rounds of Bible Scrabble or Skip-Bo before having a devotional time together and then going to bed.

As they sat chatting, their son-in-law, living below them in the same house, came up with news.

"Cheryl and five of the children have been kidnapped by Haitian gangsters!" he exclaimed. In shock, they listened as their son-in-law told them everything he knew about the kidnapping, which wasn't much.

As Cheryl's mom and dad discussed the situation, they realized there was nothing they could do except commit everything into the hands of their heavenly Father.

It was with heavy hearts that they prepared for bed. Somewhere in Haiti, their precious daughter and five grandchildren were at the mercy of a ruthless gang leader.

Chapter five

THE END OF THE DEAD END ROAD

Saturday, October 16
The Bus in the Circle

*W*ith a gangster at the wheel, the missionaries hung on as the bus continued to hurtle down the narrow Haitian roads at breakneck speed. The ride was wildest in the back seat where Sam, Austin, and Brandyn sat.

As they bounced up and down on the seats, questions popped up and down in Austin's mind. When his phone dropped to the floor, he didn't even try to pick it up. They were bouncing around too much.

Will I ever see my family again? he wondered. His little sister had reminded him before his flight to Haiti that her ninth birthday was coming up on November 1, and he *must* call her. *Will I be able to make that call? Will I even be alive?*

The gangster driving the bus suddenly slowed and pulled into a large clearing, a circle with a ten-foot-high concrete wall on one side. As the bus came to a shuddering halt, the Prado, the box trucks, and the ambulance also came to a stop, parked all around them.

Fearfully the missionaries watched as a dozen or more gangsters piled out of the vehicles and surrounded the bus with their guns.

I think they are going to shoot us, Wes thought from his vantage point at the front of the vehicle.

Oh, no, Kay thought. *This is not like that other hijacking. These gangsters aren't just borrowing the bus. Something more sinister is afoot. They brought us back here to kill us. If they just wanted to rob us, they would have done it by now.*

But instead of shooting them, the gangsters began evaluating their catch more thoroughly. By turns, they opened the side door to peer inside. They seemed especially fascinated by Laura, the eight-month-old baby in Melodi's arms.

They laughed and chatted as they smoked and drank, obviously overjoyed with the humans they had stolen. Many of them seemed to be high on drugs. It was clear to the prisoners in the hot bus that the gunmen were undecided what to do with them.

Not wanting to miss an opportunity, those who could speak Creole told the gangsters about Jesus. They handed them copies of a small Creole booklet titled *Flanbo Verite A (The Torch of Truth),* which Sam had been reading to practice his Creole.

Several gangsters came up to the driver's side of the bus next to the fourth row of seats. They stuck their heads in the open window right in front of Matt, who sat closest to the window. They looked around at the people and began pointing. They pointed at Matt's wife Rachel and at Ryan's wife Melodi, both close by. Then the one gangster elbowed the other, laughing.

"Madanm mwen."

Matt had only been in Haiti about five months, so his Creole was limited. But he understood this clearly.

The gangster had just said, "That's my wife."

"Words cannot describe the feeling of helplessness and despair that goes through you at a time like that," Matt said later.

For about forty-five minutes, the gangsters laughed and gawked and smoked as the missionaries grew increasingly hot and thirsty. The gangsters again asked for cell phones and money but did not demand that they be handed over.

One of the gangsters then opened the back hatch of the bus, where Sam, Brandyn, and Austin sat. They saw Austin's phone, which had dropped on the floor earlier, and pocketed it.

One of the men began rubbing Austin's head, feeling his hair. Then he rubbed his nose. "My head is in the sky! My head is in the sky!" the gangster repeated over and over.

Austin, still inside his first twenty-four hours in the country of Haiti, wondered what he would encounter next.

Worst of all, there was still no sign of Dale.

Dale in the Ambulance

On the floor of the ambulance, Dale stared at the top of a box truck, which was all he could see.

He had been ordered into the back of the ambulance and told to sit on one of two bench seats, with guards on each side. As the ambulance bounced down the road behind the bus, Dale prayed and watched the passing scenery. He wanted to remember the countryside in case it helped him identify his location later.

Apparently the guards noticed what he was doing, as they began waving their guns at him and motioning him to get down on the floor of the ambulance. Unable to see any scenery now except the treetops,

Dale prayed for his sixteen friends in the bus ahead of him. He especially prayed for protection over the girls.

Dale didn't take his own situation lightly, however, and prayed for himself as well. He expected to be taken deeper into the backcountry and shot. He pictured the gangsters tossing his body under a Haitian bush. He begged God for the courage to face such a fate without fear. "I was ready to die," he remembered later, "but it was hard not to let fear take control. I was constantly in prayer."

When the ambulance slowed, Dale sensed that the vehicles had entered a clearing. He could no longer see any treetops. All he could see was the top of a box truck. Although he could not see the bus, he suspected it was close by.

Again he battled fear. Was this open space, unhindered by trees, an execution yard? He imagined the gangsters unloading the bus, lining up his friends, and shooting them one by one.

Bang!

The sound sent shock waves of fear through Dale's body. He had no idea what had made the noise, but it sounded like a gunshot. His heart sank.

Suddenly the doors of the ambulance opened, and Dale's body tensed. Would they drag him out and shoot him?

No, apparently they were just checking on him, as the door slammed shut again.

Several times the gang members repeated this checkup. Each time Dale wondered if his hour had come. He also wondered what was happening to his fellow workers.

Bang!

This time it didn't sound so much like a gunshot, and relief flooded Dale. Something about the noise made him feel sure it came from the slamming doors of the box truck.

In the Bus

After about forty-five minutes, a gangster once again jumped back into the driver's seat of the bus. The vehicle lurched forward as he gunned the engine. The missionaries held their breath as he drove straight toward a concrete wall. At the last second, he swerved to the right and left the parking lot. Once more they hung on as they raced down the road—a different one than they had been on earlier.

Again the missionaries allowed themselves cautious hope. Maybe the gang was finished with them and they were being taken back to one of the main roads.

This hope soon faded when they came to a dead end and the vehicles were parked again, this time in a clearing with two small block buildings. Banks of trash were piled against the two buildings, little more than shacks, and around the edges of the clearing. They could see discarded foam food boxes, still crusty with food, in the trash, along with empty glass bottles and plastic forks.

The missionaries noticed a heavy wooden beam, about the size of a railroad tie, with holes through it like the pictures of stocks in Bible story books. A rickety contraption of tree trunks tied together with strips of cloth hanging from it suggested evil intent by its strangeness. Could it be a place to tie up people? Or a gallows?

Most disturbing of all were the gangsters. They were everywhere. They moved toward the bus like predators, cradling their guns. A few even began stripping off their clothes. One gangster held long shoestrings in his hands, as if preparing to tie up someone.

From one of the two houses, the gangsters led out two prisoners, tied hand and foot. The prisoners had to hop because of their shackles. They were skinny and bony, and their pants were falling down.

In the bus, people began praying aloud. In the second row, Cherilyn searched her heart, crying out to God. Her eyes could not stay closed forever; she had to be prepared for whatever lay ahead. "God, show me if there is anything in my life I need to ask forgiveness for!"

Oh, no, Kay thought. *We are in for it.*

Rachel, between her husband Matt and thirteen-year-old Kasondra in row four, watched the sinister scene with overwhelming dread. "I never had a feeling like that in my whole life before," she remembered. "And I sure hope I never feel it again."

Matt felt the panic of complete powerlessness to protect his wife. He saw the men stripping off their clothes, with the shoestring ties at the ready. He fully expected to die, assuming he would be shot. But this was not his most pressing concern.

"Lord!" he prayed aloud. "I'm ready to come to you. Let them do anything to me, Lord. Just protect my wife!"

At this terrible moment, Dale reappeared. The gangsters brought him over and told him to sit on the step in the open side door of the bus.

"Are you all right?" Wes asked from the front seat.

"Yes," Dale replied.

The group praised God for his safe return, overjoyed with this shaft of hope breaking through the gloom of uncertainty and fear.

A gangster stuck his head into the bus. "Give me your phones!" he ordered in English. "If I find a phone later, I will kill you!"

Dale pulled his phone out of its hiding place by the driver's seat. Ryan and Melodi considered the phone hidden inside Laura's diaper cover. It didn't seem to be worth the risk, so they handed it over. Everyone else turned in their phones as well, along with their wallets.

One of the Noecker family had a phone with a family picture stuck between the phone and the phone case. They took the phone out of the case and handed it to the gangsters. Shelden held on to the case with the picture of his family.

The gangsters saw the little boy holding the case and apparently thought it was a phone. They demanded that he turn it over.

"It's just a phone case!" Shelden yelled, gripping it tighter.

The gangsters grabbed for it, but Shelden kept hanging on.

"It's just a phone case!" he shouted again.

Finally the gangsters backed off and let him keep it.

Despite making these collections, the gangsters still seemed to be deliberating the fate of the captives. The temperature in the bus was stifling, and everyone longed for a drink of water.

Meanwhile, the leader of the gang emerged from the white Prado at the head of the procession. This was the Big Chief. He was tall with light brown skin and a scent of cologne that went before him like a herald. His arms swung out at his sides as he walked. Because he frequently cast his eyes downward, he might have been mistaken for a shy, humble man except for his expression of cold disdain when he did look up. A gold crucifix hung on a fine chain around his neck. Six inches of black plastic bands circled his wrists like bracelets, climbing up his arm toward the heavy tattoos above. A pencil mustache and goatee outlined his jaw. His name was Wilson Joseph. However, he went by his nickname, Lanmò San Jou. This nickname meant "Death Without Days." His face showed zero emotion, and his voice was quiet.

Desperate to know what they planned to do with them, Sam finally used his fluent Creole to press for answers.

"What is going on?" he asked. "What do you want from us? You have our wallets and phones. What more can you take from us? Can we leave?"

"No way. We need three million dollars."

Sam stared back at the man. "We can't give you three million dollars. We don't have it."

"Give us three million dollars!"

They began to escort people from the bus, starting with the ladies in the front. They took them to the other side of the bus and then stopped unloading as if they intended to separate the women from the men. Crying out to the Lord for protection for the women, those left in the bus watched as the gangsters lined up the ladies beside one of the block buildings.

"Out!" Sam yelled, leaping from his seat. "Everyone get out of the bus! Let me out! Go! Go! Go!"

As the rest of the group poured out of the bus in an unstoppable wave, they were herded over to where the women stood. The whole group, already praying, now began to sing. Slowly the volume increased as everyone joined in.

> The angel of the Lord encampeth round about them
> That fear Him, and delivereth them.
> O taste and see that the Lord is good!
> Blessed is the man that trusteth in Him!

"Stop singing!" a gangster ordered. They eased off a bit, then kept on. Another gangster watched them closely as he brandished an assault rifle. Nearby, Lanmò San Jou stood watching, his face impassive.

One of the gangsters walked down the line of captives, videoing them. "This is the final video of these people," he said.

What does that mean? Sam wondered. *Is this when they kill us?*

Chapter six

LOCKED INSIDE

Afternoon, Gangster Camp

*T*he gangsters took everyone's shoes, then ushered the captives into a ten-foot by twelve-foot windowless room in one of the houses. They went in the same door through which the bony prisoners had come out. The guards then shut the door, barricading it with a *thunk* of something heavy.

Some of the group sat down on the single mattress on the floor, but most remained standing. Uneasily they looked around. They noticed unmistakable bloodstains on the walls, as well as some bullet dents. The door into the next room was barred with sheet metal, covering everything except the bottom four inches. The concrete room completely lacked ventilation, and in the hot afternoon, it was stifling.

Despite the inadequate space, the temperature, and the dark brown bloodstains on the wall, there was a certain sense of relief. Just being alone together refreshed them. At the same time, they realized the truth. There was no longer any question about what was happening. They had been kidnapped.

But what did that mean? Would they be locked in this room for the whole night? If so, how would they sleep?

Sam suggested that the men most fluent in Creole sit closest to the door. They were still highly concerned about the safety of the ladies. Wes, Ryan, and Sam tried to sit close to the door to take the brunt of whatever came next.

About fifteen minutes after being crammed into the room, the missionaries heard two gunshots. They looked at each other. Had the two other prisoners been killed?

As they sat discussing the situation, as well as singing and praying, the guards popped in and out.

First a guard arrived with two more mattresses, a single and a double. Together, the three mattresses took up most of the room.

Next a guard came in with water and a bag of food. He placed this catered dinner in the middle of the room and left. The bag contained seventeen small boxes of beans and rice with vegetables on top, along with chicken. Although the water refreshed them, none of the captives felt like eating. Andre, the three-year-old, did eat a little.

The missionaries began to sing again. "The angel of the Lord encampeth round about them that fear him, and delivereth them." They sang and prayed and prayed and sang. They thought about their plans for the weekend back at Titanyen.

"Wow, the devil really doesn't want us to have Communion!" someone said.

They prayed in faith that they would be back home in the morning in time for the Communion service. And getting there in time to shower would be a nice bonus.

The group had spent the week in special prayer and sharing, making sure their hearts were right with each other and before God. This self-evaluation was practiced by most Anabaptist churches before each semiannual Communion service.

They normally held a preparatory service before the Communion service to encourage everyone to search their hearts. Today Sam felt he had experienced the best preparatory service of his life while looking down the barrels of the gangsters' guns. With death staring him in the face, there was no doubt what really mattered in life.

Soon the door opened again, ushering in a nauseating wave of cologne. Lanmò San Jou was at the door. Speaking in Creole, he ordered Ryan to call his boss and demand money for their release.

"We don't know Barry's number," someone explained. "But if you bring us our phones we can find it."

4:35 p.m., Titanyen Base

Back at the CAM base, Barry, Julia, and Ray discussed their options. They had more questions than answers. Should they plan to have Communion service tomorrow? Surely, they reasoned, the gangsters would not keep the missionaries overnight. Most likely they would be home by dark tonight. Then they could all laugh shakily and thank God for sparing them from a big catastrophe. Everyone would retire to their own beds with the incident behind them.

Barry soon received a call from the head of the United States Embassy in Port-au-Prince. This professional believed the case was a true kidnapping, but he cautioned Barry that they needed to wait for a phone call to confirm this.

"If it's a kidnapping, the gang will call you," the embassy spokesman assured Barry. "That's the whole point of kidnapping people—negotiating for their release. But it might not happen right away. The kidnappers often like to increase people's anxiety by dragging out the process.

It could be three to seven days before you hear from them."

Despite these words of caution, Barry watched his phone closely.

At 4:35, the phone rang. The caller ID said Ryan Korver! Quickly he snatched up the phone. "Hello."

"Hey!"

It was Sam's voice! Barry had not been expecting to hear from one of the team.

Good! They must be free! Barry rejoiced, thinking they had made quite a stir for nothing.

"We've been kidnapped," Sam continued.

"Are you all together? Are you okay?" Barry spoke fast, realizing it was not over yet, and that his time on the phone with Sam was probably limited.

"Yes, we're all together, and we're doing okay."

Those were the last words from Sam. Barry heard the sound of the phone being taken and then the voice of someone else.

"Everybody is in my hand," the gang leader said. "I'm in control. This is not going to be a long process. This is only going to take one day. I need one million dollars each, or I kill them all."

"We're missionaries. We're here working for God," Barry replied. "We're not going to give you money. You've got the wrong people. These are God's people you have on your hands."

"I do the talking here!" the gang leader said. "You have no business talking to me." Then he screamed, "Money, or they die!" and hung up the phone.

Barry told Ray what the gangster had said.

"No, that's not true," Ray said. "Our people are in God's hands."

That night, alone in the house he had shared with his wife and five children, Ray Noecker read Psalm 18 and felt comfort as he begged God to intervene on behalf of his family. The bed looked too big, so Ray slept on the couch, grateful that it was long enough for his tall frame.

He covered his head with Cheryl's pillow and tried to sleep, wondering if his family would be able to get any sleep.

Evening, Gangster Camp

Later that evening, as dusk settled, a Haitian American walked into the camp. He was a short, round man who spoke excellent English.

"I'm on your side," he said. "I'm here to help you."

He claimed to be a local business leader who had been harassed by the gang. "They told me to come as an interpreter," he said. "When Lanmò San Jou says 'come,' you come."

Although he seemed friendly and talked English, the missionaries weren't sure what to think of him. Should they be suspicious of his intentions?

"I'll bring you snacks and drinks and cold water," the man promised. "I'm on your side. I'm just a friend of the gang. I feel like I could get harmed for coming in here to help you guys.

"I'm here to help you," he repeated. "What do you need? Tell me anything you need. What kind of food do you need? Do you need any medication? We'll get you a generator. We'll get you fans."

"We want to go home," someone finally replied.

Going home, the man explained, was not one of the options. He made it clear that the hostages should settle in for the long haul and try to make themselves as comfortable as possible. He also said the kidnapping had been a mistake, and if there was anything he could do to get them out of there, he would do it.

"Don't kid yourself," Sam told the others after the man left. "This man is likely one of the gang leaders." He seemed so helpful, however, that they later gave him a nickname—Santa Claus.

Making themselves comfortable in the ten-foot by twelve-foot room seemed like an impossibility. Clouds of mosquitoes hung in the air like fog, and fire ants in the room began biting. The captives continued to sing and pray as darkness settled over the gangster camp. They could feel the presence of evil. *What will tomorrow bring?* they wondered.

However, there were reasons to give thanks. They were grateful for the return of Melodi's striped diaper bag. The bag was the only piece of luggage they had. All the other purses and bags had been taken by the gang.

The gangsters had taken everything they wanted from the bag, including Melodi's paper tablet and pen. But they had returned the diaper supplies, an opened bag of Oreos, Wes's water bottle, a pile of *Flanbo* inspirational booklets, a few Band-Aids, and a bottle of ibuprofen. They had also returned their credit cards and ID cards, a huge blessing.

Ryan and Wes both had pens, and Courtney, Brandyn, and Kasondra each possessed a digital wristwatch that had not been taken. After retrieving Matt and Rachel's credit cards and the small amount of cash from inside Laura's diaper cover, they stuffed everything in a small pack of tissues and put it into the diaper bag.

Most important of all, they were together. And for the moment they were safe. Cramped in his allotted square inches of space beside Rachel, Matt remembered the gangsters' pointing and the threats he had witnessed in the bus. He decided not to tell anyone what he had heard.

The captives were offered a bathroom break. The gangsters told them they could take care of business in the weeds at the edge of the clearing. The ladies refused, so a bit later the guards showed them to a cement pad at the side of the building. Three curtains hung around the small space, a shallow bid for privacy. It appeared the gangsters normally used this area as a shower but had now added a bucket to it and called it a bathroom.

They said only one person could go to the bathroom at a time. When the missionaries objected, insisting that the women go two at a time, the guards allowed this.

As darkness fell, the group continued to sing and pray. With the pause in intensity, the swirling thoughts of the captives caught up with what had happened. Many of them thought of their families at home. Their parents. Their siblings. Cheryl Noecker had four children back in the States in addition to the five with her. And her husband Ray was back at Titanyen. What had they heard? What were they thinking or feeling?

Dale looked around the room of hot, tired people. He remembered that he had been the leader of the day's outing. He had arranged the trip, and he had been driving. Was he to blame for the whole thing? He struggled internally and finally shared his thoughts with the others. His friends made it clear that he should not entertain guilt about this. They had all made a personal choice to come along.

Finally it was time to think about sleeping. The hostages evaluated their space—or the lack of it. There was simply not enough room for everyone to lie down, much less have any personal space.

The captives had heard people speaking Spanish in the next room and assumed they were other guards. "This must be a big gang with big connections," Sam said. He thought he was hearing Spanish-speaking gangsters from the Dominican Republic.

As the group tried to get settled, they were surprised to hear soft singing in Creole from under the sheet metal door to the next room. It was a song the missionaries had learned in church, and it sounded like the singing of angels. Who could it be? Surely not the guards. Although they couldn't understand where it was coming from, they accepted it as a gift from their heavenly Father, who knew exactly where they were and what they needed.

As Ryan and Melodi made plans for putting the children to sleep, Ryan considered his contact lenses. He took them out faithfully every night. But he knew if he took them out now, with no solution to put them in, he could not get them back in. He decided to leave them in.

Melodi realized that her hunch had come true—what was happening would certainly make an interesting story. But typing the email on her computer for her readers seemed like a distant dream. Maybe she could do it tomorrow.

Austin started out trying to sleep on the one chair in the room, right beside the front door. Every other square foot of space belonged to the mattresses, where the other sixteen people tried to get comfortable. Whenever one person got up or turned, they disrupted the flow of bodies. If two people traded places, both had to move quickly or the empty space would be filled by someone else. When Wes offered to sit in the chair for a while so Austin could lie down, Austin made a dive for the spot Wes had vacated and finally fell asleep. At times, the single men tried to sleep with their legs straight up the side of the wall, but this had its challenges too.

Even if the accommodations had been luxurious, sleep would have been poor. Every half hour or so, drunken guards yanked open the door, laughing and talking and shining powerful flashlights over the cramped missionaries, flooding the room with the smell of alcohol. Their noisy entrances often woke baby Laura, three-year-old Andre, and six-year-old Shelden, and their parents struggled to settle them until the next intrusion.

Thirteen-year-old Kasondra soon demonstrated a skill that made her the envy of the whole group. She could sleep in almost any position and under almost any circumstances. Her ability was a huge blessing.

Around 2 a.m., Andre began to cry. "My belly hurts," he moaned, writhing in pain. He had been the only one to eat any food the night before.

Now what? There was no room inside for anyone to start throwing up. Quickly someone pounded on the door to alert the guards that they needed help. When the door opened, Ryan stepped outside, carrying Andre. He stood in front of the chief of the guards, a man they later nicknamed Ping when he came one day with his hair in three braids sticking straight up. This reminded someone of the boy in the story of Ping, the yellow duck.

"We need to go home!" Ryan said to Ping, mustering his best Creole.

"The children can't do this!"

As if on cue, Andre vomited on the ground at the feet of the chief guard.

Ping shook his head. There was no way they could go home. When Andre refused to settle down again in the stifling heat, the guards allowed Ryan and Melodi and the children to go outside for the rest of the night. Several of the young men were also allowed to go outside toward morning.

Sam heard Ping say he didn't know what the gang was thinking when they kidnapped such a big group of white people.

Dale dozed for maybe thirty minutes the entire night and felt relief to see the darkness of night turn to day through the cracks of the wooden door.

But what would this new day bring?

Evening, Berlin, Ohio, CAM Headquarters

As the hostages tried to get comfortable in their small room in the gangster camp, a meeting began organizing at the Christian Aid Ministries main office. It was strange to be at work on a Saturday night, but the members of CAM administration felt a magnetic pull to show up, to do what they could to deal with the startling news the day had brought. There was no Saturday evening banter about the price of fuel or the best way to grill a steak.

The hallways echoed with questions. The map of the world dotted with field sites took on new meaning. On the right side of the map, under the heading "Overseas Staff," rows of faces corresponded with each location: Nicaragua. Romania. Ukraine. Liberia. Haiti. Kenya. Greece. Middle East. International Crisis. Tonight, the faces in the fifth row from the bottom were on everyone's minds. They were arranged in the order they had arrived at the Titanyen base: Westley Yoder. Kay Yoder. Sam Stoltzfus. Matt and Rachel Miller. Ryan and Melodi Korver, with their children Andre and Laura. Dale Wideman. These were the people, along with seven short-term staff, who had left to visit an orphanage and never made it home.

The CAM personnel who arrived for the meeting in person took seats in the rolling chairs of the central conference room around a group of tables arranged as a rectangle. To the left of a huge wall map of the world, people arrived remotely on a smartboard.

Tommy Wagler joined from Tennessee, and other board members signed in from around the country.

Questions followed questions. How long will the group be held? Are they being harassed or abused?

And the most agonizing question: What should we do? Everyone knew that CAM had a no-ransom policy. But there had never before been a reason to put this policy into practice.

Tommy listened to the discussion and then offered his opinion: "If we pay ransom, does that not mean the end of our operations in Haiti?"

These were difficult questions. Prayerfully the team sought the Lord and discussed options. Phil Mast expressed his willingness to travel to Haiti with his wife and daughter to provide support to Barry Grant if nothing changed. Everyone agreed that new roles would have to be developed and filled to handle this crisis, though everyone hoped the hostages would be released shortly. Maybe it was a misunderstanding— or a bad joke—and everything would be all right when the sun rose the next morning.

They finally decided that if the hostages were not freed by morning, the group would reconvene back in the conference room, making the rare decision to skip church. It was nearly midnight before the last person headed for home.

But the questions had not been answered.

And far away to the south, in a cramped room a fourth the size of the conference room, no one knew what to do either.

Chapter seven

GANGSTER CAMP

Sunday, October 17; Day 2

Gangster Camp

The next morning the captives were relieved when the guards allowed them to go outside. In the early morning light, the trash-littered clearing with its ramshackle structures looked no more inviting than it had the night before. Still, after the cramped quarters inside, it was a relief to breathe open air.

Bites from mosquitoes and fire ants dotted the exposed skin of the hostages. Already the bites were itchy and irritating.

Evaluating their surroundings, the captives wished they could go exploring around the area. But the guards did not allow this, telling them they had to stay between the two buildings. The lane on which they had come in from the south looped around both buildings and circled back to the entrance lane.

The little house in which they had been imprisoned overnight consisted of two main rooms. From their own tiny room, the missionaries now peeked under the four-inch gap at the bottom of the sheet metal door and saw that the room next to their own contained eleven captives, tied hand and foot. The captives introduced themselves as Dominicans, Chinese, and Haitians.

A porch wrapped around the east and north sides of the house, but the hostages were not allowed to go there.

The contraption of tree trunks and cloth strips that had reminded the captives of gallows sat between the two houses. It was actually an attempt at creating shade. When they fastened a tarp to the supporting structure, it created a welcome pool of shade in the courtyard between the buildings.

The second building, closest to the entrance of the camp, was boarded shut. When the missionaries peeped through the cracks into the house, they saw only a few pieces of dusty furniture inside.

The prison house was surrounded by shrubs and undergrowth on three sides, with small footpaths leading away from the clearing. From the "bathroom" on the north side of the building, the hostages could see glimpses of an irrigation ditch, with more shrubs on the other side of it. About one hundred feet down the ditch they saw a tall mango tree loaded with fruit.

"Out through there is our Red Sea," Cheryl said as she looked in the direction of the mango tree and across the brush. She gazed longingly across the many miles that separated her from her husband back at the base in Titanyen. "God is going to part that."

The hostages had never felt so much like the children of Israel. It was just that they were under the thumb of a Haitian gangster instead of an Egyptian Pharaoh.

On the southwest corner of the second house, the hostages noticed a strange tree stump. It appeared that most of the tree's branches had been partly cut off or carved away. Their captors informed them that this tree belonged to Satan. Across the lane from the second building, a broken axle with wheels lay under a tree.

A bedraggled white chicken, ugly and hen-pecked, lived in the gangster camp. Matt got disgusted at the little fowl and threw dirt clods at it. He named it Henrietta, partly because it was a little hard to figure out if it was a rooster or a hen, and that name seemed to give a nod to both genders. Along with the dirt clods, Matt gave the fowl some advice: "Go find your identity."

Some of the guards were shirtless, and most had pants so low they were nearly falling down. They usually had a knife stuck in their pants and dusty sandals on their feet. One guard wore skull and crossbones shorts. Many wore necklaces.

A man they later nicknamed Froggy arrived with spaghetti for breakfast. Froggy set himself apart from the other gangsters by his close-cropped hair, trim appearance, and crisp, neat clothes. Unlike the others, he did not let his pants hang down. He had a close-fitting necklace of multi-colored voodoo beads and a generous collection of black plastic bracelets. These black bands seemed to be a barometer of authority; the more a person had, the more advanced he was in the gang.

Froggy introduced himself in a booming voice, saying he was a Christian too. He explained that he would bring them food and anything else they needed. Since they couldn't go shopping, he would do it for them. He would be the town runner.

The hostages looked at the boxes of spaghetti. Once again no one could summon an appetite.

This concerned the gangsters. "What do you want?" Santa Claus asked. "Steak? Pizza? Hamburgers? Tell us what you eat."

"We normally eat this stuff," the hostages explained. "But we're just not hungry. We want to go home."

Everyone expected to go home later that day. Surely they would be back at Titanyen by nightfall. But hour after hour passed with no release.

Laura smiled widely at the guards, who couldn't help smiling back. The guards also offered their clenched fists to six-year-old Shelden and three-year-old Andre for fist bumps. Cheryl and Ryan and Melodi encouraged the boys to comply. They noticed that the guards followed the fist bumps by bringing the hand to their chest and circling their heart.

Froggy continued to bring supplies. Barrels of water for washing. Bags of water for drinking. Bar soap. It seemed as if they could have asked for about anything, and Froggy would have obliged.

The hostages prayed and sang to pass the time. It was a strange change from the anticipated Communion service they had expected to partake of back home.

Ping, the chief of the guards, watched and listened. He was a short, slight man with a derby hat pulled nearly over his eyes. He said he was thirty-five years old, but he walked like a much older man, reminding Austin of the halting gait of one of his relatives after a car accident. He was both pigeon-toed and bow-legged, as if his legs had spent their formative years on a horse.

Unlike the shaved sides and long top hair of the standard gangster, Ping had a forest of tiny braids under his hat. Both ears contained gold earrings, one with a cross dangling from it. Under exceptionally large nostrils, gold glinted at the back of a decayed tooth. The gold in the front of the tooth had worn away, creating a hole.

As Ping watched the missionaries singing and praying, Sam heard his soft voice from under the derby hat, "These Americans are no joke. I'm not sure why they chose to kidnap all these white people and leave them under my care."

Later in the day Santa Claus returned, as promised, with three boxes of American snacks. There were Doritos and Pringles, cookies, peanut butter, sardines, Reese's cups, even ice cream. By this time, real hunger had set in, and the captives dug into the food.

"I felt a little bad that we didn't eat their Haitian fare, but then we ate the other stuff," Ryan recalled later. "But it just took us awhile to get hungry."

The group also plied Santa Claus with questions. "Why have we been captured?"

"Money is not the main object," he said. He told them one of the founders of the gang was in prison, and the gang wanted to use the captured Americans and Canadian as leverage to get him out of prison.

The group found out that they were dealing with the 400 Mawozo gang. The self-deprecating name meant something like "400 Idiots" or "400 Men Who Don't Know How to Talk to Ladies," depending on who you asked.

Santa Claus confirmed what the missionaries had suspected. Although the gang often kidnapped people, this kidnapping was something new. Up until now, white Americans had been bypassed.

"Our gang's slogan is, 'The white people can go anywhere,' " Santa Claus said.

It wasn't clear at what point in the kidnapping the gang found out who was in the bus. But it really didn't matter now. They were kidnapped, and that was that.

But what did the gang really want? The hostages weren't sure. Was it money, as Lanmò San Jou had said? Or was it the release of the gang leader from prison?

With his competent grasp of Creole, Sam began preaching the Gospel to the guards. Although the group had no Bible with them, Sam was grateful for the inspirational Creole booklets, which contained Bible verses.

The guards openly worshiped Satan.

"If you died today, where would you go?" Sam asked them.

"To hell." There was no pause or qualification before this simple announcement. The guards claimed to be looking forward to this destiny, where they would be with the one they worshiped.

Sam told them about Jesus and called on them to repent and to leave their lives of sin. He asked them if they would be killed if they left the gang. They said they wouldn't, at least not if they escaped to another area.

Sam's mother had been right. Sam was fearlessly preaching the Gospel. Before he left for Haiti, Sam had told his journal, "I fully expect to die as a martyr for Christ someday." Under this statement he copied words from a passage written by a man later killed for the cause of Christ. "I am a disciple of Jesus Christ. I must go until heaven returns, give until I drop, preach until all know, and work until He comes. And when He comes to get His own, He will have no problem recognizing me. My colors will be clear."[1]

Sam, Wes, and Kay all spoke Creole well. Many of the others spoke at least some.

Austin, the new arrival from Oregon, realized he was useless when it came to preaching or even talking to the guards. Discouraged, he asked God what his role should be in this new setting. He felt God assure him that he could be an encourager to the other missionaries.

Kay questioned the intentions of the guards toward the women. For a few days she cautioned the other women and girls to stay inside the house as much as possible.

Grande Ronde Valley, Oregon

Less than twenty-four hours after gangsters kidnapped Melodi, her only sister gave birth to her first child, a baby boy. As Melodi's mom welcomed her new grandson, Cody Ryan, it was hard to believe that

---

[1] From "The Fellowship of the Unashamed," by an unidentified Rwandan man who was given the choice of renouncing Christ or being killed.

there was no way to let Melodi know. But as Melodi's mom wrote in her journal, the new baby was "a sweet spot of joy on this troubled day."

Melodi had recently told her mom what Ryan had said about their time in Haiti: "I wouldn't trade these last few months for anything." And Melodi agreed with him. Despite the danger and drama of living in Haiti, both Ryan and Melodi felt they were right where they were supposed to be.

It was also a comfort to Melodi's mom to remember that Melodi had always been an adaptable, resilient person. She had even dreamed of being a pioneer on the Oregon Trail. She had loved wearing the pioneer dress she had received for her fifth birthday. She had read and reread *Going West,* a picture book of a young girl in a covered wagon. She had pored over the detailed illustrations of the pioneers as they journeyed down the trail through sickness, death, snow, and a buffalo stampede.

Perhaps those early days of playing pioneer were coming true for her now. Maybe she was now the girl keeping the diary on the uncharted journey. Maybe it was just as dangerous as the Oregon

Stratford, Wisconsin[1]
At her morning church service on October 17, a grieving mom prayed during Sunday school that Melodi would have enough milk for Laura.

In the fall of 2020, Melodi, an expectant mother herself, had encouraged this young woman regarding the difficulties she was having with her pregnancy. Both women had their babies without complications. But before being kidnapped, Melodi had heard of the sudden death of the other woman's newborn son.

Now the woman who had lost her son was praying that Melodi would have enough milk for Laura.

[1] People from many states and countries sent prayers to encourage the families of the hostages. A few of these prayers, or versions of them, have been placed in shaded boxes throughout the book.

Trail. But her mother found comfort in remembering that, even in uncertain circumstances, Melodi tended to be positive and upbeat.

She would be able to help not only herself and her family, but also the whole group.

Titanyen Base

The planned Communion service was forgotten in a flurry of meetings and phone calls. Offers to help poured in from numerous sources. Barry discussed the situation with CAM administrators, an anti-kidnapping unit from Haiti, and the FBI.

Barry was glad to hear that his supervisor, Phil Mast, planned to arrive with his wife and daughter the next day.

Coshocton County, Ohio

Grace Mast went to Sunday morning church services with her thirteen-year-old daughter Olivia while Phil met with other CAM administrators and the board to form a plan. After Sunday school, she checked her phone to make sure he hadn't sent her a message. Nothing. Good. The food was warming at home, and they would still be able to host their guests for dinner. But she collected Olivia's schoolbooks from the adjoining church school, as she knew they might be flying to Haiti the next day. Olivia would need to keep up with her schoolwork while they were gone.

After the sermon, Grace headed to the vehicle. She checked her phone again. This time there was a message from Phil: "Come home as soon as you can."

Knowing the inadequacy of cell phone service in the area, Grace did not try to call him to find out why she needed to get home.

It was after twelve noon when Grace and Olivia walked through the front door of their house, followed by their dinner guests. As they breathed in the welcoming aroma of rice and beans and chicken, Phil quietly told them the news: "We have to leave by 1:30. We couldn't get the expected flight tomorrow morning to Port-au-Prince, so we have to fly to New York City today and then on to Port-au-Prince in the morning."

Grace turned the hosting over to her two older children who would not be going to Haiti. The guests graciously insisted that Phil, Grace, and Olivia eat something before starting their packing. When the Masts left for the airport, the guests were still eating.

Chapter eight

A NEW APPRECIATION FOR RUNNING WATER

Monday, October 18; Day 3

Gangster Camp

*E*arly Monday morning Matt woke up in the cramped quarters. His feet were up the wall and his head toward the center of the room, packed in among the bodies. Rachel lay beside him. *How did I get my wife into this situation?* Matt asked himself, dozing off. He was awakened a bit later by someone softly humming the tune of "The Angel of the Lord." It was Rachel, consoling herself in the difficult environment. Matt leaned over and found her face wet with tears. But Matt was encouraged that his wife's faith was strong even here.

Daylight brought Froggy with his bellowing voice and the same breakfast of spaghetti and half of a hard-boiled egg for each person. This time the hostages ate some of the food.

More supplies arrived over the next few days, making it clear to the missionaries that they would not be going home anytime soon. In addition to the three boxes of snacks they had brought earlier, the gangsters now brought an insulated cooler with a chunk of ice in it to refrigerate their juice and water. They then dragged in a couch and a love seat and unloaded a box of commercial paper towels. They also brought toothpaste and toothbrushes in a black plastic bag, which someone hung on the eaves of the house.

"All these things are for you!" Froggy bellowed when everything had been unloaded. "You're not supposed to share them with anybody else."

It seemed the gang was willing to spend money on them and get them anything they needed. Anything except their freedom.

Since it was clear that the gangsters expected them to be long-term guests, several people in the group decided it might be good to take notes. Melodi, seeing no immediate hope of typing her email, suddenly had an idea. *Why not write on paper towels?* The paper towels were white, thin, and strong, the kind

---

Willamette Valley, Oregon
Melodi's mother had gone to Christian grade school with Austin's mother. One of their former teachers, now an accomplished author, prayed for the kidnapped children of her former students.

She had fond memories of the mothers and felt gratified that both of them had learned to love writing just as she did. Perhaps she had indirectly inspired Melodi too, as she knew Melodi loved to write.

Like everyone else, she prayed for protection, for deliverance, for safety, and for the health of the children. But then she thought of something else. As a writer, Melodi must have a desperate urge to record her thoughts and feelings. Likely she had no notebook or writing supplies.

The author prayed that God would provide a way for Melodi to record her thoughts.

KIDNAPPED *in Haiti*

designed for mechanical holders.

With a little experimentation, Melodi, Rachel, Dale, and Wes began keeping diaries on paper towels. Ryan shared his pen with them. Wes also had a pen that he loaned out to them, but everyone knew to return it. He slept with it in his pocket to make sure it would not disappear.

The gangsters dug a pit twelve feet deep and three feet across close to the brush beside the second house and poured a cement slab for a toilet. They enclosed the toilet with thin blankets, with the fourth side facing the shrubbery.

Toilet paper was usually supplied, but sometimes it ran out. When this happened, shreds of cardboard substituted. Sometimes people borrowed baby wipes from Melodi's diaper bag, but these needed to be rationed to last as long as possible for Laura.

Now that the official outhouse was functional, the cement pad closer to the buildings became the shower house. The shower had a bucket of water, a metal dipper, and bar of soap. The gangsters filled fifty-gallon drums with water, from which the missionaries filled the shower bucket. There was no door on the shower pad, but the missionaries hung up a sheet to function as a door.

For the taller people, the shower curtains were only shoulder high. The tarp had holes in it, making the shower room a place of uneasy privacy. The sheet door was the worst of all. It threatened to fall open at the slightest hint of a breeze, forcing the occupant inside to be on high alert at all times.

The shower is a little corner beside the house with some worn-out tarp with sizable holes draped around some sticks, Dale wrote in his paper-towel diary. **I have a new appreciation for running water and a shower head.**

It was soon clear that Ping, the bow-legged chief of the guards, had a fastidious routine for personal hygiene. He showered with the bucket and dipper twice a day, generally stripping before getting into the shower. After his shower, he would diligently lather his body with lotion. It appeared to be a mixture of skin-lightening cream and body lotion. On at least one occasion, Dale noticed him calling over one of the other guards to rub it on a place on his back that he couldn't reach. He sometimes wandered around the camp with a fuzzy brown towel around his waist.

Ping cleaned his sandals with a brush and took pains to keep his feet clean. Compared to the other guards, his clothes were much neater and his pants less likely to be hanging down. He kept a pistol in his waistband.

The mystery of his eroded gold tooth was easily solved by watching him brush his teeth with a stiff toothbrush like those provided to the captives. Ping brushed furiously and endlessly, as if his standing in the gang depended on the cleanliness of his teeth.

Sam gave Ping one of the Gospel booklets and spoke to him about the Lord. Ping said he had grown up going to church and knew many of the Christian songs the group sang. The missionaries saw him reading the booklet from Sam. It seemed God was speaking to him.

Froggy brought a huge sack of random clothes for the captives to change into. Sam informed him that the women preferred to wear their long dresses rather than the pants and short skirts in the bag. Most of the men found pants to switch into for a second set of clothes, although they were mostly ladies' pants. Brandyn claimed a pair of pink pants with frogs on them. Matt found pants that were big enough for someone twice his size, and Wes found a pair of black dress pants that were also several sizes too large. Dale's pants were maroon pajama pants with an elastic waistband. Sam wore pants with drawstrings below the knees. None of these were standard Anabaptist garb, but at least it enabled the men to change into dry clothes after showering.

Preferring the modesty of their own clothes, the women and girls washed their clothes when they showered and put them back on wet.

This was inconvenient, but in the hot climate it often felt refreshing. Courtney, who had insisted to her relatives that she would be fine with one set of clothes in Haiti, got to put her words into action.

Melodi had made her solid blue dress for her first date with Ryan over five years before. She had always liked it.

Melodi found Andre a second pair of underwear in the bag, but they were far too big. She also found him a pair of sweat pants, but they were too big as well. She didn't like to have Andre looking like a gangster, but with the large clothes the likeness was unmistakable.

The hostages were provided with multi-colored crocs to replace the shoes that had been taken away.

Dale soon gained a new appreciation for the standard of excellence required by electricians in his home area in Ontario. The gangsters brought a generator and some electric wire. They planned to put up some electric light bulbs and fans. They were doing their best to make the surroundings comfortable for the missionaries.

Dale offered to help with the wiring, explaining that he was an electrician by trade, but the gangsters declined.

Dale watched the men place the generator off to the side of the second house. They then ran the wiring up into a tree and across the clearing to the prison house, fastening it at the corner of the shower. They strung another wire from the generator tree to the toilet and to the second house.

As Dale watched the precarious circuits being cobbled together with bare wires sticking out here and there, he simply had to look the other direction.

Some of the hostages had previously asked if they could help with the cooking or other chores to help pass the time, but the guards didn't like that idea either. Apparently the missionaries were supposed to take up space, and nothing else, until negotiations produced the results the gang wanted.

When the captives felt discouraged, they remembered that their counterparts on the other side of the sheet metal door had much worse conditions, with no fans and no freedom to move around. When these other hostages made trips to the shower or toilet, they kept to themselves. Apparently they had been ordered to remain silent.

Since the missionaries now had access to cold water after the arrival of the cooler, Ryan decided to share with the captives in the other room. To do this, he hid bags of cold water and snacks under his shirt and smuggled them into their room. He then lay down close to the gap below the sheet metal door so he could pass the things to the eleven people in the other room.

Since the interior of the room was dark, Ryan didn't think the guards would notice him even if one of them would happen to glance in. Some of the others were a bit nervous, remembering Froggy's warning that the food was only for the missionaries. To be safe, one of the other hostages usually stood outside the door, ready to sound an alarm if trouble approached. Ryan began doing this on a daily basis.

So badly wish I could tell my family we are okay! Rachel wrote in her diary. **Miss them and can't imagine how they are feeling.**

Matt's health was on the minds of the whole group. He had come without his medications.

When Lanmò San Jou arrived with his trademark escort of cologne and bodyguards, Sam petitioned him for Matt. Surely he could be released to go home, since he had a genetic condition that required specialized medications including an injection.

"He could die from this," Sam said. "It's very important that he has his medicine."

Lanmò San Jou, as expressionless as ever, agreed that Matt could go.

Sam, who preached to anyone, told Lanmò San Jou he should become a Christian.

"If you give me $17 million," Lanmò replied, "I'll become a Christian and see you in heaven."

9:30 p.m.

Later that night Matt was trying to sleep with his legs up the wall when he heard a vehicle approaching. He felt miserable, both from his condition and from the cramped quarters.

Sam, who was sleeping outside since the guards had given the okay for several of them to do that, leaped up. Lanmò San Jou had come back, intending to take Matt.

"If he's going, his wife has to go too," Sam told him.

"What? That's not possible."

"Okay," Sam said. "I can ask him, but I think he'll say he has to take his wife along."

Sam stuck his head in and called to Matt, "They're saying you can go."

"Can Rachel go too?"

"No."

"I'm not going without her."

Sam returned to Lanmò and reported Matt's decision.

"Oh, well!" The gang leader's voice was thick with sarcasm. "If he's not willing to leave without his wife, then it's not that bad."

Port-Au-Prince, Haiti

Phil Mast and his wife and daughter arrived in Port-au-Prince on Monday. After their arrival, Barry and Phil immediately headed to the U.S. Embassy for a meeting with officials.

At the embassy, Barry laid out his thoughts clearly. He respected the officials, but he wanted to make his position clear. "We believe in the Bible. We believe in the power of God. I'm not saying you don't, but we believe it in a way that we live out every day. We actually believe that God is still working."

Barry and Phil informed the officials that they were not planning to pay ransom, in accordance with the policy of their organization.

The officials were accustomed to taking care of things and providing solutions. "We have something for that," they would say when a need came up. "We can have that flown down."

Their generosity amazed Phil and Barry. It was almost as if all the resources of the U.S. government were at their disposal.

Barry continued to watch his phone, waiting for Lanmò San Jou to call again, demanding money. But no call came.

Berlin, Ohio, CAM Headquarters

High on a top shelf in Bobby Miller's office, a hand-carved wooden penholder from Haiti provided a daily reminder of the past. Bobby and his family lived in northern Haiti for years as missionaries for CAM. When they left the country, Haitian friends gave him a wooden souvenir, a carving of the outline of the country resting on wooden letters that spell *Bobby Miller.*

Bobby now served the ministry from an office in Ohio. But leaving Haiti had not removed his love for the country. He and his family still spoke fluent Creole and visited the country whenever they could.

Along with Phil, Bobby had been shocked by the discovery of sexual abuse in Haiti. As angry phone calls and emails rolled into the organization from around the country, Bobby and the other board members and administrators had sought the Lord. At one meeting after the crime came to light, a board member said he had never before seen so many grown men weeping at once.

Now, in the fall of 2021, no one had expected CAM Haiti to be in the news again. But that's what was happening. The headlines said it all:

CNN:

17 AMERICAN AND CANADIAN MISSIONARIES KIDNAPPED BY GANG MEMBERS IN HAITI

Forbes:

17 AMERICAN MISSIONARIES HELD HOSTAGE IN HAITI AFTER BEING KIDNAPPED BY GANG

The Washington Post:

AMERICAN MISSIONARIES AND FAMILY MEMBERS KIDNAPPED IN HAITI BY '400 MAWOZO' GANG, GROUPS SAY

Once again the phone lines to the Berlin office were jammed. The media pressed for answers. Sarcastic callers wondered why children were taken to such dangerous places. A few angry people made reference to the abuse scandal, indicating that the Haitian team was getting what they deserved. Most, however, pledged support.

Chapter nine

B-O-R-E-D

Tuesday, October 19; Day 4
Gangster Camp

A **boring day,** Wes christened Day 4 in his diary. To get a little exercise, the captives walked in a circle in the small area between the two houses.

The gangsters roamed around, their pants hanging low, dressed in sleeveless shirts or T-shirts. Many had the trademark shaved heads with long hair on top. Some of them had to hang onto their pants with one hand to keep them from falling completely down. The gang seemed to be a little low on guards, and Ping, the chief guard, looked tired.

Cheryl, the oldest member of the group, finally had enough of the low-riding pants. She called to one of the guards to pull up his pants, making the motion of pulling up around her own waist.

When the guard quickly pulled up his pants, all the missionaries clapped and cheered. It seemed the guards gave Cheryl a little more respect because of her age.

Austin, Kasondra, Brandyn, and some of the other Noeckers sometimes talked to the guards in English. The guards would answer back in Creole. This had the potential to be funny for everyone, but especially for those who knew both Creole and English.

However, the guards did not think it was funny if the Creole-speaking missionaries spoke English. They wanted the Americans who were able to speak Creole to speak it.

As Tuesday wore on, Ping sat on a chair with his gun, fighting sleep.

Matt, wearing extra-large white pants from the sack of donated clothes, noticed a broken mud flap by Ping's feet. With some imagination, it looked a little like a pistol. He walked right up to Ping and picked up the mud flap, then held it in his arms like a gun, with Ping staring at him in amazement.

"You can go to sleep," Matt said in his best Creole. "I'll guard."

He turned to face the others, looking like a prison convict in his ludicrous pants. "You may not run away!" he told them, brandishing his "gun." "I'm here to guard you."

For the first time since their captivity, all the missionaries had a good laugh. What a blessing to have Matt with them! Even Ping laughed, once he figured out Matt's joke.

That evening Dale noticed the guards snap into high alert. The missionaries had no idea what was going on, but the guards began loading their guns and running around. Everyone wondered if there would be a gun battle.

Suddenly a vehicle pulled in and something popped. For a second, Dale thought the noise was a gunshot. Whether the hostages were about to be shot or freed, Dale didn't know, but he thought it might be the end of their captivity. Surely this hum-drum existence could not go on much longer.

But when nothing came of the tension, Dale resigned himself and decided maybe it would be the weekend before they were released. Could they last a whole week?

Dale decided to try the love seat for sleeping that night. The guards still allowed some people to sleep outside. The only problem with the love seat was that it was about half the length of his body. As Dale struggled to get comfortable, one of the gangsters came over, motioned him off, and demonstrated the proper way to sleep on it.

After the demonstration, Dale lay back down. His next challenge was to keep from getting eaten alive. The mosquitoes, as usual, filled the air like a bloodthirsty smog. To protect as much skin as possible, Dale took a piece of extra clothing from the bag the gangsters had brought and tried his best to cover both his head and his feet with it. Soon the same guard returned. This time he patiently showed Dale that the piece of clothing was a skirt with multiple layers. By spreading out the fabric, it was long enough to cover both his feet and his head. The gangster then proceeded to tuck the pieces of fabric around Dale's feet and head.

Dale offered a prayer of thanks to God. He had never expected to be tucked into bed by a gangster. It was certainly a lot better than abusive treatment.

Walhonding, Ohio

Matt's family, like all the others, waited in an agony of suspense for updates. But Matt's younger sister comforted everyone with her insight. "Knowing Matt," she said, "when people are down, he's going to make some kind of dry, comical remark. He'll say something, maybe about the food, to get people laughing."

Matt's mom remembered the day when Matt, as a young boy, had been disciplined for cutting off the fringe of a black and white rug. When asked why he did it, Matt justified his behavior by pointing out that the rug reminded him of a skunk.

Hopefully, she thought, *my daughter is right and Matt is still going strong.*

8:30 a.m.–4:30 p.m.
Berlin, Ohio, Haiti Hostage Crisis Team

Bobby Miller took minutes in an all-day meeting concerning the hostages.

The newly formed Haiti Hostage Crisis Team was now responsible, along with the board of directors, for making decisions regarding the hostage situation. David Troyer, the general director of Christian Aid Ministries, and other members of the executive committee were on this team, as well as Phil Mast, who joined remotely from Haiti, and Bobby Miller.

The average age of the committee was forty-nine. They were all married with at least three children, with an average of five. Some had grandchildren. Every member of the committee of nine had been to Haiti for at least a short visit.

The team had organized themselves into roles. James Yoder was to be the main contact for the families of the hostages. Jay Stoltzfus would be the one to inform the staff at Christian Aid Ministries of any new developments and lead out in the daily prayer meetings for the kidnapping situation. Weston Showalter was to be the main contact for the media, while Bobby would be the secretary, being responsible for summarizing the discussions on paper.

More information kept trickling in about the nature of the 400 Mawozo gang. The group, which originated in the countryside east of Port-au-Prince, had recently expanded from stealing cars to stealing people. They were known for kidnapping religious workers as well as large groups. Officials estimated that the 400 Mawozo gang was responsible for 80 percent of all recent kidnappings in Haiti. Although they did not typically torture or abuse their captives, former hostages described minimal food and less-than-comfortable conditions.

In the middle of this traumatic day, a former executive committee member who no longer worked with CAM arrived with pastries and coffee. Greatly moved by the crisis, he wept and prayed for the team and everyone involved, strengthening and encouraging the others.

9 p.m.–2 a.m., CAM Board of Directors Meeting

At 9 p.m., about the time the gangster tucked Dale into bed, Tommy Wagler assembled the board of directors for another meeting. Like Barry and Phil, Tommy went into the meeting feeling confident that no ransom should be paid.

Like the Haiti Hostage Crisis Team, the CAM board consisted of nine Anabaptist men, with one man holding a position on both the crisis team and the board. Most, like Tommy, had served on the mission field in the past. Tommy was raised by missionary parents in Belize and had served in Kenya with his wife and children. Others had served in Paraguay, Romania, Ukraine, Cambodia, and Disaster Response Services for emergencies in the United States. All but one had visited Haiti, and one board member had lived there for some time.

The board members had day jobs too. There was a schoolteacher who also ran a duck farm, an accountant, a landscaper, a stainless-steel tank fabricator, a retiring general contractor, a retired farmer, a software developer, and a doctor. Tommy ran a small-equipment rental business.

As the group discussed the no-ransom policy, they realized they were not as committed to the policy as they had thought. Should a decision made when nothing was at stake be followed to the letter when lives were on the line? All the board members agreed that if the no-ransom policy was the only Biblical way to handle the crisis, it should be maintained. But did the teachings of the Bible prohibit complying with unscrupulous thieves to save lives? Was it wrong to give gangsters money in return for people? Or to comply with a robbery to protect life? Was there a precedent in the Bible?

When the meeting ended in the wee hours of the morning, no final decision had been made. Most of the board members had jobs waiting for them in the morning, and it was time to close the meeting.

Wednesday, October 20; Day 5
Gangster Camp

We have been singing and praying for the last hour, Dale wrote in his diary. Sitting underneath a palm branch shelter, somewhere in Haiti but we're not exactly sure where.

It was hard to believe that another day was dawning in captivity.

Ryan had spoken for everyone when he emerged from bed that morning singing new words to the tune of the well-known children's song "The B-I-B-L-E."

"I'm B-O-R-E-D, I'm B-O-R-E-D, I know I am, I'm sure I am, I'm B-O-R-E-D!"

In his mother's words, Ryan was experiencing what for him was "the worst punishment in the world"—nothing to do.

Most of the songs they sang, however, were inspirational Christian songs stitched together by memory. Melodi, especially, excelled at this, quoting verse after verse of Christian songs and hymns so the others could be reminded of the words. Austin also taught them a new song, "One More Miracle, Lord,"[1] with Melodi helping to piece the verses together:

> Lord, you walked the silver sands of the Galilean sea,
> You healed the crippled boy and made the blind to see.
> There's a need within my heart, have compassion now on me.
> I am asking for one more miracle, Lord.
>
> Lord, I thank you for your love, for your blessings and your care,

---

[1] © 2004 by Flo Mitchell. Used by permission.

You heal my little hurts, you hear my whispered prayer,
For you watch o'er all your children, all the time and everywhere,
And I'm asking for one more miracle, Lord.

Lord, I come to you today; is there grace enough for me?
Please take the storms away, or come and strengthen me;
If the miracle you send is to walk more close to thee,
Then I thank you for one more miracle, Lord.

Chorus:
Just the touch of your hand on my sin-weary soul,
Gentle touch of your hand and I know that I'll be whole.
There's a need within my heart, have compassion now on me,
I am asking for one more miracle, Lord.

It was hard to sing this song. Oh, it was easy to sing "Have compassion now on me," "Please take the storms away," and "There's a need within my heart." The hostages felt an acute neediness they had never known before. However, the words of the third verse sobered them.

Was it possible God had brought them to this gangster camp not to deliver them but to draw them closer to Himself through their difficult experiences? The missionaries knew that sometimes God answered prayer by delivering people out of trouble, and sometimes He answered prayer by giving people strength to face their troubles. By singing that last verse, they gave up their right to freedom if that's what God chose. They sang this song almost every day, along with "The Angel of the Lord." Most mornings they started with "I Owe the Lord a Morning Song."

Most of the songs were sung in English since the Noeckers and Austin knew little Creole. But the group was able to sing "Everything's All Right in My Father's House" in Creole.

Andre often picked "The Angel of the Lord" or "Little Black Sheep." Shelden's favorite was "I Have Decided to Follow Jesus," and he picked it every day. Other songs sung frequently included "Between Here and Sunset,"

"Open the Wells of Grace and Salvation," and "Unto Thee, O Lord."

This last song put the words of Psalm 25 to music, almost exactly as they appear in the King James Version. Matt in particular identified with the words of this psalm. He felt solidarity with David, the writer. Had David's situation been similar to this gangster camp when he wrote those timeless words? Had he also been fearing for his life and the lives of those he loved?

The captives were surprised that they could not remember more Scripture passages from memory. They had all memorized portions of Scripture in school or for other reasons. As a teacher for three years, Melodi had asked her students to memorize the first chapter of James, memorizing verses and coloring pictures to accompany the Scripture. By the end of the year, the young students had a book of verses and pictures based on the first chapter of James.

But it was more difficult than they had expected to pull up those passages.

The captives discussed how their muscles would become flabby from disuse if they did nothing but sit around.

"Except our wrists!" Courtney pointed out. "From running the fans." Of course, the parents fanned their children a lot when they were hot and miserable, but other people helped with this too.

The captives washed their clothes in a black tub. The wire running from the tree above the generator to the corner of the shower made a clothesline of sorts, so the men hung their wet clothes up to dry.

A blessing in this situation was that many of the hostages had experience in doing laundry without modern conveniences. During their time in Kenya, the Noeckers had not even had a wringer washer, but had scrubbed their clothes by hand. So while washing clothes by hand with questionable water was not exactly convenient, it wasn't as hard as it might have been. Cherilyn in particular enjoyed scrubbing clothes and offered to help the others.

The gangsters tried to supply the baby with diapers. They brought different sizes, sometimes newborn and sometimes toddler size. Thankfully, Melodi had been using cloth diapers and diaper covers, so these could be washed and reused as needed.

Andre had to be content with wearing the huge underwear whenever his other pair was being washed.

"I don't like this orphanage," Andre said to his mother. "I want to go home."

"Yes, I want to go home too," Melodi agreed. "Shall we pray and ask Jesus to take us home pretty soon?"

The hostages often thought of their families and homes and wondered how the news of the kidnapping had affected their loved ones.

I wonder what my parents and siblings are thinking, Dale wrote that night, his mind floating back to the hobby farm in Ontario where he had grown up. Wes thought of his home on a Tennessee plateau, with his mother's bakery close by and the outdoors he had explored as a child with his twin brother Weston and younger sister Carol. Kay thought of her Ohio home, her siblings and nieces and nephews. Sam thought of Pennsylvania and his brothers, who were sure to be worried about him. Matt and Rachel had each other, but they missed their families, knowing they must be terrified. Ryan and Melodi thought of their cozy home in Wisconsin, with

Ahaura, New Zealand

While the hostages slogged through long, hot afternoons in the gangster camp, a woman milking two Jersey cows halfway around the world remembered them in prayer.

It was springtime in New Zealand. As she milked the cows in the lean-to shed, she prayed for the hostages, especially for the mothers. She prayed that God would give them wisdom as they cared for their children in less than ideal circumstances.

Ryan's family close by. They wondered how Melodi's family in Oregon was doing.

The Noeckers wondered what was happening to their father and husband, Ray, back at Titanyen. And what about the four sisters back home in Michigan who had not come along to Haiti? Austin thought of his family, especially his little sister whose birthday was fast approaching.

With all this time to think, their homesickness grew.

Matt remembered an old lady from the time he had worked in the nursing home who repeated, "I just wanna go to bed, uh, bed, uh, bed." Matt revised her slogan to apply to the gangster camp. "I just wanna go to home, uh, home, uh, home!" Soon others were repeating the slogan. "I just wanna go to home, uh, home, uh, home!"

For all his humor, Matt was not doing well. Now on the fourth day without his prednisone, his ankles and fingers had begun to swell. Concerned, the other captives had a special prayer meeting for him.

Only one person of the seventeen felt completely at home: Laura. The eight-month-old had everything she needed—her mother, her father, her brother, and the same food source that had always sustained her. She also had a new family of admirers, captives and captors alike. Although she suffered from the fire ants and the hot, cramped

---

Lancaster City, Pennsylvania

A young mom rocking her eleven-month-old daughter thought of the baby held hostage in Haiti. As the recliner rocked back and forth and the baby fell asleep, the mother thought of how much her daughter's appetite had increased recently. Would the kidnapped baby in Haiti have enough food?

She prayed in the rocking chair, and again when she and her husband knelt beside their sofa before going to bed. She specifically prayed that God would give the gang a special compassion for the baby.

KIDNAPPED *in Haiti*

quarters, she was too young to make the connection between these discomforts and the gang that held them captive. She was at peace.

Perhaps because of this peace, Laura was a beacon of hope and happiness to the entire group. Dale described her as the hero of the group, and the best part of the tedious days. Laura could make the toughest gangsters smile, and everyone benefited from this. She loved the onslaught of attention and was always ready to entertain. While all the others suffered from unmet needs, as far as Laura was concerned, she was right at home.

Kay also had a distinct advantage, but in a different way. During the years when she had helped Julia care for her children, Kay often experienced boredom during afternoon naptimes. While Julia and the children slept, she had nothing to do. There was no one around to talk to and no bookcase full of books. She had learned to be content in sheer boredom.

Now, in the gangster camp, she realized that God had been preparing her for this day.

Kay also remembered that the men had talked about how they should be willing to preach in dangerous places. They had always wanted to get the Gospel out to unlikely people. Kay herself had wondered if they were doing all they could to share the Word of God.

Now they had gangsters to preach to. Kay suspected that Barry would also be using this opportunity to share the Gospel. As she pondered these things in the boring camp of the kidnapped, she gained reassurance and courage.

That evening it rained for two hours, turning the dusty yard into a muddy mess. The banks of trash glistened with fresh drops of rain. Since the hostages didn't like to stay inside unless they had to, many of them huddled under a tarp the gangsters had supplied. Ping inched his way around the camp, anxious to keep out of the mud. The cleanliness of his sandals was a big issue for him. They received a brushing almost on par with his teeth, whether they needed it or not.

As the missionaries prayed before going to bed, lightning flashed and thunder rumbled. Somehow it was comforting to see God's power in a place as foreign as a gangster camp.

That night Sam woke up with a nagging sense of evil. In some ways the gangster camp had felt that way ever since their arrival, but tonight Sam sensed something more. He wondered if Satan worship was happening close by. Unable to change his surroundings, he turned to God in prayer. Finally, feeling the presence of evil leave, he went back to sleep.

But not every midnight moment was discouraging for Sam. In the evenings, he often preached to the other captives, to the guards, or to whoever would listen. One night Sam heard someone in the other room crying out to God and confessing his sins. He hoped his words had encouraged and strengthened the fellow prisoner he could not see.

Chapter ten

INTERVALS OF BOREDOM AND TERROR

Thursday, October 21; Day 6
Berlin, Ohio, CAM Headquarters

*C*AM announced this day as a special day of fasting and prayer. "It is not only for the hostages, but also for the kidnappers, the government authorities, and the ongoing suffering of millions of Haitians," the announcement said.

Morning Prayer Time, Titanyen Base

Ray found morning devotional time at Titanyen powerful and encouraging. Even with their small group, the men sang songs together.

One day Phil shared a thought that Ray kept in mind for many days. "I often pray that the will of God will align with my will and that the captives will be set free. However, I need to remind myself to align my will with God's will and pray for His will to be done."

7:30 a.m., Gangster Camp

It's early in the morning, Dale wrote in his diary. The sun is just beginning to dry out the mud. Another boring day stretches before us. It's hard to see these men bound by the devil. I could really use a Bible right now for some inspiration. Not having access to one makes me more sympathetic to believers in restricted countries.

Living in a gangster camp, the group decided, was sheer boredom interspersed with intervals of sheer terror. With almost nothing to do, it was hard to feel motivated about anything. The group spent much time praying and singing, but overall there was just not much to do.

The hostages sensed a pattern emerging. After rising, they had a time of singing and prayer. Froggy would arrive anytime between nine and two with the first meal of the day. If Baby Laura was asleep when he arrived, his booming voice invariably awakened her. Spaghetti was the standard fare for breakfast, with half a hard-boiled egg each. Sometimes the menu included bread or avocados.

Froggy often had a young assistant with him, a boy of about eleven or twelve years old named Bigotry.

"Why aren't you in school?" Melodi asked him occasionally.

He always had an excuse of some kind. Either school was not in session or there was some other reason. The group felt sorry for Bigotry. What would it be like to grow up in such an environment? They noticed that he even helped distribute drugs to the other gang members. What chance did this young boy have to stay drug-free himself?

Throughout the day, the captives prayed, sang, and asked God to deliver them. As the days passed, they began to fight discouragement. *Surely we'll get out of here soon,* they thought. *Maybe by the weekend. But what if we don't? Does anyone know for sure where we are or what is happening to us?* Hidden in the Haitian bush, the group felt very alone.

Supper was rice and beans with fish sauce or cooked vegetables, arriving anytime between 4 p.m. and 8 p.m. The captives held another time of prayer and singing before retiring for the night. At this time, the guards made a point of closing all the doors and windows.

As time went on, the hostages concluded that the gangsters had no interest in killing them. Living hostages were clearly more valuable to them than dead ones. And why would they bring fans and snack foods to people they planned to kill?

Kay and the other ladies also relaxed. It seemed the guards did not mean to harm them, so they began to move out of the house more freely.

But as the threat of murder and abuse wore off, another appeared. Sickness.

Of course, Matt's condition was a constant concern. Pain lit up the nerves in his joints and fingers.

Cheryl too was getting sick and struggling with severe pain due to an inflammation. Her condition seemed to be deteriorating rapidly, and everyone was worried.

Andre, who had vomited the first night, had occasionally vomited since then and sometimes cried of stomach pain.

Matt's wife Rachel struggled with gluten sensitivity, which did not mesh well with morning spaghetti. The group finally helped support her by saving a portion of rice and beans from the evening meal for her to eat in the morning. They also saved some for Shelden and Andre, who needed something in their stomachs before breakfast, which sometimes didn't come until 1 p.m. or later.

Melodi felt okay, but as a breastfeeding mother who weighed only 120 pounds when she arrived at the gangster camp, she was almost always hungry. She wondered if she was receiving enough food to keep herself and Laura well nourished. And would Laura stay in good health despite the countless fire ant bites she received during the night?

Ryan's contacts had stayed in his eyes now for six days straight. This was something he would never have dreamed of doing at home.

Then a new health danger appeared. As the hostages scratched the mosquito and fire ant bites on their feet and arms, some of them broke open. Soon the bites became festering wounds. They grew red, hot, and swollen, with pus forming in them.

The guards explained that the canal water contained microbes, small invisible bugs and worms. When the hostages took their bucket showers, these microbes entered the open sores and worked their way under the skin.

Together the group prayed for health for everyone, especially for Matt. They also tried to convince the gang to let Cheryl leave. Lanmò San Jou came and took a look at Cheryl, but he didn't seem concerned.

2:47 p.m., News Release

The *Los Angeles Times* reported the following on the gang leader's threats:

> The leader of the 400 Mawozo gang that police say is holding seventeen members of a kidnapped missionary group is seen in a video released Thursday saying he will kill them if he doesn't get what he's demanding.
>
> The video posted on social media shows Wilson Joseph dressed in a blue suit, carrying a blue hat and wearing a large cross around his neck.
>
> "I swear by thunder that if I don't get what I'm asking for, I will put a bullet in the heads of these Americans," he said in the video.
>
> He also threatened Prime Minister Ariel Henry and the chief

of Haiti's National Police, Leon Charles, as he spoke in front of open coffins that apparently held several members of his gang who were recently killed.

"You guys make me cry. I cry water. But I'm going to make you guys cry blood," he said.

5 p.m., Gangster Camp

Two gunshots popped in quick succession. Six-year-old Shelden was terrified, and fear struck the hearts of the others too. Some of the guards quickly left the area, and those who stayed paced nervously.

When the sun went down, the group of missionaries huddled under the tree trunk shelter with palm leaves for a roof.

That night sleep eluded most of them. They lay awake listening to Andre screaming and moaning because of his stomach pain.

Friday, October 22; Day 7

"I feel like a stale pretzel," Austin announced the next morning. Many of the others felt the same. Some, however, wished they only felt that bad.

Ryan and Melodi had not slept much at all. Nor had anyone not gifted with Kasondra's skill of sleeping through anything.

Very bad night, Melodi wrote. **Cherilyn took Laura outside for several hours towards morning. Saw seven shooting stars and many satellites.**

Cheryl felt even worse than the day before. She had hardly slept and was in terrible pain. It was so bad that she pounded the walls of the house in her distress.

"It was bad," her daughter Cherilyn recalled later. "She was flat out on the bed."

At morning prayer, the group prayed that Cheryl could be released to go to the hospital. Perhaps they could all be released with her. Only God knew.

Slowly the day dragged on, with various people entertaining hope for deliverance. The group sprawled on mattresses, couches, and chairs outside. Some of them showered.

The guards did not seem to be listening to the pleas for help for Cheryl. Finally Cheryl didn't know if she could go on.

"I need prayer," she said. "I can't handle this. It is just too much for me."

The group surrounded her, laid their hands on her, and prayed. Back home in Michigan, Cheryl might have gone to the doctor's office or the emergency room. Here there were no options like that, and the group cried out to God for one more miracle.

Feeling the desperation of sickness with no access to medical care, many of them began to think seriously of escaping.

Wes noticed that by now only a few guards carried their guns openly around the group. And the guns they did have were not exactly the latest model. One was a shotgun with a bent barrel held together with a zip tie. Another was an old-style assault rifle. Ping, of course, still carried a pistol in his back pocket, or sometimes in the waistband of his underwear.

The single men discussed the situation. It would be easy for one or two of them to slip away into the brush. The guards were not watching all of them all the time. Likely one or two of them could remain unnoticed for several hours.

"What would you do if I escaped?" Sam asked Ping one day.

Ping gave Sam some fatherly advice. It was a bad idea, he said. He explained that if the missionaries all escaped, the guards would be shot. If Sam tried to escape and was caught, they would shoot him. And if Sam or a few of the others escaped successfully, the remaining hostages would be shot.

Even though no one was sure if these threats were real, it put a damper on their thoughts of escape. They also remembered Barry's coaching to think and act like a team. They would stay together.

I'm really wondering what my family is thinking by now, Dale wrote in his diary. I feel much better about a safe deliverance than I did the first few days. However it happens, I hope the gang doesn't receive any money from the government, CAM, or our families. If we get out of this alive, I hope CAM Haiti keeps operating. I'm not ready to go home because of this.

The group spent a lot of time in prayer, pleading for deliverance.

2:30 p.m., Berlin, Ohio

Christian Aid Ministries invited those following the situation to send words of encouragement for the families of the hostages to a designated email address.

Ladysmith, Wisconsin

Ryan's mom shared with the church ladies how much Melodi's message a few weeks earlier had meant to her.

"Ladies, Melodi told us several weeks ago that Ryan said he wouldn't trade the last three months for anything! It was just such a confirmation that Ryan and Melodi are in the middle of God's will! It's such a comfort. God knows exactly what He's doing! Stand still and see the salvation of the Lord—and pray!

"I know very well this could end in death, but I believe the words in a song we sing: 'How sweet would be our children's fate, if they like them could die for thee!'"[1]

Evening, Gangster Camp

Lanmò San Jou stopped in for a visit. With him was his second in

---

[1] From the song "Faith of Our Fathers."

command, a man later nicknamed Pop-A-Wheelie Chief because of his penchant for popping wheelies with almost any vehicle or bike he drove. One day while trying to drive on the back wheel of his motorbike, he almost decapitated himself on the electric wire that doubled as a clothesline. Santa Claus, who could help with communicating in English, was also along.

Lanmò, loaded with black bracelets and cologne as always, explained that he wanted the hostages to call their boss and pressure him to pay the ransom. The missionaries said they didn't know the number.

While the gangsters went to find a phone, the captives made a plan. They needed to memorize the phone number in case they ever got a chance to call Barry themselves. Haitian telephone numbers consisted of two sets of four numbers. When someone handed him the phone, Ryan told the first set of numbers to one person and the second set to someone else. With this number secure, they could record the number in the journals and all of them could set about memorizing the eight digits.

Even though he didn't understand English, Lanmò put the call on speakerphone so he could get in on it as soon as possible. The sound of a phone ringing filled the air in the gangster camp as the group breathlessly waited for Barry to pick up.

"Hey, how are you?" It was Barry's voice!

"We're hanging in there."

"Are you all together?"

"Yes, we're together."

Borneo, Indonesia

"Just want to let you know that we are praying for the release of our seventeen brothers and sisters still held hostage in Haiti.

"We are sure that the Father will protect them, the Holy Spirit will comfort them, and Jesus will give them peace—and together with the host of heaven will free them eventually.

"Many blessings and love for all the families of the seventeen as well."

"The whole world is praying for you!"

By this time, it was clear to Lanmò that no pressure was being applied. Incensed, he grabbed the phone and ended the call.

It hadn't been long, but hearing Barry's voice and the comfort that prayers were ascending around the world refreshed the group and brought emotions to the surface. They were not alone! Tears of joy slid down their faces.

Later Santa Claus came to check on Matt's medical condition. He promised to try to get some medicine.

Santa Claus reiterated that the group was held hostage because of the imprisonment of their leader. **This gang wants him released, so we are here till he is released unless God works a miracle,** Rachel wrote in her diary.

That night the captives in the next room had a concerned question: "Why didn't you sing today?" The missionaries hadn't realized that their discouragement had been so obvious.

7 p.m., Titanyen Base

That night, with a number supplied to him by government officials, Barry called Lanmò San Jou.

Lanmò explained that the kidnapping had nothing to do with CAM or Barry. Instead, the gang leader was angry with the Haitian government.

"They give us these guns, they pay us to do their work, and then they come in here and arrest us and shoot us. Those were my men in the caskets," he said, referring to the video he had released. "They're going to have to pay."

He wanted the top leader of the gang, a man named YonYon, released from prison.

"That is out of my control," Barry said. "If you want someone from the government, you have to kidnap someone in the government."

CAM Board

Tommy Wagler, chairman of the CAM board, spoke to a group of Anabaptist pastors and educators about ransom. The group did not feel that paying ransom was necessarily wrong, but they conceded that not paying ransom was also a valid option.

The families of the hostages were also raising questions about ransom. Does the Bible teach against it? What if the families paid some ransom? Would this make things hard for CAM in the future? Other family members felt strongly that paying ransom would indicate a failure to trust God.

Tommy and the rest of the board braced for a big meeting the next day.

Chapter eleven

FOOD DISCUSSIONS AND SPIRITUAL BATTLES

Saturday, October 23; Day 8

Gangster Camp

A week ago, we were getting ready to head to the orphanage, Dale wrote in his diary on Saturday morning. He was covered in mosquito bites, as usual, but grateful that he wasn't being held in a country where malaria was prevalent.

The good news for the morning was that since yesterday's prayer for Cheryl's health, she had begun to feel much better. What a blessing to feel God moving on their behalf! There had been no medical help, but God had answered their prayers and relieved her suffering. The hostages thanked and praised God.

Their medical concerns had not disappeared, however. On almost everyone, the mosquito bites continued to become infected from the contaminated water, creating boil-like, festering sores. But to have one person experience relief brought a renewed spirit to the whole group.

Froggy had not provided the group with combs. To comb their hair, the women resorted to plastic forks. It was a poor excuse for a comb, so they did their best to make their hairdos last for several days. Wearing a veil helped conceal some of the hair problems.

There were also no razors. The men felt their facial hair growing, and saw it on others, but neither the women with the fork-combed hair nor the men with the untrimmed faces could see the effect of these changes on themselves—there was no mirror.

To pass the time, the group walked in circles. The guards still wanted the hostages to stay between the two houses. To keep them from straying too far, the guards hung a tarp between the buildings at the east end.

One day, after a rain, Ryan removed the tarp so the breeze could come through and dry out the mud. His plan worked quite well until the guards came along and put the tarp back up.

So instead of walking around the prison house, they had to walk in circles. Loop after loop of the same scenery, the same banks of trash, the same two buildings, and the same outhouse was depressing.

I'm so ready for some privacy, Rachel wrote in her diary. **Privacy is definitely not a thing around here.**

In the afternoon, a pattern was emerging. By about 4:00, most of the hostages' thoughts and conversation turned to the food they wished they could have. The standard fare of spaghetti for breakfast and rice and beans for the evening meal kept them alive, but it never seemed quite enough. And usually there was no meat or vegetables.

Sometimes the food came in seventeen portions. At other times Froggy brought a six-quart kettle of rice that needed to be dished out into foam bowls. Courtney was always quick to jump up and do the dishing out. Melodi noted that, in addition to a servant heart, Courtney had a good eye for judging how much food should go into each bowl to divide it equally.

Cherilyn became the silverware washer. Although other people did wash the "dishes" sometimes, she was the one who did it most often.

Melodi, eating for both herself and Laura, could always have eaten more. When possible, others shared with her. Kay often slipped her hard-boiled egg portion to Melodi at breakfast, under the pretense that she didn't really like them. This was consistent with Kay's way of living. When the group gathered on the couches and chairs, Kay "preferred" sitting on an upturned bucket rather than on the couch.

After returning home, Kay admitted the truth to her mother. "I often just didn't eat much because I knew the others needed the food more than I did. There was just not enough to reach around."

The snacks that Santa Claus brought helped, but they posed their own dilemma. Should they eat them up as quickly as possible, assuming they would be going home soon? Or should they ration them in case they still had many days ahead of them?

Austin or Cherilyn would often start the conversation about food. Cherilyn would mention the Thai curry dishes her mother cooked. Or Austin would talk about the pizza his mom would make every Saturday night, or the seafood chowder she made at Christmas time. She would probably be making pizza this Saturday night. She might be starting to prepare it already, thousands of miles away. Too bad she couldn't deliver. As he described the dripping pizza sauce or the cheese stringing off each bite, others thought of the foods they loved.

"Oh, is this the time of day when we start talking about food again?" someone else would say.

Wes and Dale craved peanut butter. Of course, a bowl of it mixed with pancake syrup would be best, but just one big spoonful would do.

Wes knew without a doubt that his mother was back in Tennessee baking cookies and pies for local stores. What a pity she couldn't add this gangster camp to her route. But usually Wes was quick to find a different conversation when food came up.

"I tried to change the subject," he said later, "because I couldn't handle it."

In general, the men craved meat. Any meat. The women dreamed of leafy salads with strips of chicken or steak, a generous shower of real cheese, and a drizzle of dressing.

Much rhapsodizing about food, Melodi wrote that afternoon.

"What do you want for your first meal when we get home?" she asked Ryan. She tried to picture what she had in her freezer back at the Titanyen base. She knew they had cheese. The Noecker family had brought cheese from the States, a special treat not available in Haiti, and had given everyone some. They also had bread. They decided their first meal back at the base would be egg sandwiches with cheese.

Melodi knew she was likely not eating enough calories for a breastfeeding mother, even with the donation of Kay's hard-boiled egg at breakfast. But Laura did seem to be getting enough. She was a happy little girl, and for that Melodi was grateful. Little did she know that specific prayers of people around the world were being answered.

9 a.m.–5 p.m., Berlin, Ohio

The CAM administration rallied its members for an all-day Saturday meeting. The meeting revealed that despite the no-ransom policy, some of the CAM board and other leadership, as well as some members of the families of the hostages, thought ransom could be appropriate depending on the situation. After lunch each member took a turn sharing his personal thoughts. Bobby Miller recorded minutes as usual, sorting through the extensive conversations to condense them into something legible.

As they considered the ransom question, board chairman Tommy Wagler and the rest of the group in Ohio felt the weight of making a decision that affected the lives of other people. Tommy sensed that no matter what they decided, some people would be unhappy. While others could discuss these

things without making a decision, Tommy and the board did not have that luxury. They had to reach a conclusion.

The meeting ended with another idea. Since the gang had publicly claimed an interest in advancing the health and wellness of their own communities in Haiti, perhaps they would accept humanitarian aid instead of money.

10:15 a.m., Titanyen Base

Lanmò San Jou called Barry again on Saturday. He was no longer demanding $17 million—only $14 million.

"We aren't paying money," Barry said.

"No money, no white people."

Sometimes when Barry talked to the gang leader, he wondered if there was a second person involved. But the government officials reminded him that the man was often high on drugs, which could account for variations in his voice and tone. Lanmò lived a dark life, practicing a type of black voodoo that most Haitians, even those who practiced voodoo, did not approve of.

"Don't forget," Barry told Lanmò, "you're dealing with people who serve Jesus."

"Don't forget, I serve King Lucifer."

Sunday, October 24; Day 9
Gangster Camp

"Would I still be able to love and forgive if I buried a child here?"

Ryan's hypothetical question struck Melodi's heart. She didn't burst into tears, but she felt them threatening. Both Laura and Andre had cried for much of the night, and by this morning both she and Ryan were exhausted. Kay had taken a turn with Laura for an hour or two around midnight to give Melodi a break.

At morning prayer, Melodi choked up as the group prayed around the circle. Thirteen-year-old Kasondra crept over to her and put her arm around her shoulders.

"Thank you, Kasondra," Melodi said. "You're a brick!"

Austin shared a short message, after which the group sang and prayed until the spaghetti and hard-boiled eggs arrived.

To pass the time and add inspiration to the surroundings, Cherilyn wrote Bible verses on the blue walls inside the house. Beside the outside door she wrote, "The fear of the Lord is the beginning of wisdom." In the back corner she wrote out John 3:16. Straight in from the door she wrote, "The angel of the Lord encampeth round about them that fear him, and delivereth them. O taste and see . . ." Here her pencil ran out.

After more walking in circles for exercise, Wes and Dale scratched a checkers board into the dirt. They had noticed bottle caps lying around in the dirt, so they collected enough caps in two colors for a game of checkers.

The hostages had discovered several tailless lizards running around the compound. The little creatures ran so fast they were almost impossible to catch. When they finally grabbed hold of one, it just shed its tail and kept running. They all laughed, knowing it could grow a new one. Brandyn and the other men and boys especially tried catching them. But the wiry little creatures, even the de-tailed one, evaded their grasp.

A gangster with orange dreadlocks told Sam that the gang only wanted money in exchange for the hostages. "They are not asking for a prisoner release," he said. "Just money." Could it be that there were two opinions in the gang?

On Sunday evening, after a long, boring day, the hostages looked up in amazement to see their own vehicle driving into the gangster camp. Could it be that the Lord had answered their prayers and they could go home?

They soon saw that the ride was for five people in the other room. Although it was disappointing to not get released, the missionaries were encouraged to see other people going free. In addition, the night was cooler and the clouds of mosquitoes slightly less oppressive.

A persistent sense of evil permeated the camp. Many things reinforced this feeling—the cigarette smoke hanging in the air, the cocaine circulating among the guards, the continual cursing and arguing, and the prostitutes that came and went. The hostages wondered, however, if there was some deeper reason.

Whenever the guards could get their solar-powered radios to work, ugly music vibrated across the camp. The music reminded those who understood Creole that not understanding Creole was a blessing in some ways. One of the gangsters informed the missionaries that the black bracelets worn by most gang members were good luck charms to provide safety. Apparently Lanmò San Jou and the other leaders needed more protection than the lower-level members because they wore many more bracelets.

By now, Froggy's claims to be a Christian rang hollow. With the voodoo beads around his neck, the hostages were beginning to suspect him of being the camp witch doctor. In addition to bringing them supplies, he carried on a brisk trade with the guards, selling them cigarettes and cocaine.

Whenever Froggy pulled into the camp, loud, violent music usually blared from his vehicle. If he had nothing playing when he arrived, he made sure to turn it on at high volume before getting out with the food or other items.

Beyond the evil they could see and hear, the missionaries sensed a hidden darkness, as if they were stepping into a hornets' nest of unseen demons. Perhaps Satan had been the only god worshiped in this place for years, and suddenly his archenemy, Jesus Christ, was being worshiped through prayer, singing, and preaching. Thousands of prayers were also pouring toward the gangster camp from around the world.

Not only did the guards calmly announce that they served Satan and planned to go to hell, but they did it with a smile on their faces. "I'm going to hell after I die" or "Satan loves us" seemed to be acceptable, even pleasant, realities.

The missionaries hated the deception the guards experienced, and Sam and others preached relentlessly about God's love, even when mocked by Lanmò San Jou. Some of the Haitians believed that Haitians are inherently sons of the devil, while white people are sons of God. The missionaries tried to refute this belief, telling the guards that God loved them and was calling them to something much better than their life of sin.

"During the first few weeks, we did more spiritual warfare than I have ever done in my life," Sam remembered. "It was literally exhausting."

One day Brandyn found a snake. Sam had a habit of calling creatures such as lizards and tarantulas his "pets." Not to be outdone, Brandyn picked up the snake. When he put it back down, some of the others began throwing rocks at it. Brandyn protested against the harassment of his "pet" and tried to block the rocks.

When the guards noticed what was going on, they became upset. "Don't kill the snake!" one of them said. "If you kill the snake, Satan will bite you."

The forces of evil seemed very real in the gangster camp. Most disturbing of all, the little boys seemed to be behaving strangely.

Andre continued to wake up in the middle of the night, screaming and crying. Sometimes it seemed logical. "I'm hot. I'm hot," he would say, and Melodi would try to comfort him. Sometimes she felt like screaming too. The relentless heat, the mosquitoes and fire ants, and the cramped quarters were hard for anyone to endure. Andre also often complained of stomach pain.

But there seemed to be something more. Ryan and Melodi didn't want to see a demon behind every bush, but they were beginning to wonder if some sinister power wasn't having an effect on their son. Andre was now three years old, and though he still cried when he was sick or tired, they had always been able to calm him down.

"It felt like there was something different going on," Melodi said later. "It seemed like he was being unreasonable, as if he didn't even hear us. He seemed out of control, just crying and screaming."

Shelden also had unusual fits of crying.

Melodi kept her thoughts to herself, but she wondered, *Is some kind of spiritual darkness attacking the children?*

Sam listened to the children and wondered the same thing. "We began to cry out in the name of Jesus Christ," he said later. " 'O Lord, deliver us!' we prayed. 'Fight the powers of Satan!' "

Others would wake up in the night too and sense the presence of evil. One night Rachel woke up Matt. "I'm scared," she said.

Matt blinked, adjusting himself to his surroundings. "Shall I pray for you?" he asked.

"Yes."

There was no privacy, and Matt didn't want to wake up anyone else. He put his arms around his wife and whispered a prayer, asking God to help her feel His presence.

"I feel so much better," Rachel said.

Sunday Service, Titanyen Base

On Sunday morning, those still at the base in Titanyen gathered for church. The group was small: Barry and Julia and their five children; Phil and Grace, with their daughter Olivia; and Ray Noecker. A few others were also there to support them, including a construction worker and the Shenksters, an Anabaptist family from the Blue Ridge International for Christ mission in Port-au-Prince.

Ray's daughters from the United States wanted to join their father, but government officials strongly advised against more people going to Haiti.

After singing, Phil shared a devotional. Usually a calm and reserved man, he felt excited this morning as he talked about the spiritual battle they faced. His animation and enthusiasm stirred the others to engage in the spiritual battle through prayer. Lanmò San Jou had stated it clearly: he served Satan and the missionaries served God.

This was not a battle of money or a war of wits. It was a battle in the unseen realm, in principalities that did not appear in an atlas. No human sword could defeat this foe. Only the armor described in Ephesians 6 could win out.

Ladysmith, Wisconsin

"While I still beg God's protection for them," Ryan's mom wrote for her husband to share with their church, "I am learning to ask more for spiritual blessings.

- For strength to endure.

- For faithfulness.

- For love in the face of mistreatment.

- That I can learn, remember, and live by the lessons God is sending my way.

"We all want to grow, and God helps us grow, but the wrapping paper is usually PAIN."

Ryan's mom had no idea what question Ryan had asked himself and Melodi that morning in the gangster camp.

2:00 p.m.–7:30 p.m., Berlin, Ohio

The crisis team met again in the central conference room for another long meeting. They were joined by Tommy Wagler, the board chairman. Most of the men arrived in their Sunday dress shirts. They took their seats around the square of tables. The general director, David Troyer, sat diagonally across from the door, close to the overhead computer screen. His son Phil and Jay Stoltzfus joined him on the left leg of the tables. Mike Hershberger, Tommy Wagler, and Weston Showalter took positions on the back table, facing the screen. Bobby Miller sat on the right-hand leg of tables, along with the three Jameses: James B. Mullet, James Yoder, and James R. Mullet. Phil Mast, in Haiti, joined virtually part-time, along with other board members.

The team had had an exhausting week. Now, on their day of rest, they had to be at the office again instead of at home on their recliners. There would be no ping-pong games with the children for James Yoder, and James B. Mullet wouldn't be playing hide-and-seek or Settlers with his grandchildren.

They started the meeting with a song, "Come, Gracious Spirit, Heavenly Dove." They sensed a deep need for the presence of the Holy Spirit. The men were moved as they sang the song in harmony.

As the song ended, Bobby straightened out of his prayerful pose and reached for his laptop. There would be plenty of minutes to take. The work ahead was more taxing than heavy physical labor. There were agonizing decisions to be made—decisions that could affect the lives of seventeen people.

The team felt good about the idea of offering food boxes to the gang. In addition to this, they discussed the topic of allowing anonymous volunteers to pay ransom. A dizzying number of people had offered to help, and it was tricky to make sense of it all. Government officials had asked the large team to make a decision soon. They were losing time.

Tommy, the board chairman, explained that the board had agreed to stay the course with no cash payment for now, but they were open to re-examining the cash ransom option if the situation presented no other practical alternative.

5 p.m., Titanyen Base

Barry called the gang leader again and spoke to a different gangster boss.

"Where's the money at?" the man asked.

"We don't pay money," Barry said. Barry broached the topic of humanitarian aid, but the gang leader insisted that only money would do.

Chapter twelve

PRAYER FOR DELIVERANCE

Monday, October 25; Day 10
Gangster Camp

O n Day 10, the group decided to add a third prayer time to the routine of each day. Brandyn set an alarm on his watch for 1 p.m. This prayer would have a focus. They would specifically ask God for deliverance.

For the children, daytime went better than nighttime. Wes and Melodi told the children stories, drawing on the vast number of books and stories they had read. Matt teased Andre and Shelden, playing with them.

Little Laura, though she had her moments of crying, basked in the attention of her suddenly large family. She explored the world around her as if she were on a global tour. Every new sight was a wonder of the world, and every new person was a dignitary.

She began her daily tour, chirping merrily, around 5:30 or 6:00 as the others awakened. Since Laura was hungry for breakfast, Melodi awakened then as well, whether she felt like getting up or not.

The Noecker girls, who had dreamed of starting a baby orphanage, often took Laura outside after Melodi had fed her. The baby bounced back and forth between people, although Ryan and Melodi requested that she not be given to the guards.

By morning prayer time, usually starting around 8:30-9:00, Laura was ready for a nap. Courtney often put Laura to sleep. She seemed to have a special touch that convinced Laura it was naptime, and Laura would fall asleep in her arms. Often one of the other girls braided Laura's hair where it grew longest at the top of her head. She would sleep through all of prayer time, usually lasting an hour or two.

Although the guards didn't hold Laura, they came right up to her face, and she would smile and laugh at them. She would fiddle with their beards or grab their jewelry with her iron baby grip. She soon learned that the sound of an approaching vehicle meant the arrival of another admirer, usually one of the gang leaders. She would flap her hands excitedly.

Andre had also adjusted by now, although he still asked to go home at times. He sometimes took up Matt's mantra from the nursing home, repeating, "I just wanna go to home, uh, home, uh, home!" Repeated by a three-year-old, this phrase became even more hilarious. When Matt teased him, Andre would say, "Matt, Matt, Matt, that's enough out of you."

Andre had not made this up on his own. The men had a habit of repeating each other's names. Matt would say, "Wes, Wes, Wes," or "Sam, Sam, Sam," or "Dale, Dale, Dale."

But it was extra funny when Andre said it.

Henrietta remained a member of the family too, even though Matt still found the chicken's appearance disturbing.

Austin too had a run-in with the mangy chicken. One night he and three of the other men were sleeping on a double mattress outside. Finally Austin concluded that it was just too tight. He slid to the ground to sleep about six inches away from the mattress.

Henrietta was not sleeping, however. Since the guards had taken down her normal roosting spot, she roamed around at night. About every half hour, she made her way past Austin. But rather than go around him on the side where there was plenty of room, she insisted on walking between him and the mattress. In the morning, Austin found scratches on his arm from one of her passages.

One day during prayer time, Kay saw Henrietta approaching some food under Rachel's chair. To keep the chicken from getting the food, Kay threw something at her. The chicken, right beside Matt, squawked loudly.

Startled, and suddenly becoming aware of Henrietta, Matt jumped, throwing up his legs and almost falling off his seat. This incident did not improve Matt and Henrietta's relationship.

When Wes and Melodi got done telling stories to the children, they often started talking about books they had read. Austin, an avid reader, and some of the other book lovers also bobbed in and out of the conversation.

Of course, no actual books were available, but their memories served them well. Those who had read the story retold it as best they could, with each person contributing scenes and memories to the discussion. It was a great way to pass the time.

Of particular interest was the discussion about the book *In the Presence of My Enemies*. This book detailed how a radical Muslim gang had kidnapped American missionaries Mr. and Mrs. Burnham and others in the Philippines. They had also been with an organization with a no-ransom policy.

The American missionaries in the Philippines had been held for an astonishing length of time. Although none of the missionaries recalled exactly how long, they were pretty sure that it had been at least eight months.

Because the Burnhams were Americans, they were held for political ransom, a situation similar to the way Santa Claus had described their own position. In the book, the kidnappers were eventually willing to accept ransom, and a ransom was paid. However, the kidnappers did not release the missionaries, instead asking for more ransom. They were moved from place to place as the gang and the Filipino army fought multiple gun battles. Over time, some of the hostages were released while others were killed. Eventually they were nearing starvation. When the Filipino army moved in to rescue them, all three remaining hostages were shot, with only one surviving.

Although there didn't seem to be much danger of being shot by the 400 Mawozo gang, the simmering illnesses and the worsening sores nagged at everyone's thoughts. *Surely,* they concluded, *this won't go on much longer. Surely we will get out of here soon.*

The only trouble was, the missionaries in the book had said the same thing—month after month.

As Wes, Austin, and Dale lay outside late in the evening, they discussed the problem of talking about the guards. Whenever someone in the group mentioned one of the guards by name, the guards wanted to know what they were talking about and demanded a translation. So why not come up with nicknames for all of them?

As the mosquitoes swarmed in the hot night, they assigned a nickname to each guard. The head chief, Lanmò San Jou, became Beanie, while one of the guards who was always losing his clothes became Eeyore. There was also Carrot Top, Henry, Johnny, and Charlie Horse.

Earlier that evening when Santa Claus had brought some snacks, the hostages had sung the song "There Is a God" while he videoed parts of it.

No one could figure out on which side Santa Claus really was, or if he was on a side. Could it be that he was just bringing them food and English conversation out of the goodness of his heart? If it really was an act of goodness, it was certainly out of place in a gangster camp.

We were confused after he left, Rachel recorded, **because he says we are here because of government issues, but all the gangsters say we are here until they get ransom money.**

Berlin, Ohio, CAM Headquarters

CAM announced a 24/7 prayer chain on their website. "Those who would like to pray daily until the situation is resolved are asked to send in the fifteen-minute time period in which they would like to pray."

Central Conference Room, CAM Headquarters

This long meeting commenced with a reading from Psalm 55: "Give ear to my prayer, O God, and hide not thyself from my supplication!"

The meeting began with a reminder of the urgency of making a final decision on how to negotiate with the gang. Government officials wanted to know soon and indicated that if no ransom was paid, they needed to negotiate on a different level. This could possibly end in a tactical approach, endangering the lives of both gangsters and hostages.

Speaking for the CAM Haiti base, Phil Mast suggested it might be best to refuse payment of any kind, both monetary and humanitarian, in keeping with their policy. He and Barry saw the confrontation as a spiritual battle between good and evil that would not be won with material things. He advocated simple faith in God. However, he indicated a willingness to carry out whatever the team in Ohio decided.

Concern was raised that refusing to pay a ransom might encourage the government to forcibly rescue the missionaries. Was it sensible to risk human lives over an issue that was not spelled out in Scripture?

Not everyone agreed. Some believed paying a ransom would have a negative impact on all missions in Haiti. Others believed it would be worse if the hostages were killed or abused because of a refusal to pay ransom.

"There were tense moments," Weston Showalter recalled later. "There were times that some of us unloaded."

David Troyer, general director and founder of Christian Aid Ministries, suggested that a group of administrators travel to Haiti to get a better understanding of the situation and to support the team at Titanyen. Others pointed out that government officials did not think that was a good idea because of the political unrest.

The team finally concluded they would rather be proactive and offer humanitarian aid now, rather than wait until some of the hostages had been abused or killed.

They hoped the gang would accept the aid and release the hostages. If this did not happen, they would have to face the cash ransom question head-on.

Titanyen Base

Barry continued sharing the Gospel with Lanmò San Jou whenever he could.

"You need Jesus," he would say. "We love you!"

One time the gang leader paused, then replied, "I love you."

Another time the gang leader called and said, "Come and get them," then hung up.

Barry called him back. "Where?"

"You know where I am."

"No, I don't."

"Don't forget the money. Just give us a little money. We have wives and children."

The FBI commended Barry for his conversations with Lanmò. "Barry, you're doing a very good job," they said.

Barry felt he was building a relationship with Lanmò. He felt confident that God would work through this contact, just as He had with the gang leaders around Titanyen.

"But we had to admit that the negotiations weren't going anywhere," Barry remembered later. "We weren't negotiating."

Chapter thirteen

DECISION DAY

Tuesday, October 26; Day 11

Titanyen Base

*B*arry and Phil, on the ground in Haiti, had reservations about offering the gang humanitarian aid. They did not think any concessions should be made. They had made this clear to the embassy on the day of Phil's arrival, and Barry had repeatedly told the gang leader that no money would be paid. He knew each of the captured people personally and was sure they were not expecting ransom.

Phil, too, as he had shared with the Titanyen staff on Sunday, felt strongly that they were engaged in a spiritual battle. He believed God required only a simple faith, and then He would do the work.

Barry, however, understood chain of command. When he received the new instructions from Ohio, he called Lanmò to offer humanitarian aid.

The gang leader didn't answer the first few times, but then he picked up about an hour later. "Where is the money?" he asked.

Barry said he can't talk until he knows if the hostages are okay.

"They are okay," Lanmò said. "Where is my money?"

Barry then brought up the offer of food boxes. Since the gang claimed to care about their communities, their wives, and their children, would they be open to humanitarian aid?

Lanmò San Jou cursed, then replied, "I did not ask for food."

Gangster Camp

The hostages, however, would have been happy for more food. **The snacks disappeared like I have never seen before,** Rachel wrote in her diary.

The checkers games had advanced from squares scratched in the dirt to squares on the mattress. A flurry of checkers games had motivated this improvement. The pieces were still bottle caps.

The gangsters brought Dale his phone, asking him to sign into it and reset it to factory settings. Dale complied, since he wasn't given a choice. He realized the phone would likely be sold or appropriated by one of the gangsters.

The boredom lifted slightly when the missionaries noticed that the guards were agitated about something they had heard on the radio. But no one could figure out why.

They had no idea that Lanmò San Jou had just hotly refused an offer of humanitarian aid in exchange for their release.

The topic of escaping continued to surface. Sam had been an early proponent of coming up with an escape plan. When the group started to deal with sickness, he had dismissed the idea for a time. But it was like trying to hold an inflatable boat under water.

Sam's theory was that if he got shot while attempting to escape, he would go to heaven and be better off anyway. While no one doubted this, most of the others were not so sure this was the right approach.

Kay thought escaping sounded scary but exciting. She wasn't going to plan out the logistics of it, but she knew she would go along if the others decided to do it. If they were all going to die trying to escape, she wanted to die with them.

Dale thought it was a great idea, but he couldn't justify leaving if it endangered the life of the guards, most of whom were straightforward about their eternal destiny: hell.

Austin wanted to have a clear sign that God wanted them to escape, rather than relying on a man-made plan.

Ryan wanted to escape with his wife and children, but he was nervous about the realities of escaping with an eight-month-old baby and a three-year-old.

Melodi drew on her memories of books and stories she had read about kidnappings, missionaries, and prisoners of war. She liked the audio story she had heard of a kidnapped missionary pilot who had escaped by running to his plane and flying away. She knew that the missionaries in the book *In the Presence of My Enemies* had discussed escaping too.

However, planning an escape for their own group was an entirely different matter for Melodi than reading about it in a book. She wasn't against the idea, but it scared her, and she preferred to stay out of the conversations. She definitely wanted God's direction. Having a good story to write about was not worth risking the safety of her two small children.

Matt and Rachel were not pushing for an escape plan but wanted it to be an option. If the Lord opened that door, they wanted to go through it.

Cheryl thought talking about escaping was a good way for the men to pass the time, but she was inclined to wait for a sign from God, as were some of her children.

Wes loved to theorize about logistical operations. He had grown up reading about people escaping from prison. He especially remembered the book *The Great Escape,* an account from World War II when members of the U.S. Air Force escaped from a German prison camp by digging a tunnel under the fence.

There were a few assumptions everyone agreed on. First, it was best to stay together, as Barry had repeatedly emphasized in team meetings at Titanyen.

Second, escaping would be out of the question if some people were sick.

Third, even if they did escape the immediate area, it would be difficult to get back to the CAM base without running into gangsters or people sympathetic to them.

But many other things were not clear at all. If an escape was planned, what form should it take? Should they dig a tunnel or should they just walk away? Would the guards actually shoot them if they got caught? They knew they were worth more to the gang alive than dead. But when guns were pointed, they could easily go off.

Although escaping was obviously risky, the alternative was also weighing on their minds. What would happen if they did not escape? There were several possibilities. Someone might pay a ransom and the gang would release them. This seemed doubtful, since they all knew CAM had a no-ransom policy. And the $17 million the gang was demanding was out of the question. Another possibility was that the U.S. military might come in to rescue them. Or—and this seemed like the best option—God could choose to miraculously deliver them, sending an angel to save them as He had delivered the Apostle Peter from prison.

There was hesitation about the prospect of military action, since everyone in the group believed in nonviolence. They weren't sure how they would feel if that happened, though they knew the Bible said that rulers do not bear the sword in vain. The Apostle Paul, who had written that passage, had suffered abuse and mistreatment from many people. But he had also sometimes appealed to his Roman citizenship for protection.

Would it be a sign of deeper faith to simply trust God and let Him deliver them in His own time?

Over in Titanyen and far away in Ohio, Barry, Phil, and the CAM Ohio team were having a similar debate.

Berlin, Ohio, CAM Headquarters

Bobby Miller's minutes of the meeting that day had no start or end time, just a cryptic heading: "All Day."

With the offer of food rejected, Phil Mast suggested that they tell the FBI they are done negotiating. CAM could then step completely aside and let the government take over in whatever way they saw fit.

Or, Phil went on, if CAM was going to eventually agree to negotiate with money anyway, it should be pursued immediately so the government officials know what was happening.

Everyone knew that was true. It was time to come to a decision. They also agreed that if they did allow ransom, Barry and Phil would not have to do the negotiating since they had told the kidnappers no money would be paid. It was a matter of integrity for them.

An FBI agent and a crisis adviser joined the meeting virtually for an hour or so. The FBI agent said no Americans kidnapped during the past few years in Haiti had been harmed, but most had been released by ransom. "People who refuse to pay ransom can expect their loved ones to die," he said.

He cautioned that negotiating with larger amounts of food could take months, while negotiating with money could facilitate the release much more quickly, perhaps within a week. He said they knew of a third party who was willing to take care of the negotiations.

When the adviser stated that paying ransom does not encourage more kidnappings if the amount paid is not too high, Tommy Wagler pushed back, stating that he thinks history shows it does. The adviser replied that unless no one ever pays any ransom, kidnappings will continue.

The adviser also discussed the slow pace of making decisions. "There are too many people in the meetings and too many committees, so decisions are taking too long. The authorities are feeling pressure to do something."

Weston later recalled the agony of those meetings when decisions had to be made but not everyone was on the same page. "There were many, many tears in the meeting room. Our hearts were all tender and in great agony at times."

Although the meeting had already lasted all day, the leadership decided a decision would have to be made that night.

At 5:25 p.m., Tommy Wagler sent a message to his wife: "Please pray for us . . . It promises to be a long evening and intense."

The White House, Washington, D.C.

National Security Advisor Jake Sullivan gave a report on the Haiti hostage situation in a White House press conference and ended by saying, "The children aspect of this is something the President is quite focused on, to make sure they're taken care of and they get home okay."

12:04 a.m., Berlin, Ohio

Tommy Wagler exited the central conference room at the end of the board meeting and jumped into his vehicle. He had an hour's drive to get home. He sent a text to his wife that he was on the way.

His mind couldn't stop circling. It had been hard, but they had finally come to a decision: they would allow a donor to pay ransom for the release of the hostages.

Tommy, as chairman of the board, had prayed many prayers in the last ten days and heard many perspectives from many people. He hated to make a decision that went against the wishes of the team on the ground. He knew Phil and Barry felt that the spiritual battle would not be solved with payment and that the Holy Spirit was leading them to simple faith and trust in God. They were sure the kidnapped missionaries were prepared to meet God. And in a worst-case scenario, they were ready to die. They did not expect to be ransomed.

Tommy respected their sincere beliefs and could see their point. He had also been against the idea of ransom. But Tommy was now going home to his wife and children. The other board members all had children too, at least four each. Some had grandchildren. Tommy liked to play Settlers of Catan with his children. The software developer liked to go on bike rides with his children. The accountant liked to play Monopoly with his. The teacher's children loved when he read them stories. The landscaper's children liked the Farming Game, along with the real-life farming of tending their goats. One of the grandfathers on the board, a retired farmer, liked to play hide and seek with his grandchildren. Another grandfather, a physician, enjoyed reading to his grandchildren.

It is one thing, Tommy reflected, *to make a decision about our own lives and our own children. But that's not what we're doing. We're making a decision for others who are unable to do so.*

This was the dilemma the board and the crisis team faced. To ask the seventeen hostages, without being able to communicate with them, to potentially die for a policy or position not spelled out in Scripture was something the board found they could not do.

Reluctantly they agreed to allow ransom to be paid. They hoped the authorities were right, and the hostages would be home soon.

Chapter fourteen

"DELIVER US!"

Wednesday, October 27; Day 12
Berlin, Ohio

*C*AM announced an official day of prayer and fasting for the hostages, kidnappers, and other oppressed Haitians.

Grand Ronde Valley, Oregon

The day of prayer and fasting was also the birthday of Melodi's mother. Her daughter with the new baby invited her over with a few friends. The birthday woman limited her food intake to one small scone, wanting to be part of the prayer and fasting for the kidnapped group.

Titanyen Base

The worst moment in the whole kidnapping ordeal for Barry was finding out that CAM had agreed to allow ransom to be paid. Not only had he repeatedly emphasized to Lanmò San Jou that no money would be paid, but he also did not feel at peace with the idea of paying ransom. Would God work on their behalf if they were taking matters into their own hands in this way? Barry feared that the decision makers at CAM had relied on the advice of secular experts who pushed for action rather than waiting on God.

In the coming weeks, Barry discussed the faith and works issue with many people. He knew the debates in Ohio had been long, with many hours of discussion.

"If we are doing everything in our power, does God still work?" he asked later. "I don't know. But I don't feel comfortable in saying, 'God, I want to do everything I can.'"

Phil was disappointed too. With Lanmò San Jou's words about serving King Lucifer, he had felt a confirmation that this was a spiritual battle—to be fought with spiritual weapons, not money.

Everyone involved wished they could talk to the hostages themselves. If the hostages said, "We're fine here. Please don't pay ransom," that would have made a difference. Or if they said, "Please get us out of here, no matter what it takes," that would have mattered too. But no one really knew what was happening in the gangster camp.

As the day of prayer and fasting came to an end, the action was just beginning at the hostage house.

Late Evening, Gangster Camp

Inside the cramped room, Melodi lay down beside Andre and Laura to help them fall asleep. As she lay there with her children, thoughts bounced through her mind. *It's October 27. My mother's birthday. Oh, I wish I could talk to her!*

Melodi had learned a lot from her mom during her growing-up years. As the family moved to Washington to help with the Russian school and then to Belize for several years, Melodi had observed her mom sacrificing things she could have had if they had always stayed at home. Also, Melodi had gained her love for writing from watching her mother write.

Before their trip to the orphanage, Melodi had picked out a birthday card for her mom. She had addressed the envelope and started writing in the card, but she hadn't finished it. She wished she had gotten it into the mail.

She wondered what kind of birthday her mother was having. If only she could send her an email, a paper note, a telegram—anything! It wouldn't have to say much, just a few words, something like, "We're hanging in there. I love you. We are praying for you." Melodi knew being held captive was probably harder on her parents than it was on her and Ryan and the children.

Andre and Laura were almost asleep when Froggy's vehicle pulled into the camp, the radio blaring. Tonight the booming program was an evening news station. Shelden was already asleep.

From the "shower house" where he was making use of the dipper and bucket, Sam heard the radio announcer saying in Creole that the United States military was coming to Haiti to free the seventeen hostages. Wes, who also understood quite a bit of Creole, picked out some of it too.

The guards were visibly rattled and ordered the hostages to pack up. They burst into the house and shooed the children off the mattresses. Froggy began tearing down wires and fans.

Shelden, still dazed from being awakened, was confused about what was going on. And so was everyone else. As the missionaries gathered in a group, they were both terrified and excited. What was happening? Were they going to be freed?

It was dark by now. Really dark. There was almost no moonlight, and the electric lights were gone. The chairs and couches were gone too, so the group stood in a circle, talking and praying and singing as the guards rushed around in the dark, loading the vehicles.

As bad as this gangster camp was, they did not want to move to a new location. What if someone had discovered their location and was planning to rescue them? Also, they had found a certain routine. Since some of them had been permitted to sleep outside, the crowding was less severe.

In addition, when Cheryl was sick, she had seen a vision of an angel coming to free them from this gangster camp. The angel had parted the bushes and helped them walk back to the Titanyen base.

As they prayed and sang, the group did not feel that God was going to let the gang move them.

Suddenly, with no explanation, the guards jumped into their trucks and roared away.

The group praised the Lord as they thought of being freed and taken back to the base at Titanyen. Besides their own anticipation, they imagined how excited Ray would be to see his wife and children! And how Barry would praise the Lord and welcome them back! All those people around the world who were praying would start praising God instead of pleading with Him. Surely God would deliver them tonight. They begged Him to do it, praying aloud for the grace to be back at the CAM base before the sun came up the next morning.

Then we spent some time singing and sharing and confessing, Wes wrote in his diary. I don't think our singing was ever so good. We felt very encouraged, and we poured our hearts into the songs.

The bubble burst, however, when the guards came rushing back. With no explanation, they quickly loaded everyone into a truck. The nervousness of the guards rubbed off on the missionaries as they climbed into the trucks. What was the gang planning to do with them? Was this the end? Would they be taken to a ravine somewhere and killed?

Dale was not as concerned about being killed as being moved to a location where they could be locked up. Driving through the pitch-black Haitian countryside only added to the drama of uncertainty.

Being killed was high on the list of possibilities in Melodi's mind as she clambered into the vehicle with her husband and children. *If they kill us, I hope they shoot us,* she thought. *That would at least be fast. I hope the children go with us.*

Cheryl and her children didn't think of immediate death, but they wondered if the group would be separated. Along with everyone else, they cried out to God, asking Him to prepare them for whatever came their way. Cherilyn again asked God to search her heart, as she had done the day of the kidnapping.

As the trucks headed farther back off the main road toward the mountains, they passed through a deserted village. Dale noted a few men who looked like off-duty gangsters standing around.

Finally they arrived at their destination. It was too dark to see much, but it was clear that the new house was boarded up and full of dust. However, it offered more space than the tiny room in the other place. In another positive development, the gangsters returned the missionaries' shoes—a real blessing.

Much as they had not wanted to move, the captives admitted that it was nice to have more room. This house had four small rooms, with the missionaries in the two bigger ones.

As the hostages surveyed their new surroundings, Lanmò San Jou rolled in, smelling as sweet as always. He had a box of medication with him, including prescription medication for Matt. It was a liquid instead of the pill form Matt usually used, but it was the right kind. The other medication, the one he injected himself with, was still not included.

The box also contained several other kinds of medications, such as pain relievers and Benadryl.

As the group tried to make themselves comfortable in the new house, the guards kept getting in the way, shining their lights around the dark house. Matt finally reached the end of his patience. As one particular guard kept crossing his path, Matt gave him a piece of his mind, "Mr. Zigzag, go get lost!"

Of course, the guard couldn't understand his English, but everyone else burst out laughing. After all the stress and fear, the laughter was good medicine. And from then on, that guard was known as Zigzag.

A short time later, still inside the house, Zigzag got out a cigarette and prepared to light up. When he struck the first match, it didn't light. Wes began praying that the next match wouldn't light either, as he really didn't want to sleep in a house full of cigarette smoke. Austin then joined in, praising God as match after match failed to light. The guard tried every match in his box with no success.

Finally, at about 11 p.m., everyone was ready to settle down. Ryan went to bed with his contacts still in. It was Day 12.

Despite the extra space, it was difficult to sleep. With no fans running, the place was blistering hot. And no one was allowed to sleep outside.

For some, the uncertainty was more disturbing than the heat. Would they be passed from place to place like the missionaries in the Philippines? Was the U.S. military really planning to rescue them? And who was in charge of their case? Was it the U.S. government or was it Christian Aid Ministries?

Also, what did the gangsters really want? Was it money? Or were they demanding the freedom of their leader?

Matt and Rachel Miller were the first two hostages released. Here they are shown in the hospital at the military base in Cuba.

The group of twelve back at the CAM base in Titanyen after hiking out on December 16.

Happy reunion with Haitian staff at the Titanyen base.

The Noecker family is reunited at the Titanyen base after the escape.

Sam, Wes, and Dale standing in the mechanic shop at the Titanyen base.

Photo credit: AP Images / Odelyn Joseph

Barry is overjoyed about the morning's events and congratulates his friend from the Associated Press for being the first reporter to show up on that memorable day.

Photo credit: AP Images / Odelyn Joseph

The two youngest hostages, Andre and Laura, ready to head with the others to the airport for the flight to Miami.

Photo credit: AP Images / Odelyn Joseph

The convoy taking the former hostages to the Port-au-Prince airport.

The Coast Guard plane that brought the last group to Miami.

The former hostages are all reunited in Miami on December 17. L-R: Sam, Wes, Matt, Dale, Rachel, Ryan holding Andre, Melodi holding Laura, Austin, Cherilyn, Brandyn, Kasondra, Courtney, Cheryl, Ray (was not in captivity) holding Shelden, Kay.

Dale holding his paper towel diary.

Sam receives a hearty welcome from his brothers.

Some of the CAM staff from the Berlin, Ohio, office singing "Nearer, My God, to Thee" at the press conference on December 20.

The former hostages reunited at a reunion in Michigan in February 2022.

CAM's field director and family: Barry & Julia Grant, holding Elizabeth.
Front L-R: Bethany, David, Andrew, and Abram.

CAM's country supervisor Phil Mast with
his wife Grace and daughter Olivia.

Chapter fifteen

PALM TREE PRISON CAMP

Thursday, October 28; Day 13

Gangster Camp B

*B*anana trees, cultivated fields, coconut palm trees, and mango trees surrounded the new house. When the captives awoke in the morning and ventured outside to look around, they were refreshed and encouraged by the beauty of the area. In the midst of captivity and fear, what an unspoiled paradise!

"Under different circumstances," Ryan said later, "I think I could live there."

Laura woke up early, so Melodi took her outside before most of the others were up. As she drank in the refreshing scenery, she noticed Carrot Top, one of the guards, feeding a small dog. Carrot Top had earned his name by the burnt orange hair on the top of his head. Like most of the other gangsters, he cut his hair close on the sides, but let it grow long on the top. He dyed the top of his hair orange.

Carrot Top seemed to have some affection for the dog, whose name was Sòlda.[1] Carrot Top opened a can of sweetened condensed milk for the little dog and poured it into a tin. Next he chopped up a bunch of salami for him.

Haiti abounded with roaming dogs. At night they could be heard barking incessantly.

Out in the fields, they could see farmers hoeing the soil. Unlike most of Haiti's fields, these appeared to have few rocks in them. The workers started before daylight, took a break at midday, and then worked a little again in the afternoon. Chickens and turkeys wandered by with their chicks.

A little boy tied seven goats around the hostage house every morning, collecting them again in the evening. Other children walked past on their way to school, following the footpath that led past the house. People also passed on their way to market, their donkeys loaded with goods.

The boy who herded the goats stood and stared at the white people. When one of the hostages said something to him, he plugged his ears with his fingers and dropped his eyes to the ground. Then, when no one was looking, he took his fingers out of his ears and watched again.

The hostages noticed a farmer passing by with a horse and three cows, all fine-looking animals. He cast sympathetic glances at them. Obviously, the local people knew that the missionaries were being held by the gang.

The guards found a farmer to pick coconuts for the hostages. After a steady diet of starch and oil and refined foods, the fresh fruit tasted marvelous, and they made a feast of coconut milk and meat. They also

---

[1] "Soldier" in Creole.

praised the Lord for a nicer location. Mosquitoes still feasted on them, but there weren't as many. And the whole atmosphere seemed less evil.

Apparently, the U.S. Army is planning to intervene, Dale wrote in his diary. **I don't think we'll be here for the whole weekend. My spirit feels lifted today. The peaceful place and beautiful nature are good for the soul.**

Ryan too was in a good mood, refreshed by the scenery and the fresh air. He walked around the house, noting that all the windows were shuttered, with a stick holding each shutter in place.

Ryan had always had a knack for fixing things. In his teenage years, his mother had announced at the breakfast table one morning that her Kitchen Aid mixer was not working properly. Only two speeds worked: low and high. Although he had never seen the inside of a mixer before, Ryan dismantled the tool. When he put it back together, his mom tried the settings and found that every speed worked.

If we have to stay here, why not make the conditions as good as we can? Ryan thought. He grabbed one of the sticks holding the shutters in place and wrenched it off. The shutter opened. He moved on around the house, ripping off sticks and opening shutters. One was too high to reach, so he left this one closed.

Ping, the head guard, was not pleased and scolded Ryan severely.

Sam made a comment about Ryan's Home Improvement, and the name stuck. Ryan also seemed to have landed himself on the guards' blacklist. They had learned that whenever anything was fixed or altered, Ryan was likely responsible.

During the day, about five armed guards watched the hostages. Several new guards appeared at this location, including the one already nicknamed Zigzag by Matt. At nighttime, reinforcements arrived. Even though the group was locked into the house around 6 p.m., there were from seven to ten guards around with big guns.

As they had done earlier for Dale, the gangsters brought Ryan his phone and asked him to enter his password and reset it to factory settings. Ryan said he needed to ask his wife about the password. He slipped away to find her in the house—and on the way sent a hurried text to Barry.

"We are okay. Barry, how much longer?"

Titanyen Base

Barry stared at his phone. Was this really a message from Ryan? It said it was, but someone else might have his phone.

"Are you still all together?"

"Yes, we're all together."

"Are you encouraged?"

"Yes! Keep praying."

Ryan dropped a pin, but to Barry it seemed to be in the middle of nowhere.

Barry was sitting beside Phil, who was talking to an official. He asked Phil, "What should I ask?" He wanted to ask what Ryan thought about paying ransom, but clearly that was a risky question if he didn't know for sure if it was Ryan.

"Ask him if they got the meds," Phil suggested.

"Did you get the meds?"

"Some."

This did not seem conclusive to Barry.

"What do we do Wednesday nights?" Barry asked. Surely Ryan would not have forgotten the Wednesday evening games of Knock Out on the basketball court.

There was no reply.

Barry was encouraged by the conversation, but he kept thinking about the message: *"Barry, how much longer?"* What did it mean?

Barry pondered the words, sifting them for meaning. *Is there something I can do?* he wondered.

Gangster Camp B

Holding Ryan's phone, Ryan and Melodi tried to stall as long as possible. But outside the door, Froggy was demanding speed. As Ryan put in his password, a message flashed to the top of the phone.

"What do we do Wednesday nights?"

Ryan and Melodi puzzled over this. What did Barry mean? Was he saying that churches were praying for them at their mid-week prayer services?

"Give me the phone!" Froggy was demanding in no uncertain terms. Reluctantly they returned it without answering Barry's question. They later reported their brief conversation with Barry to the group.

"Oh, Knock Out!" Kay said.

Oh. Knock Out.

Friday and Saturday, October 29, 30; Days 14, 15

Late Friday evening the guards chased the hostages inside. No one was quite sure why, but there were flashlights out in the fields. *Could it be a rescue?* But nothing came of it. It seemed someone was stealing goats. More excitement came on Saturday morning when there was a burst of gunfire while the missionaries were singing. Everyone was quickly herded inside until things quieted down.

A tall, lanky guard with an angular face was becoming a regular at the new place. His voice was loud and obnoxious, and he was not afraid to use it. The missionaries named him Mr. Attitude.

Mr. Attitude had a blanket he liked to use for sleeping on the porch, and woe to the man or woman who dared infringe on the dignity of this personal item.

One morning Melodi came out onto the porch and carefully stepped over Mr. Attitude's blanket. He turned on her in a rage, demanding to know why she had stepped on his blanket. Melodi patiently explained that she had not, pointing to where her feet had landed.

Mr. Attitude would not be placated. Finally Melodi said, *"Bonjou,*[2] Mr. Attitude," and walked away.

On another occasion, Ryan actually stepped on the blanket. He didn't notice his transgression at the time, but later there was a distinct footprint on the blanket. Ryan apologized and got down on his hands and knees to brush away the damaging evidence.

Austin also stepped on the blanket one day. This time Mr. Attitude blew up. "I should just shoot both of your feet!" he yelled. He pointed his assault rifle at Austin's feet.

"Sorry," Austin said.

But Mr. Attitude did not seem to accept the apology.

Not only did Mr. Attitude pester the hostages, but he also got on the nerves of the other guards, who didn't seem too fond of him.

Mr. Attitude told them he was twenty-three years old and had been with the gang since he was fourteen.

The guards mounted a solar panel on the roof of the house to provide power when the generator wasn't working. Using the solar panel, the fans would run for five to six hours.

Dale, who had especially disliked the need to be on high alert in the tarp shower at the first place, appreciated having a shower room here with a roof and walls. It was one of the four small rooms of the house. They still had to use a bucket and dipper, however. To create a drain, Ping chopped a hole in the concrete outside wall with a broken adjustable wrench. **So we could sweep the water out uphill after we showered**, Melodi noted in her journal.

Although privacy had improved, the door still fell short of impressive. **Somewhat unreliable**, Dale described it in his white paper towel diary.

The bathroom facilities at this new location had taken a step down, however. Instead of an outhouse, there was only a block wall a few feet

---

[2] "Good morning."

high in a weedy area behind one of the buildings. The hostages nicknamed it the Wailing Wall.

"Where are you going?" someone would ask.

"To the Wailing Wall."

Zigzag arranged almost daily for a farmer to get them some coconuts. First the farmers pierced the coconuts, allowing them to drink the water. After that, they cut the stiff rinds so the meat was accessible. Not everyone was fond of coconuts, but they all knew fresh fruit was good for their health.

Andre, however, really loved coconut water, and Melodi had to keep an eye on him or he would drink more than his share.

Zigzag bent over backwards to provide the group with coconuts and mangoes. He also sometimes brought little dough pies called *pate.*[3] He even spent his own money to buy a few treats for the missionaries.

Everyone loved the *pate,* although Zigzag usually brought only a few. The crescent-shaped pastries were filled with spicy coleslaw or meat, then fried in hot oil. They were a favorite all over Haiti. People made them in their homes and sold them on the streets. Kay had enjoyed them different times in her years in Haiti, but they had never had them on the CAM base.

Pop-A-Wheelie Chief also brought more snacks. Some of these were anything but fresh. Huge cardboard boxes arrived full of food. It appeared they were intended for wholesale use, so the group suspected they may have come from a captured box truck. Small bags of Doritos filled one box, while another box was full of vanilla cakes, individually packaged in clear plastic containers. These cakes quickly became moldy, but they were a treat when they first arrived.

The hostages appreciated the food, but the snacks also reinforced the fear that they would not be going home soon. On the day they had been kidnapped, they had expected to be released that night. Then

---

[3] Pronounced PAH-tay.

they thought, *Maybe tomorrow.* Then it was, *Surely this week.* Then, *Surely this weekend.*

If we had been told we'll be here for two weeks, Dale wrote, **we would have thought we can't do it. The Lord is carrying us through.**

Again the topic of escape came up. This new location was much more open, and it seemed it would be easy to just walk away. The only drawback was that they would be visible for about five minutes before they could duck behind something and get under cover.

Someone suggested that since they frequently walked in circles anyway, they should try to calculate how long it would take the whole group to walk a mile. The men stepped off one of their loops and then timed themselves. They estimated it had taken them sixteen minutes to walk a mile, or a little less than four miles an hour.

How long, they wondered, would it take to get back to the highway if all went well? Not long, they agreed. It seemed so close, yet impossibly far away. They also discussed walking back to the orphanage they had visited.

Carrot Top continued to take good care of Sòlda. None of the other guards seemed to like the dog, so the missionaries concluded he belonged to Carrot Top.

"Sòlda is my best friend," Carrot Top said once or twice. If the missionaries came out in the morning and found Carrot Top sleeping, it was common to find Sòlda curled up on his stomach.

One day the hostages heard Sòlda howling bloody murder. They found Carrot Top prying open the dog's mouth and squirting in citron juice. "I'm deworming him," he explained.

One night when the fans were not working, Austin lay on the floor trying to sleep. Sweat poured off him. As usual, the guards had shut all the doors and windows. Austin, who preferred a cool place to sleep, hated it. In addition, he missed the soothing hum of the fans.

Highly frustrated and unable to sleep, Austin rolled over. It was time to pray, he decided, and present his list of complaints to God.

Through the doorway, he could see into the next room where Matt and Rachel and Cheryl's family slept. Austin saw Cherilyn sitting against the wall, obviously awake as well.

"Are you melting over there yet?" he asked.

"I'm just imagining I am in a refining fire," Cherilyn replied. She explained that she had been praying and had given up her right to be free. "If God is going to free me, it is up to Him."

Challenged by this, Austin retracted the list of complaints he had prepared for God. Instead, he placed his circumstances and his longing for freedom in God's hands. As he prayed, he found peace in knowing that God would free them in whatever way He saw fit.

Ryan's position on the guards' blacklist was solidified when Andre woke up in the middle of the night crying with a bellyache. Since Melodi was also sick, Ryan wanted to take care of Andre without bothering her.

Sensing that Andre was almost ready to vomit, Ryan made a beeline for the side door nearby. It was blocked by a barrel of water, but at Ryan's kick the barrel went flying. Instantly the guards surrounded him, talking furiously. Ping's normally soft voice grew loud with anger and frustration at this further evidence of Ryan's Home Improvement. The next day Ping nailed the door shut.

> **Chassell, Michigan**
> Three-year-old Bradley prayed almost daily for Andre and his family. Sometimes his mother walked into a room to see him kneeling by the bed or in front of the couch, praying.
>
> "Lord," he prayed, "be with the people in Haiti. Let them come home and keep them safe. And help them be able to eat. And help the bad men to love Jesus and let them go."
>
> His older sisters, six and eight years old, prayed for "the kidnappers that kidnapped the kidnapped people."

1:30 a.m., Moorefield, Ontario

Dale's mom was asleep, dreaming. In her dream, a baby was crying. She woke up and shook herself. How could it be? She still heard a baby crying, but there was no baby in the house.

"Is it one of the hostage children?" she asked God.

The crying continued, so she continued in prayer.

"God, please comfort the child."

Immediately the crying stopped.

Sunday, October 31; Day 16

On Sunday, Day 16 of captivity, the missionaries invited the guards to join their church service, but they declined. Under the mango trees, the group talked about heaven. Everyone felt a longing for that place of freedom and peace.

They noticed the man who walked past daily with the horse and three cows. Today he was dressed up and carrying a Bible, evidently on his way to church.

By now the little herder boy had stopped plugging his ears when the group talked to him. They even managed to slip him food when they had extra snacks, which he enjoyed. One day they got the bright idea to ask the boy if he could get them a phone. He seemed agreeable, but they had forgotten to specify that the phone needed to come from an outside source. The boy walked over to the guards and asked if he could have one of their phones for the missionaries. Obviously, that effort ended in failure.

During the 1 p.m. prayer meeting for deliverance, someone noticed a plane circling high above. The group knew there were flight paths close by. It had become a fun pastime to shout out the identity of the planes approaching the Port-au-Prince airport. "Sunrise!" "Jet Blue!" "American!" Even Shelden and Andre took up this sport, though they could not identify the planes.

But this plane seemed smaller than an international jet, and it was clearly circling. Brandyn waved a bright shirt, as if drying it off, in an effort to draw attention. Then the group walked in a figure eight for a while. But there was no visible response from the plane. Although it was impossible to know what the plane was doing, the group felt their hopes rising. Maybe someone on the outside world did know where they were.

In the afternoon, a new guard arrived and Ping gave him gun training. Watching the gun training was a pleasant diversion for the hostages. The group named the new guard Rookie. The training ended with Ping and Rookie wrestling in the weeds, a welcome bit of comedy.

Like Ping, Rookie had grown up in church. He had been baptized into a mainstream evangelical congregation. Desperate circumstances had now inspired him to join the gang.

"Why couldn't you farm?" one of the hostages asked him.

"I don't have any land," he said. "And I have six children to feed."

Sam still talked to Ping about salvation sometimes, and he said he wanted to become converted.

"But I can't while you are here," he told Sam. "Because I have to guard you."

Sam knew he was counting the cost. "Chief, if you don't repent today," he said, "I'm afraid you will never do it. The Bible says, 'Today is the day of salvation.' You can't just keep putting it off like this."

Monday, November 1; Day 17

Monday, Day 17, was another boring day.

A few of the men did push-ups, creating a bit of distraction to pass the time. Even Carrot Top and Rookie joined in.

Austin noted the date with deep sadness. It was his little sister's birthday—and there was no way he could call her.

By now over two weeks had passed, and there was still no sign of deliverance. Once again the topic of escape came up. Austin, who had newly surrendered his freedom to God unless He acted on their behalf, was not ready to make plans to escape. A few others also felt this way, and a division began to emerge in the group on this issue.

"We called ourselves the little church," Sam said later. "And we had church problems."

Cherilyn recalled the challenges of learning to get along in the tight quarters. "It was not always easy," she said. "There were people from all different backgrounds, many of whom had not known each other well before the kidnapping. Giving up privacy and personal space meant we saw both each other's low points and high points. One day someone would say something offensive or hurt someone's feelings. But there was no choice except to forgive and get along. There was nowhere to go, no way to avoid anyone. It was a lesson I felt God was teaching me."

Lanmò San Jou came in the evening and assured the hostages that it wouldn't be too much longer before they could go home. However, his evil, sweet-smelling presence was so repulsive that everyone felt heavy when he left.

Titanyen Base

Many practical tasks found themselves on Grace Mast's to-do list. Food was spoiling in the refrigerators at the base in Titanyen. And the government officials wanted luggage ready to go for each hostage in case of a sudden release.

Barry's wife Julia did not have much extra time between caring for five small children. However, the Shenksters from Port-au-Prince continued their stay at the Titanyen base to support the remaining staff. While her husband supported the men on the base, Mrs. Shenkster pitched in to help Grace. The two ladies scraped moldy food into the trash, defrosted freezers, and packed luggage. It was an odd feeling to pack someone else's bags, but the women were able to find basic necessities and passports for most of the kidnapped missionaries.

Worse than the physical tasks was the psychological strain of waiting for something to happen.

Grace wrote in her journal, "Waiting-waiting-waiting . . . for the captives' release!"

Berlin, Ohio, CAM Headquarters

Although the decision had been made to accept the anonymous ransom donation and the third-party negotiator, the meetings did not end. With government authorities predicting a swift release, plans had to be made for what would happen when the hostages got out. Would they be evacuated to the United States immediately? Would the Titanyen base have to be shut down?

Also, much red tape was involved in officially authorizing the anonymous donor to proceed with negotiations for the hostages' release. To honor the donor's wishes, CAM agreed not to request details about the amount of ransom or the results of the negotiations.

Nor had the struggles for unity on the CAM board and crisis team ended. The members still weren't all on the same page.

"Had some go around," the meeting minutes reported, "about team structure, conflicting opinions, and striving for mutual respect as we hash through hard issues."

Chapter sixteen

"YOU NEED TO BE SET FREE"

Tuesday, November 2; Day 18

6 a.m., Gangster Camp B

*A*s the days wore on in captivity, it was easy to wonder if God knew or cared. And did anyone else know or care? Surely their families did. But was anyone doing anything? Was there no way to bring this ordeal to an end?

Some of the hostages gained strength and hope by watching the sunrises and sunsets. Most of the Noeckers liked to do this, and Austin often joined them.

On the morning of November 2, Sam was also outside. Discouragement was pressing in, and he needed some time with God. In search of solitude, he went around the corner of the house to pray, as alone as one could be in the presence of the guards.

After praying for a time, Sam saw movement out of the corner of his eye. Froggy stood under the last mango tree in the row. He was reaching down and screwing a cork onto what looked like a wine bottle in a black plastic bag. The cork had strange-looking wires running through it. Froggy suddenly glanced up and noticed Sam watching him.

"This is the devil's stuff," he said. "Don't touch it, or it's going to bite you!"

The challenge was unmistakable. Since Froggy practiced voodoo as a religion, Sam knew this was no joke. He debated what to do next. He had no way of knowing that back in the United States, just minutes before, someone had been praying against the voodoo practiced by the kidnappers.

Sam remembered hearing a sermon titled "Get in the Way of Evil." The pastor[1] had emphasized that Daniel in the Old Testament was not afraid of getting in the way of evil. He didn't care if he was tossed to the lions. "If I do not engage with the enemies of truth and morality," the pastor had asked, "do I really get in the way of evil?"

By now Froggy had disappeared.

"O God, what does a Christian do with threats like

5:30-5:45 Prayer Time

During a woman's early morning prayer slot, she was led by the Holy Spirit to pray for Haiti and the kidnapped missionaries. As she prayed, the Lord brought three things specifically to mind to pray for:

1. Salvation for the kidnappers.

2. That they would *drop the chains* that hold them captive.

3. That the stronghold of voodoo in the country could be broken.

Later in the morning, a friend called her and said she had a burden to pray for Haiti. She immediately began to pray, and without any hints, she prayed for the same three things.

---

[1] Val Yoder.

this?" Sam prayed. "What should I do? God, I believe we are called to get in the way of evil."

After Froggy had left, Sam walked over to the sunrise watchers and explained what had happened. "What should we do about it?" he asked them.

"I'd take that bottle and throw it as far as I could," Austin suggested.

"Would you like the honor of doing it?"

"Sure!" Austin enjoyed playing disc golf. Why not practice his throw?

Dale stepped onto the porch just then and joined the group as they walked toward the bottle.

Sam picked up the bottle. "Satan, I rebuke you in the name of Jesus!" he said. "Lord, protect us. Cover us with the power of Jesus Christ!" He then handed the bottle to Austin.

With a look of determination, Austin hurled the witchcraft symbol as far as he could into the adjoining field. Sam's eyes followed the bottle, watching it burst open when it hit the ground. He thought he could see red fluid spilling out. Brandyn remembered that after the bottle landed, fluid spewed out like water from a garden hose. As they turned away, they could see the bottle lying out in the field.

11 a.m., Berlin, Ohio, Family Conference Call

As he had done for the last two weeks, James Yoder from Christian Aid Ministries met the families of the hostages on a morning conference call. Every morning he provided any updates that were available and read some of the messages of encouragement that had arrived.

James wished he had more to share, but there was no breaking news. No hint of any imminent action on the part of either negotiators or gang members. In short, there was no indication that the hostages would be home anytime soon.

The news that did break on November 2, 2021, was not the kind to share as encouragement. *The Caribbean Times,* a New York City newspaper, reported the murder of a Haitian professor who had been abducted on the same day as the CAM missionaries. Now, after the professor's family had paid some of the ransom money, the gang had killed him.

"Meanwhile," the article concluded, "the seventeen United States and Canadian missionaries kidnapped for more than two weeks are still being held by their abductors, who are demanding US$17 million ransom. Police here are being assisted by officials from the Federal Bureau of Investigation (FBI) searching for the missionaries."

6 p.m., Gangster Camp B

The day passed more swiftly than sometimes because the hostages had a goal: housecleaning. With the bathing water brought to the camp in large barrels, they washed the walls and mopped the floors. Ryan forced open some windows to allow more air to move through.

Sam had been on high alert after they had thrown away Froggy's bottle, but as the day wore on, he relaxed. They had committed their action to the Lord, and there was nothing more to do about it.

Dale reported seeing three snakes, but beyond that no evil befell the group during the day. The plane they had seen the last two days circled in the sky above them again.

As darkness fell, the seventeen hostages gathered under one of the mango trees outside the house for their evening worship time. The surrounding fields and landscape gradually disappeared from sight. Soon they would have to go inside for the night. Day 18 was history. Or was it?

"He's coming!" Brandyn said to Wes, who sat close by.

Sure enough, Froggy was making his way to the last mango tree in the row, flashlight in hand. Although the hostages did not remember seeing the bottle before that morning's episode, it was apparently part of Froggy's daily ritual. They saw the beam of his flashlight bouncing across the ground under the tree. Then they heard his angry voice, questioning the guards.

"*Kot bidon?*" (Where's the bottle?)

Apparently the guards did not give Froggy the answer he wanted, because he headed toward the circle of missionaries.

"Samuel! *Kot bidon?*"

Although Austin had thrown the bottle, Froggy automatically fixed his fury on Sam because he was the most fluent and most vocal Creole speaker. Sam always got blamed for any problem except for "home improvements," which were well known to be Ryan's work.

"We threw it away," Sam replied.

"No! No!" Froggy's voice bellowed. "Where is it?"

"We threw it away."

Froggy lunged toward Sam as if possessed.

"Satan, I rebuke you in the name of Jesus Christ!" Sam cried.

Froggy moved back as if struck with a brick.

Someone in the group began a song, and the others joined in. While they were singing, a guard walked up with a shotgun. Froggy took it and leaned on it, appearing to listen to the song. Encouraged, the hostages kept singing. Occasionally Froggy would start yelling at the end of a song, demanding to know where the bottle was and accusing Sam of stealing it. But someone always had another song ready, and the rest joined in, drowning out Froggy's angry tirade. They sang children's songs, choruses, hymns. Anything to keep Froggy calm.

Finally Sam suggested they move into the house for the night. It was time to bring a close to the evening.

But Froggy was not done. He walked to the house, blocking the doorway.

"Tell me where the bottle is." Froggy's voice was cold. "Samuel!"

Furious, Froggy once again lunged at Sam.

Again Sam rebuked Satan, and Froggy jerked back.

We didn't know what he was going to do, but he looked and sounded like he wanted to kill Sam, Dale wrote in his diary the next day.

As the group continued to pray, crying out for God's help, more guards arrived at the scene. Chaos reigned.

"I need to have that bottle before the light of dawn!" Froggy yelled. "If I don't, we will beat you!"

Ping, the chief of the guards, soon arrived. "If you don't tell us where the bottle is, we will beat you without stopping until you show us where it is."

"I am ready for that," Sam said. "Go ahead. Start beating me."

Ping pulled a pistol from his waist. "Samuel, do you know what this is? It is a gun. Do you know what guns can do?"

Sam smiled. "Chief, I am not afraid of you."

Brandyn and Ryan stepped up beside Sam as the guards kept shouting. "You're not going anywhere until you show us where the bottle is!" they yelled. "Show us or we will beat you! We will kill you!"

"Go ahead. I'm ready to be beat. I'm ready to die. All you'll do is send me to heaven."

"We will not let you into the house until you tell us where the bottle is!" they fumed.

Melodi and Cheryl decided to go inside with their young children, while some of the other ladies sat down on the porch. All of them continued to pray. But the men refused to budge from Sam's side. They supported each other, praying aloud.

"Those men were angry enough to kill us," Ryan remembered later. "And yet they couldn't touch us."

While Froggy raged at Sam, the other guards ran around, searching for the bottle. They looked behind the house and searched the newly dug outhouse that had replaced the Wailing Wall.

Sam had never seen Froggy so angry. He knew this could be the night he would have to give up his life for Christ. Sam stood in the center of a half circle. Froggy, blocking the door to the house, faced him, furiously angry. Dale, Austin, Wes, and Brandyn stood on one side of Sam, while Ryan stood on the other, along with several of the ladies who had not gone into the house.

Once again Froggy came toward Sam, yelling. Brandyn and Ryan, one on each side, put their arms around Sam.

"Satan, I rebuke you in the name of Jesus Christ," Sam said again.

Froggy stopped, close to Wes. Whenever the group prayed or called on Jesus, Froggy seemed unable to continue his attack.

Wes put his hand on Froggy's shoulder. His calm, quiet voice carried more authority than Froggy's yelling. "Look, you're the one who is bound in chains. Satan has bound you, and you need to be set free."

Froggy turned to Wes, listening. He almost seemed to have forgotten about Sam. Brandyn remembered a verse he had memorized from Proverbs: "A soft answer turneth away wrath." The truth of the verse was playing out in front of him.

Wes went on, "You need that bottle to protect yourself. But we have angels to protect us."

Wes's calm voice deflated the furious man for a moment, but Froggy soon marched into the house to search for the bottle there. The missionaries followed, gathering in the front room. Froggy soon burst out of the back room, empty-handed. He yelled at Sam again, incensed that he had not been able to find the bottle in the house.

Wes joined the others in prayer, crying out to God. He felt that something was going to happen. Something had to happen. With the others, he prayed for deliverance. Perhaps God would blind the eyes of the guards. Maybe this was the night they were hoping for. The night to escape and run back to the base at Titanyen. The night to walk off without a backward glance.

After lots of shouting, chaos, and tension, the guards finally went back outside. A few minutes later Eeyore stuck his head in the door.

"Do you have any cookies?" he asked.

Everyone laughed nervously. Tight muscles loosened and people let out shaky breaths. Melodi jumped up. She grabbed the stale vanilla cookies and a box of snack-size Doritos. Setting the cookies on top of the Doritos, she shoved the whole thing out the door.

The box soon came flying back in. Apparently not all the guards were excited about a peace offering.

Eventually, perhaps partly due to the cookie interruption, things quieted down. Sometime later they heard the guards outside telling Froggy something. Had they found the bottle?

Some of the group stayed up to pray and sing for several hours until they felt at peace that God was going to take care of them the rest of the night.

While the battle raged that evening, two more emails arrived in CAM's inbox.

8:14 p.m., Email Prayer

"Abba, Father, we pray for your hand of calm upon these hostages while they wait for rescue. We pray your powerful Holy Spirit will lead the terrorists to release all the hostages while changing their own hearts to accept your Son's salvation though His sacrifice and your grace. In Jesus. Amen."

8:57 p.m., Hampton, Connecticut

"Grace and peace be multiplied unto you. You are in our thoughts and prayers all the time! We pray especially for your safety and for your release. We don't understand God's ways, but we know He has a purpose in all of this. Love and prayers."

Chapter seventeen

SETTLING INTO A ROUTINE

Wednesday, November 3; Day 19

Gangster Camp B

*T*he next morning there was no sign of the bottle in the field.

"You were very naughty last night," Ping told Sam. "You should be tied up." Overall, the guards seemed peaceful.

Froggy, however, refused to talk to the hostages when he brought the morning spaghetti. He did finally say that Ryan and Sam were bandits and that he would kill them.

When Lanmò San Jou found out what had happened, he told the guards they weren't watching the captives closely enough. After this, the hostages were herded into the house at 6 p.m. sharp. In this way, Froggy could perform his voodoo practices with no followers of Jesus

Christ to interfere. In the morning he took care of the bottle before the hostages were up.

With this system, the hostages saw the black bag and the bottle only a few more times. Once Froggy was seen carrying it, and another time Cheryl saw it under the mango tree as at the beginning.

The hostages later recalled the snakes they had seen the day before. Was it possible that destroying Satan's bottle had caused an influx of snakes? Cherilyn recalled that this had happened in Thailand when the people destroyed an idol.

Whether or not snakes were connected to it, the bottle incident left its mark on the group.

"I was completely drained through the whole process," Ryan told the others later. "I can't understand it."

"It was a huge faith booster for us," Dale recalled. "But we also felt very physically drained after it was over. I believe the guards had more respect for us and our faith after that. They saw that our God is more powerful than their master."

"It felt so sharply like there was a line between good and evil," Melodi remembered. She could imagine angels flying about the group that night. "The men wanted so badly to hurt us. And they couldn't."

But besides being exhausted, the group felt grateful to God for seeing them through. The power of Jesus had conquered. They were not free from captivity, but compared to their captors, they were free in spirit.

As if his tongue had been loosened by the cookies from the night before, Eeyore had news to share the next morning: "The United States government is talking to the Haitian government about you. I don't think you will be in captivity much longer."

Ryan and Melodi were becoming concerned about Andre's spirit. Their little son had always loved his dad. Whenever Ryan came home,

Andre had been overjoyed. Now he was developing a strange aloofness toward Ryan. At the same time, he wanted to spend time with Froggy, a voodoo worshiper, and insisted he was a good man.

It also bothered Ryan and Melodi that Andre cried only at night, as if the light of day healed his sickness. What kind of sickness came on only at night?

Ryan and Melodi had encouraged Andre to greet the guards and Froggy with fist bumps. This had seemed perfectly fine when they had first arrived at the gangster camp.

Now they evaluated this greeting more closely and decided it needed to stop. They weren't sure why Froggy and the others touched their hearts after the fist bump. But could that be a way for Satan to get into the lives of the children? They told Andre to quit doing fist bumps with the gangsters.

Thursday, November 4; Day 20

It was Wes's turn to wear the pink froggy pants that Brandyn had saved from the sack of clothes. He sat outside in them, writing in his paper towel journal and watching Ping working on a door.

Home improvement did not appear to be Ping's strong point. He had replaced the door upside down, with one hinge on backward. Since Ping had made it clear that he did not want assistance, the hostages, including Austin, the construction worker, just watched. With Rookie's help, Ping finally got the door on the right way. But the hinge was still on backward, so the door tilted to the right. To solve this problem, Ping hacked away at the jamb to make more room for the crooked door.

Wes, Dale, and all the others were delighted when a jar of peanut butter showed up in the snacks. It didn't take away the craving for strips of freshly grilled steak and chicken, but it was a welcome treat.

At morning prayer, Ryan and Melodi shared their concern about the fist bumps. Cheryl agreed and asked Shelden to quit participating in this greeting too. "If you want to greet them, you have to shake their hand," she told him. The whole group focused on praying for the children's protection.

The sores on Wes's feet were growing worse. What had started as a mild case of athlete's foot had become infected from the bath water, and by now he could hardly walk. Many of the others also struggled with sores.

Noticing Wes's plight, Cheryl wrapped the sores on his feet with Band-Aids. She told the others what they had learned when Ray had sliced off one of his fingers on a table saw. Someone had told them to soak his hand in water infused with ashes. Perhaps if they could convince the guards to allow them to make a fire, it would work for the sores they were battling.

Friday, November 5; Day 21

"Happy birthday!"

Melodi had never expected to spend her twenty-eighth birthday in a gangster camp. As a child, Melodi's mom had always made her birthday a special day. Melodi remembered cake and presents and sometimes a party.

At morning prayer, the group sang "Happy Birthday" for Melodi. Later in the day, Cherilyn used peanut butter to frost one of the vanilla cakes in the clear plastic containers. With a pin, she scratched "Happy birthday, Melodi" in the peanut butter, then stuck in a match for a candle.

Although the cake had begun to mold, Melodi greatly appreciated the thought behind the gesture. The peanut butter was a treat.

The harsh voice of Mr. Attitude the guard was enough to make a person long for special birthday treatment. When Melodi began to wash a piece of Laura's clothes in a small yellow bucket, Mr. Attitude insisted that she fill the big washtub with water and soap instead.

"Why should I fill the whole washtub for one little piece of clothing?"

But Mr. Attitude insisted, so she filled the big tub of water to wash the one piece.

Mr. Attitude did not like when Melodi talked English. "You know Creole," he snapped at her. "You're acting like you don't understand what I'm saying."

"Well," Melodi told him, "I can understand a little bit, but you need to talk more slowly and not yell so loud. Then maybe I can understand you."

It was clear to the group that the farmer who passed the hostage house daily sympathized with their plight. They exchanged greetings with him every morning and afternoon.

Finally Sam decided to write him a letter asking for help. Would this kindly gentleman who walked by with his Bible on Sundays be willing to assist them? Maybe he would let them borrow his phone.

When the man walked past, Brandyn handed him the note, written in Creole on a white paper towel. The farmer took it discreetly and kept on walking with his animals.

When the farmer returned that afternoon, he positioned himself where the guards couldn't see him and made a slicing motion in front of his neck.

The missionaries understood. Even though he would like to help, the gang would kill him if they found out. It was too great a risk.

With some persuasion, the guards allowed the hostages to start their own fire for medical use. It was nice to have something to do for once. Gathering the wood and getting the fire going brought back memories of past camping trips and cozy nights with s'mores and friends.

When Froggy arrived with lunch, he announced that he had been in a meeting with the big chiefs. What that meant, no one knew.

Supper that night was a meager meal of white rice and sauce. **Everyone went to bed hungry,** Rachel wrote.

The number of guards at night continued to be about twice as many as during the day. Later that night, five of the hostages stepped outside at the same time to go to the restroom. Only one guard was close by, and he frantically began to shoot into the air, thinking they were escaping. The other guards quickly came running.

Grande Ronde Valley, Oregon

Melodi's mother wished she could send her daughter a card for her birthday. They had been praying that she would be released before her birthday. But here they were, unable even to talk.

Saturday, November 6; Day 22
Gangster Camp B

The missionaries decided it was time for an accountability meeting. Back at Titanyen, this happened every month on the first Saturday for the men. The women had their meeting the first Monday evening of the month at Kay's house where they drank tea and talked while the men watched the children. They would share with each other how things were going in their walk with the Lord. If someone was struggling, the others would pray for that person.

The hostages concluded there was no reason they couldn't keep up the tradition here. After all, their schedule was not pressing. The only change was that they ran both the men's and women's meetings at the same time.

Later in the day, they finally got a kettle of water boiling with wood ashes in it. Wes soaked his feet in the water, and Cheryl bandaged them up again. The wood ash created a lye solution and the warm water improved circulation. Perhaps Ray's lost finger had not been in vain.

Although it had been difficult for the little boys to quit fist-bumping the guards, it seemed to be helping. Andre's attitude and demeanor had changed significantly for the better. After the greeting was banned, Shelden told them that the fist bumps were the guards' way of "connecting with my heart." Cheryl thanked God that they had put a stop to it.

Sunday, November 7; Day 23

Lanmò San Jou arrived with his trademark expressionless face, a cloud of perfume preceding him. About the only time anyone had seen any emotion on his face was when he laughed at Sam's preaching.

The "big chief" talked to Ping for a long time. Then he came over and gave his phone to Sam, saying someone wanted to talk to him.

"What is your name?" the person asked in English. "How are you doing?"

"Sam Stoltzfus," Sam replied in English. "Who are you?"

"I am the negotiator. We are working to have you released."

"Speak Creole!" Lanmò San Jou snapped.

"What are the last four digits of your social security number?" the caller continued.

Sam began rattling off the numbers, but before he had finished, Lanmò snatched the phone away from him and gave it to Ryan.

"What is your name?" the person asked.

"Ryan Korver."

"Do you speak English or Creole?"

"English!"

"Can you give me the last four digits of your social security number?"

"No!"

The person asked again, and again Ryan declined.

Lanmò grabbed the phone and walked away, leaving the missionaries staring at the retreating gang leader's back.

"Did you actually give them your number?" Ryan asked Sam.

"I don't think they heard it," Sam said.

The group stewed about this for some time. What was the point? Had the gang figured out that they weren't getting any money, so now they wanted to steal their identities and drain their bank accounts?

But later Ping shared some good news with the group: "In four days you will be going home."

Thrilled, the hostages discussed this new development. Had the gang leader been released from prison? Or had a ransom possibly been paid? The missionaries tried to temper their excitement with realism. They knew that few things happened on schedule in Haiti. But Ping seemed excited, and surely he would not have misunderstood.

"My mom's birthday is in three days," Kay told Ping. "I want to tell her happy birthday."

"You're going to be leaving soon!" Ping assured her. "You might be a little late to tell her happy birthday, but you're going to be leaving, and you can tell her soon."

Wes soaked his feet again in the water mixed with ashes. He was in more pain than ever.

Ladysmith, Wisconsin

After the phone call with Ryan, officials drove out to meet Ryan's parents.

They played back the recording of the conversation with Ryan and Sam.

"Is this your son speaking?" they asked. "He did not answer our proof-of-life question."

"Yes!" they said. "Absolutely!"

Ryan's parents felt encouraged. His mom said Ryan sounded just like the same determined son she had always known. He sounded strong. Not beaten down or discouraged.

Monday–Wednesday, November 8–10; Days 24–26
Gangster Camp B

Excitement about an imminent release remained high. Wes could hardly walk, though his feet seemed to be improving with the ash soaks. Home seemed so close. The group discussed having a reunion sometime after their release.

Ryan's Home Improvement went on another service call. With a pry bar, Ryan finally managed to reach the shuttered window that was above his head and wrenched it open. Ping's normally soft voice grew loud when he was angry, and this time he almost exploded.

"You wreck everything I make!" he screamed. "You are not a mechanic!"

Ryan felt a bit remorseful. He wasn't sure where the line was between helping his family and being respectful of Ping's wishes.

To their chagrin, the group discovered that Kay's birthday had been the day after Melodi's, on November 6, and no one had celebrated it. To make up for this deficiency, they sang "Happy Birthday" to her three times.

Just another long, long day, Rachel wrote in her diary.

That night it rained. Ryan and Melodi awoke to find their mattress in a puddle from the leaky roof.

The next day the missionaries watched an old lady tottering by on the road. Shortly after she passed them, she met a farmer who began beating her. The group of missionaries couldn't do much, but they jumped up and began yelling at him to stop. Thankfully, he did.

The guards heard the commotion and came over. They explained that the lady was a thief and therefore deserved such treatment.

Zigzag soon arrived with mangoes. It wasn't clear if the mangoes were intended for the guards or for the hostages, but Andre saved the day.

"Mangoes!" he shouted. "Thank you very much!"

What could Zigzag do but hand them over?

Zigzag was quite faithful at finding a farmer to knock down coconuts for them. However, he didn't always oblige. One day Brandyn got tired of waiting and took matters into his own hands.

Wearing the pink froggy pants, he climbed one of the coconut palms when no guards were watching and began raining down coconuts.

Charlie Horse, a guard with a swinging, singsong voice, saw Brandyn in the tree and began yelling. He was afraid Brandyn would fall and break a bone.

Mangoes and coconuts aside, the burning question for the group was whether they would actually be released on Thursday.

Pop-A-Wheelie Chief soon arrived on his motorbike. "I had an accident yesterday with my motorcycle," he informed them, pointing to a bruise on his shoulder. Pop-A-Wheelie Chief's driving was legendary, so this was not a huge surprise to anyone. He seemed to take great delight in demonstrating his wheelies to the group every time he came to the camp.

Sam decided to address him directly. "When are we going to leave?" he asked.

"If it would be up to me," Pop-A-Wheelie Chief said, "you would be gone by now. But it's not up to me. I don't know when it will happen, but not this week."

The news was a big letdown. *But maybe he's wrong,* they decided. *Maybe he just doesn't know.* Still, his message dampened the excitement that had been building.

The missionaries decided to fast the next day about whether they should try to escape. Soon it would be a whole month since their captivity. Perhaps God wanted them to act on their own.

After the decision was made to fast, someone made a dire prediction: "Just watch Froggy bring scrambled eggs and bread and avocados tomorrow morning."

And that's exactly what happened. The next morning everyone stared in disbelief, almost drooling with hunger, as Froggy arrived with their breakfast—eggs, bread, and avocados. This was terribly hard. After days of boring spaghetti, it was almost more than they could do to pass up the treat. But they held on and kept fasting.

The guards seemed subdued and unhappy. The hostages suspected they were disappointed that the release had been canceled.

We had a longer praise and prayer service, Rachel wrote. **We talked about walking out and it got a little heated. There are varying opinions.**

On the subject of escape, most people fell into one of three categories:

First were those who had no question about it. They were ready to risk their lives to do it. Sam had made it clear from the beginning that he wanted to escape. Rachel had once said that if she and Matt did not show up at prayer meeting, they had walked off.

Another part of the group loved to talk about escaping but had reservations about actually making an attempt. Wes loved discussing and planning, but he felt that an escape should involve careful forethought. If they attempted an escape and it failed, they might be shot or chained hand and foot. Wes felt sure they had only one chance, and he didn't want to mess it up.

Kay was ready to jump on board if others did the planning. She didn't want to push it, but if an escape was attempted, she wanted to be along. She prayed that the group could come to an agreement.

Melodi, as a mother of two small children, found the idea of escape frightening. She tended to step away from any such conversations that got too serious.

Dale was willing to try it, but the consequences for the guards troubled him. "If you escape," Ping had told Sam, "all of us guards will be shot." *Will their blood be on our hands if we escape?* Dale wondered.

There was also a third group—those who did not even want to talk about escaping. They believed God would show Himself strong when He chose, and human reasoning should not interfere. Since surrendering his right to freedom, this was Austin's position, along with Cherilyn and some of her family.

Sam finally had enough of the conflict. "If nothing happens in the next week," he told them, "I'm leaving. My health and sanity depend on it. It's better to risk death than to stay. Whoever wants to stay can stay, but I'm leaving."

No one said much. Dale worried about Sam, but some of the group agreed with him.

Sam later prayed about this and realized that God was stronger than the mental turmoil he feared. He apologized to the group for his strong words. When his self-imposed deadline rolled around, he stayed. Although the division over escaping appeared to be insurmountable, everyone agreed that they must all stay together.

"If we ever had a church split," Wes remembered, "it was over that subject."

That afternoon a big jet circled above the house. Carrot Top loaded his shotgun and starting making phone calls, but nothing came of it.

Later in the day, shots rang out in a field nearby. Ping fired into the air and then herded the hostages inside. They later found out that some gangsters had been stealing goats. It was just part of their normal life—taking what they wanted from the people around them.

Titanyen Base

On the day the hostages fasted, Ray worked on a letter to his wife. He had no way to get it to her, but it helped him process his thoughts. Hopefully someday she would read it.

"I love you, dear. Twenty-six days. So much has happened, and on the other side, so little."

He told her his daily routine. They had breakfast at 7:15, then morning prayer time with the men on the base. Even though there were just a few of them, they continued to sing together. They especially enjoyed the song "The Solid Rock."

"In those early days the singing was so powerful and encouraging," he wrote. "Now singing is a commitment, an act of worship and faith. We often pray that God will put a song in your hearts." He explained to her that the twice daily meetings with the families of the other hostages had been long and informative at the beginning. Now there was usually not that much to share.

He explained that the CAM base would be closing for a time at least, and that he was trying to summon the energy to pack their things. He told her he slept in his clothes every night, then showered and changed in the morning.

"I must admit," he wrote, "we did laugh a few times about Courtney having only one dress."

Thursday, November 11; Day 27

Thursday morning, the hopeful day of release, dawned much too early at 4 a.m. The guards were extra loud, so it was difficult for anyone except Kasondra to sleep much longer. In addition to the noise of the guards, the distant beating of heavy drums played in the background.

Wes didn't mind nights. Like Kasondra, he usually slept well, and sometimes he would dream he was back in Tennessee. He would wake up and report to the others about his night.

"I was home!" he would say. "We went hunting last night."

For Wes, sleep was an escape from the tedium of life in the gangster camp. Matt warned him that this could be a disadvantage. "Wes, Wes, Wes!" he said. "You wouldn't wake up if an angel did come!"

The problem with morning was that it meant they were still twelve hours away from any news. By this time, they knew that all important things happened at night.

They bugged Ping about the release. After all, it *was* the fourth day. Ping didn't seem happy about the situation, but he confirmed that the plans had changed.

Instead of being a joyful day of being released, it was a day of trials. To begin with, they were out of drinking water for much of the day. They were also concerned about Cheryl, who was sick with a high fever.

The guards talked with the missionaries for a while, telling them that the airport in Haiti was shut down because of all the unrest.

"The roads are blocked," they said. "You wouldn't be able to get to Titanyen even if you were released."

Friday, November 12; Day 28
9 a.m., Basement Conference Room
Berlin, Ohio, CAM Headquarters

Morning prayer for the kidnapped missionaries continued each day. Jay Stoltzfus led these prayer times, with another staff member leading the singing. Jay offered the staff new information about the kidnapping situation whenever he could. After the announcements, the staff divided into groups of two or three to pray, scattering around the basement.

With many of the executive committee occupied with the hostage crisis, other staff had to step into unfamiliar roles to keep the organization running smoothly. Unsung heroes walked the halls every day as the leadership was forced to attend to the crisis. Jay did his best to provide encouragement and support wherever he could.

Gangster Camp B

No water, no diapers, no TP, Melodi wrote. Praise the Lord that Cheryl is doing better this morning.

As always, the topic of escape bobbed to the surface again. Would the guards really be killed if they escaped successfully? Someone brought up the Bible story of the Apostle Peter. An angel had delivered him even though sixteen guards had lost their lives for failing to do their job. But perhaps an angelic deliverance was different than a human effort to escape.

Although she said nothing, for the first time Melodi was beginning to wonder if escape might be the only way out. When she had heard Sam say that he was going to leave, it had sounded possible. One or two young men slipping away when the guards weren't watching seemed easy enough. But seventeen people? Melodi felt her stomach tighten at the thought. Her childhood dreams of being the brave pioneer on the Oregon Trail were becoming too real for comfort. But maybe it would come to that.

Some of the group thought it took more faith to just sit and wait on an angel from God than to attempt an escape. What would it be like if an angel swooped down and picked them up and dropped them off at CAM's gate? Others thought faith usually involved action, trusting that God would direct them as they began moving.

"I just prayed that God would make it clear," Kay remembered.

9:30 p.m., Titanyen Base

Barry and his family had just fallen asleep when his phone rang. Jerking awake, he snatched it up.

"Tonight is going to be the night," the caller said. "The donated ransom has arrived, and we're sending our guy out to do the drop. Be ready for the call."

Oh, at last! After almost a month of this nightmare, it was coming to an end! The darkness of the Haitian night transformed into a soothing atmosphere of hope. With great excitement, Barry dialed Phil. They met at the vehicles, ready to drive away at a moment's notice.

Forty minutes after the first call, Barry's phone rang again. The moment had arrived. Barry answered, every nerve alert and ready to go.

"Never mind," the caller said. "It was called off."

Saturday, November 13; Day 29
Gangster Camp B

By Saturday, a pall of disappointment had settled over the hostages. They were well past Ping's prediction of being released in four days.

The guards reported fighting within the gang. Perhaps there had been a release in the works, and the fighting had stopped it. But if release had been that close, surely it could not be much longer.

At daylight, Matt came into the house, whispering, "The guards are all sleeping. Should we try to escape?"

For a few minutes they considered the possibility, but before they could get organized, Sòlda, the little dog, woke Ping up. Ping was a diligent guard when awake, so their chance was gone.

That morning after their time of prayer and singing, Sam brought up the subject. "Listen," he said, "this morning we had a chance to escape, and we missed it. Could we agree that if this happens again, it would be a sign from God that we should go?"

Remarkably, everyone seemed open to the idea. As they continued to discuss the possibilities, Wes drew maps in the dirt with a stick. When they were done discussing, they swept away the maps, just in case the guards would see them and get suspicious.

I think people are on board for the most part, Rachel wrote. It seems like a huge step.

Melodi also wrote about it: Discussion went better than anything previous and it seems all are agreed that if everyone is out it may be a sign from God to start walking.

Since Froggy hadn't brought enough drinking water again, they boiled some of the washing water to drink. Ping was not happy. They didn't know if he was angry with them for boiling the water or with Froggy for not bringing enough.

"We're Americans," someone explained to Ping. "We drink more water than Haitians."

The ashes and warm water recipe had worked wonders on Wes's feet, and he could walk easily now. He even crawled into the loft over the porch of the house to explore it. He emerged with a metal implement, telling the others he had found a paint stirrer. He offered it to Ryan for his use in further home improvements. As the group looked over the tool, they discovered that it was actually a branding iron.

Had it not been for Andre, the day might have passed in deep gloom. Carrot Top was chatting with Andre, who could now speak and understand some Creole. Carrot Top asked him what the English word was for "goat."

"It's an H," Andre said, just being funny.

Pleased with his lesson, Carrot Top began calling the goats in the neighboring field "H," until he was corrected.

"Oh, how we laughed!" Sam remembered later. "That is still one of the better memories."

Discouragement crept over the hostage house like patchy fog. What was happening? Anything? Had CAM and the gang reached an impasse where no further progress could be made? They had already been in captivity for four weeks, almost a month.

The hostages found that they needed each other. One day one person would be lost in a fog of despair and the rest would reorient him, reminding him of eternal truths. The next day that person would see clear sky again, but someone else would feel down, and the roles would switch.

On Saturday night, as the group tried to sleep, they again heard the pounding of voodoo drums not far away, along with violent music and people yelling. They knew they weren't close to Mt. Carmel, but it reminded them of the prophets of Baal, facing off with Elijah.

Chapter eighteen

FAITH AND WORKS

Sunday, November 14; Day 30

Gangster Camp B

*E*ven as the hostages' lives seemed to have stopped, the sun continued to rise every morning as if everything were business as usual. On Sunday, November 14, its rays shone down on a tired team.

They were tired not from physical labor, but from psychological stress. They were tired of the boredom, tired of the endless days. They were tired of eating greasy spaghetti for breakfast and snacking on moldy cake. They were tired of being hungry. Although none of them had started out overweight, they were all dropping pounds as the days passed. Ryan was tired of wearing his contacts day after day. Even Courtney had to admit that wearing the same dress for thirty days wore on one's patience.

Most of all they were tired of hoping for release, only to have those hopes dashed day after day. They had learned from the guards that the gang was fighting in Port-au-Prince. Perhaps that was why their release had been called off. It was impossible to say.

When they gathered for their Sunday service, the topic usually developed out of their experiences. They often talked about food. They couldn't help it. They also talked about stories of God's deliverance.

God had miraculously delivered the children of Israel from Egypt, but the deliverance had not come for 400 years. And when it did come, it took a long time. King Pharaoh had said he would let the people go, but then he had changed his mind—much like the gang had just done.

I sure hope the Lord isn't planning to keep us here for forty years! Dale thought.

Sometimes the hostages felt like the children of Israel eating manna in the wilderness. They had no idea what God's big plan was, but He always met their daily needs. They had enough food, and the children were doing better at night. They were also thankful that Cheryl's sickness was better and that Matt was doing relatively well despite his chronic illness. And Wes's feet were much better.

Yes, God had answered many of their prayers for food, water, or protection. But for some reason He did not seem to be answering their prayers for deliverance.

How, they wondered, did faith and works relate to each other? Moses had believed God's word, but he had also gone to work, risking his life by angering the monarch. In the end, Pharaoh had driven them away in fear and anger.

In the New Testament, followers of Christ were persecuted and killed, but the Apostle Paul had also claimed his Roman citizenship to his advantage several times.

The discussion about whether to eat extra food immediately or save it for later was an ongoing part of this faith and works topic.

Melodi was a proponent of saving valuable items like peanut butter and making them last as long as possible. If she could give Andre and Shelden a spoonful of peanut butter in the morning, the day seemed to go better.

In one of these faith versus works discussions, they wrestled with whether they actually believed God would deliver them. "Maybe we should act more like we're trusting that God will deliver us," Melodi suggested one day.

"Yes, let's just eat up all the peanut butter!" one of the peanut butter lovers suggested.

Melodi laughed. "Good point."

When Ryan first heard Lanmò San Jou asking for $17 million, it had seemed laughable. "Good luck, pal," he had felt like saying. There was no way it would happen. The gang had tried to pressure the hostages to beg for ransom, but they had determined not to do this.

Perhaps the gang realized this. Although the hostages still received enough food to get by, the gang was no longer as generous as they had been at the beginning. As the guards and gang leaders grew more irritated, some of the hostages began to wonder why someone didn't just pay some money to get them released.

They knew, however, that CAM had a no-ransom policy. "All of us had been told before we went to Haiti that CAM doesn't pay ransom," Wes said.

But did the no-ransom policy mean that no one else could pay some ransom? Surely the gang would take less than $17 million. What if some businesses each contributed $5,000? It would take only twenty of them to come up with $100,000. They didn't want their families to have to do this, but if people could donate anonymously through CAM, then maybe it would work.

The group wondered if paying ransom would actually accomplish anything. As in the book *In the Presence of My Enemies,* the gang seemed to be asking for more than just money. And there was no way CAM could get someone out of jail. If that was the demand, they might as well settle in and get used to being imprisoned. Indefinitely.

But no one in the group was that pessimistic. They decided to pray fervently to be free by Thanksgiving Day. What a wonderful Thanksgiving gift that would be! Besides being a holiday, Thanksgiving Day would mark the forty-first day of their captivity.

The missionaries talked about the significance of the number forty in the Bible. Jesus, Moses, and Elijah had all fasted for forty days. And the children of Israel had wandered in the wilderness for forty years. This number often signified a time of suffering followed by a time of triumph. Jesus triumphed over temptation, Elijah went to heaven in a fiery chariot, and the children of Israel watched the walls of Jericho fall down.

Would God allow the number to hold true for them? Surely He wouldn't allow them to be held longer than forty days.

The day before, Froggy had found a scar on Sam's arm. He had been pretty sure Sam had a GPS embedded in his arm. Matt then showed Froggy the scar on his arm where he had cut his main artery as a child. "That's where my GPS is," he said, grinning.

The gang was worried about a GPS because they were afraid the U.S. government or some other authority would be able to track them down. Froggy said he had heard that all Americans have an embedded GPS.

No day was complete without a discussion about food. Sometimes certain restaurants came up. Matt described what he would order at Subway the next time he got the chance: a sweet onion chicken teriyaki flat bread with sweet and sour sauce, a little bit of ranch and chipotle sauce, jalapenos, lettuce, tomato, and onion. He thought of biting into that sandwich almost every afternoon.

Also, he said, the next time he got to Miami he would instruct whoever picked him up at the airport to stop at the first restaurant they passed. And the second. And the third. And the fourth. He wanted something from each one—Subway, McDonald's, Hardee's, Sonic—whatever was on the route.

On other days the food discussed was pizza. Or burgers. Or desserts. Everything sounded so good. The Noeckers had traveled extensively and liked to cook the foods they had learned to love. They especially enjoyed Thai food.

Cherilyn craved chai or tea. In Kenya, when she had stayed in a friend's mud hut, she would wake up to warm tea on cool mornings. Here they were living in the outdoors similar to Kenya, but there was no morning beverage.

I felt weak and hungry all day, Rachel wrote.

On Sunday night, the violent music and pounding drums seemed closer and louder than usual.

Monday, November 15; Day 31

The next morning when Austin stepped outside to look at the sunrise, he stopped short. All the guards were gone except one—and he was sleeping. Turning around, he hurried back inside. "Hey, Sam," he said, "all the guards are sleeping!"

Sam quickly notified everyone. "Get your shoes on! Are you ready to go? The guards are all sleeping!"

For a moment, Kay thought her prayers for clarity had been answered. Perhaps this would be the day.

After praying together, they decided that if nothing changed in fifteen minutes, at 7:45, they would head out. With excitement and fear they packed bags of water in their clothes, put on their shoes, and gathered the few things they needed. It would be a bold move, walking out through gangster territory in broad daylight.

After gathering in a circle, they prayed a final prayer for God's protection.

"Well, it's 7:45," Sam said. The group almost stopped breathing. Were they really doing this? Then they looked across the field, and there they came. Two guards.

The group wasn't sure whether to be relieved or disappointed. But everyone agreed that God had been very clear that today was not the day, and this direct message encouraged them.

Even though the chance was gone for that morning, cautious hope spread through the group. Temporarily at least, they had all agreed to escape. Perhaps they weren't so far apart in their beliefs as they had thought.

Breakfast that morning was meager.

"He brought only enough food for two little piglets," Kay said.

The missionaries shared more ideas for having a hostage reunion when they got out of captivity. Someone suggested they should all guess which day they would be freed. Whoever picked closest to the right day would be responsible for hosting the hostage reunion back in the States. They were pretty sure that was where they were headed once they got out.

Matt predicted they would be released that night. Sam said tomorrow. Ryan and Melodi picked Wednesday. Wes said Thursday, and Dale said Friday. Cheryl's family picked together, choosing Sunday, November 21. No one wanted to think any farther into the future. It was too painful to contemplate being in captivity into December.

Except for Kay. Her prediction was Christmas Eve.

"Kay!!" the group protested. They hoped she was just being unreasonable because she didn't want to host the reunion.

That night, at 11:30, the group heard the same violent music blaring in the distance and soon realized it was coming closer. It was a radio in a vehicle, headed their way.

The vehicle came all the way up to the house and stopped right outside, the radio belting satanic music full blast.

As Melodi lay awake, she heard Froggy's bellowing voice outside, along with the voice of a woman. They were both yelling. She nearly jumped as she recognized names. "Samuel Stoltzfoo, Samuel Stoltzfoo." And then an eerie chant, almost a shriek: *"Tonbe! Tonbe! Tonbe! Tonbe!"* (Fall, fall, fall, fall.) The words were repeated over and over.

In the next room, Rachel had been listening to the racket for a while without really hearing it. Commotion happened so often at night that most of them, even those without Kasondra's sleeping skills, had learned to sleep through lots of racket. However, as Rachel awakened more fully, she realized that some of the others were awake and talking. Matt had just raised one of the shutter windows, frustrated with the noise. Outside he could see a truck backed up almost against the house, all four doors wide open, the music blaring. But he couldn't see anyone.

"I was going to rebuke somebody," Matt remembered.

"Matt! Matt!" Cherilyn called to him. "Close the window! Close the window!"

Matt closed the window.

"They're trying to curse us," she said. She had heard the gangsters outside killing a cat.

Matt, Rachel, Austin, Cheryl, and Cherilyn banded together to pray. They prayed against the evil presence and the satanic blaring music. They prayed for hours.

Around 2 a.m., Wes awakened for the first time. Hearing the violent, blaring music, he called through the front door to Ping, who was sleeping on the porch, to either turn down the music or shut it off.

Seconds later the music ended. The group praying inside praised the Lord for this answer to their prayer. Then Wes walked in and explained that he had just awakened and had told Ping to turn off the music. It was still an answer to prayer and a great relief to have some peace and quiet. But everyone got a good chuckle about how Wes helped end the music without having any idea that others had been praying against it for hours.

Overall, the spiritual darkness at the second location was more intense than at the first one.

"Satan was very real in that place," Ryan remembered.

Chapter nineteen

PESTS AND PRAYER

Tuesday, November 16; Day 32

Gangster Camp B

*I*t was once again the sixteenth. With sinking hearts, the hostages realized they were entering their second month of captivity.

The tyranny of waiting weighed heavily on the group, but they tried to be faithful in the few things they could do. They continued to pray for deliverance by Thanksgiving Day, the forty-first day of captivity. They prayed that God would disrupt the evil deeds of the gang. They prayed for one more miracle.

They prayed again for Cheryl's health, as well as the health of the entire group. For some, the infected sores were getting worse. Although the sores on Wes's feet had healed after soaking in a kettle of ash water, there was no way to soak infected wounds on other parts of the body. Cheryl's ankles had begun to swell too.

The afflicted people put aloe vera on their sores and wrapped them in bandages. This angered the guards, who insisted the sores must be kept uncovered to allow them to scab over and heal.

The missionaries kept singing "I Owe the Lord a Morning Song," "One More Miracle, Lord," "The Angel of the Lord," and many more songs.

That night the rice and beans disappeared so quickly that Ryan decided the meals needed improvement too. He took the empty pot to Froggy.

"If we don't have anything else but spaghetti and rice and beans," Ryan told him, "we need a *big* bucketful."

Froggy sent for more rice and beans, and forty-five minutes later a second pot arrived. The hostages ate some and put some in containers for the next day.

As they settled down for the night, a scream rang through the house. People jerked awake, sitting up. It was too dark to see clearly, but they recognized Cherilyn's voice. "Something just walked across my forehead!"

A big ruckus started, with people asking, "What was it?"

Cherilyn didn't know, but judging from the size and furriness, she suspected it might have been a tarantula. Someone fumbled for the battery light on one of the fans

---

Rawlings, Virginia

In the middle of the night in mid-November, a woman dreamed as she slept in her log house on the banks of the Nottaway River. In the dream, she heard a girl scream. She woke up, chills all over her. She was almost certain she had actually heard it. This sensation was immediately followed by an urge to pray for the safety of the hostages. After several minutes, the urge passed and she felt at peace again.

"I don't know if God used that prayer in any certain way," she said, "or if He gave me that dream so I would pray at that time."

and switched it on. Sure enough, sitting on the diaper bag was a large, hairy tarantula.

"Things really escalated then," Matt remembered.

Someone went in for the kill but missed.

"That thing has to be dead before we go to bed!" Cherilyn said.

The spider engaged its eight fat, furry legs and shot under a mattress. Someone carefully raised the mattress while someone else took aim again. This time the blow was fatal. After collecting and disposing of the pieces, everyone went back to bed, hoping their heart rates would soon resume a normal pace.

The next night the group was sitting in the house praying before going to bed. Cherilyn sat close to the doorway where she normally slept. Out of the corner of her eye, she saw movement. Another tarantula was racing along the side of the mattress.

"There's another one!" she shrieked.

Volunteers leaped into action again. Desperate, the tarantula raced toward a hole in the doorframe and disappeared before anyone could smash it.

This was bad. How could Cherilyn sleep with this creature just inches below the floor, ready to emerge at the slightest whim? Someone poured water into the hole, hoping to flush out the spider, but nothing happened. Finally, with no other ideas presenting themselves, they stuffed plastic trash bags into the rotted area, hoping to keep the spider in the hole.

After lying down on the bed again, Cherilyn heard a noise. She put her ear toward the spider hole. First there was a buzzing noise, then a rustle of plastic being chewed. There was no doubt—the tarantula was trying to eat its way out of the hole.

"It's chewing!" Cherilyn yelled to the others. Several of the men returned, pulled out the trash bags, and vainly tried to extract the spider. They finally decided it would take the spider a long time to chew its way out, so they stuffed the hole again—and Cherilyn tried to forget it was there. But for several days, when everything was quiet, she could hear it chewing. Thankfully, it never made it out.

Melodi hated tarantulas too, but the thing that really made her skin prickle was the gnawing and scurrying of rats roaming about looking for food. One night she heard one feasting on some moldy cake stored next to the mattress where her family slept. She did not sleep well the rest of the night.

Smaller creatures also harassed the group. Although the mosquitoes and bugs were slightly more tolerable at this location than the first, they were still bad.

"Of course, we didn't smell good, so gnats were swarming all over us," Matt remembered.

Matt slept beside an outside door. The guards had barricaded it, but the bottom six inches had rotted off. Just before dawn, mosquitoes would swarm in through this gap in search of warm blood. One day Matt counted thirty mosquito bites on one arm.

Even in the midst of bites, bugs, furry spiders, and satanic music, the missionaries found things to laugh about. One time they teased Charlie Horse, the guard with the singsong voice, about what would happen if the U.S. military came to free the hostages. Matt did a live show of what Charlie Horse might look like as he tried to run away while smoking a cigarette. Then he picked up a piece of coconut and said, "Oh, look at little Charlie Horse." Austin, sitting on the empty cooler, leaned back in his seat and laughed so hard that he and the empty ice chest flipped over backwards. Everyone else then laughed even harder.

It was just silly humor to pass the time, but it was good medicine. Charlie Horse, though he realized the hostages were just teasing him, didn't think it was very funny.

To see what would happen, Brandyn gave some Benadryl to Sòlda, Carrot Top's dog. It didn't seem to affect him, but the next day he slept almost all day, as if the medication had been delayed. After seeing Sòlda zonked out, someone suggested a new escape idea. Why not slip the guards a little Benadryl, then walk off while they were having a deep sleep?

This idea was pursued a little farther. Sam took Benadryl one night to test it and could not be roused, even with hammering right over his head.

But everyone finally agreed that drugging the guards was simply too aggressive, so this idea withered and died.

2:23 p.m., Washington D.C. White House Press Briefing

Question: "It's been a month now that sixteen Americans and one Canadian were kidnapped in Haiti. What has the administration been doing?"

Ms. Psaki: "Well, we've had—we have a significant presence on the ground, including with law enforcement officials from the FBI and others, who are working constantly to bring these individuals home.

"I wish I had an update for you today. I know everybody is seeking an update. But unfortunately, there's nothing I have to report at this moment."

Wednesday and Thursday, November 17, 18; Days 33, 34 Berlin, Ohio, CAM Headquarters

"Encouraging letters concerning the hostage crisis have now arrived from forty-five states and fifty-five countries," CAM reported.

Another day of prayer and fasting was announced for November 18.

"We invite believers around the world," the website statement read, "to join us in seeking God for His mighty hand to work. We request ongoing prayer for those being held, the families of the hostages, government officials who are assisting, and the kidnappers themselves.

"Great is our Lord, and of great power: his understanding is infinite" (Psalm 147:5).

Gangster Camp B

The hostages had no idea that a day of prayer and fasting had been scheduled for the next day when they planned a 24-hour prayer chain. They started at 9:30 p.m., with each adult praying for half an hour. When the half hour was up, the person who had been praying passed the watch to the next person in the predetermined order.

They prayed for deliverance. They wanted it as soon as possible, but especially by Thanksgiving Day, now just a week away. They prayed for the health of the group, especially for Cheryl and Matt and Andre, who still struggled with sickness. They prayed for strength, knowing they were all losing weight. They prayed for wisdom to know if they should try to leave. They also prayed for the salvation of the guards.

They intended to keep the prayer chain for only twenty-four hours, but by Thursday evening, as people around the world continued to pray for them, they decided to keep their prayer chain going. Why quit? It wasn't as if they had a busy schedule to work around. Eventually they changed the night segments to one hour instead of half an hour so no one would need to wake up twice in one night. Sometimes a link in the chain snapped when someone fell asleep during the allotted prayer time. But mostly it kept on, much like the 24-hour prayer chain for the hostages organized by CAM.

One night soon after the prayer chain was started, Dale finished his thirty-minute prayer slot around 2 a.m. and poked Sam, sleeping nearby on a mattress. Sam, who normally awakened fairly easily, did not respond. Dale shook him gently, then harder, but he still got no response. Sam was in a dead sleep.

Dale hated to awaken anyone from such a refreshing slumber, but he knew Sam wanted to participate in the prayer chain as much as anyone, so he kept trying. Sam finally jerked awake, mumbling and confused. Dale couldn't help laughing as Sam stood up and hit his head on one of the fans. Next he stepped on an empty water bottle with the cap still screwed on. The cap shot off with a sound like a gunshot.

By this time almost everyone was sitting up, mumbling, trying to figure out what was going on. And why was Dale laughing so hard? He was not known for breaking into helpless fits of mirth.

About this time, Dale reached up onto the little shelf above the door to grab something. He knocked off the small piece of mirror that someone had found and it fell to the floor, shattering. By this time Sam was fully awake and ready to pray.

"I really laughed myself to sleep that night," Dale remembered later. "It was a dramatic way to hand over the prayer watch."

Dale was glad he didn't struggle with falling asleep during his prayer time. Compared with some of the others, he felt he was doing quite well with his responsibility. One night he took his watch early in the night and began to pray. Five or six hours later, he awoke with a start—and a fresh dose of humility.

Friday, November 19; Day 35

As tired as the hostages were of captivity, they couldn't stop being grateful for the beautiful scenery at this second location. The sunrises and sunsets were particularly splendid. At the first hostage house, the brush and shrubbery had obscured the sunrises and sunsets. Here both horizons were plainly visible.

"It was perfect," Cherilyn said. "All you needed yet was the ocean."

One morning Cherilyn and several of her siblings and Austin went out early to watch the sunrise, as was their habit. Rookie, the guard who had been brought up in an evangelical church, came walking up, terrible music blaring from his phone.

"Turn it off!" Austin said.

"Oh, okay." Rookie fiddled with his phone, switching through different channels. All of a sudden, the phone started to play beautiful Christian music in English.

Smiles broke like the sunrise across the faces of the hostages.

"Is this okay?" asked Rookie.

"Yes!"

Another aspect of nature manifested itself during morning devotions. Matt was praying, with Ryan and Austin close by. Matt heard a splattering noise on the branches above him and felt wet droppings land on his head and drip down on his lap.

"Hey!" Matt said, glaring up into the mango tree above him where the woodpeckers liked to hang out. "You disrespectful creature!" Then Matt continued praying, "God, I'm not sure why you allowed that," as everyone else tried to rally their composure.

Ryan, Dale, and Austin suffered slight splatters as well, but Matt took the brunt of it. Matt finally continued his prayer, thanking the Lord for birds.

That evening the missionaries were suddenly ordered to pack up for another move. Once again they went through the emotions—the fear, the uncertainty. Had something happened that was pressuring the gang to hide them in a more obscure location?

To their surprise, they were soon bumping down the same dead-end road they had taken on the day of the kidnapping. They parked beside the same house they had been in earlier. It was dark, but they knew the irrigation ditch was just north of them, with the tall mango tree off to the left.

This time the gangsters allowed them to occupy both rooms of the house, as the eleven other hostages were gone. They moved out several current prisoners and prepared to transfer them elsewhere. Ryan wished he could talk to the captives and assure them that the second location was nicer than this one, assuming that was their destination.

This time they were not allowed to exit through the door they had used before. Only the front door, leading out to the wrap-around porch, was to be used. The back door was barricaded with a rock and a 6 x 6 wooden rail.

Even with two rooms instead of one, no one would have described the accommodations as spacious. There was just enough room for everyone to lie down. It was good to see the verses Cherilyn had written still on the walls. On the green walls of the second room, where they had never been before, they found a list of words. They were in two columns, one in Creole and the other in English: Hope. Faith. Belief. Love. God. Happiness. Fidelity.

Apparently the person doing the writing had dreamed of other home improvements as well. On one wall, a large screen TV had been sketched. In the opposite corner, there was a sketch of a pillow.

They also spotted their old friend, the de-tailed lizard, now starting to grow a new tail.

Chapter twenty

BACK AT THE RED SEA

Saturday, November 20; Day 36
Madras, Oregon

*I*n the weeks preceding their daughter's wedding, Austin's parents had discussed whether they should postpone the event. Austin's mom could not believe that Austin was still a prisoner. They had felt sure he would be out in time for the wedding and had decided to go ahead.

As the congregation sang the song "Be Still, My Soul," tears streamed down the faces of Austin's family. Afterward Austin's dad got up and spoke a few words about the pain of not having Austin present. This helped diffuse the elephant in the room, and the family felt able to focus on the young couple and celebrate the day.

Gangster Camp

When the hostages woke up the next morning, they received another pleasant surprise: they could see around much better. The irrigation ditch and mango tree, which had been barely visible the other time, could be seen much more clearly from the north side of the house where they now exited.

Beyond the ditch and shrubs, gangly papaya trees reached toward the sky, clusters of fruit clinging to their rough branches. Blocks of cultivated fields spread toward Goat Mountain far in the distance. Somewhere around that mountain, their quiet, comfortable homes waited for them on the CAM base.

Thinking about his sister's wedding made this a hard day for Austin. He knew he should be a part of the special singing group for the occasion. How many more special days and holidays would pass while they languished in this gangster camp?

For two of the group, that question was about to be answered.

That afternoon Matt stepped away from the group briefly to use the bathroom. When he came back, he could barely walk.

"I wasn't feeling well this morning," he told them. "Now I'm really sick."

Matt's outlook on his situation was matter-of-fact, but morbid. "If this is sepsis, as I suspect," he told the others, "I might not be here for more than twelve or eighteen hours. But at least maybe you can go free if one of us dies."

Rachel stared at her husband in horror. *Is he going to just sit there calmly and say he is ready and willing to die?*

Everyone gathered around Matt and begged God to heal him. They laid their hands on him while some prayed aloud.

Matt deteriorated rapidly and was soon burning with fever. He lay on his bed, shaking and partially delirious. His heart rate was 150, and he was experiencing chest pain.

Frantically Rachel considered the first-aid options in the diaper bag. She found the ibuprofen and a tablet of amoxicillin and made Matt swallow them.

Then Rachel called for Ping. In her limited Creole, she told him that she and Matt needed to leave—now. "I don't want him to die."

Ping promised to make a phone call. A flurry of visitors started arriving after this. First was Lanmò San Jou, rolling in on his wave of cologne. Before he reached Matt, Cheryl accosted him. "You have to do something!" she told him in no uncertain terms. Matt had gone down so quickly that everyone felt sure he was dying.

"I know. I know!" Lanmò pushed his hands out in front of him as if fending off her question. Those watching were amazed to see a flicker of concern cross his face.

When the chief reached Matt, he found Rachel weeping. She repeated that she didn't want Matt to die, and they needed to leave. Lanmò looked at her and nodded his head. Rachel was amazed at his attention. He turned around, however, without saying a word.

"Wait!" Rachel said to him. "Can we leave?"

He nodded his head briefly, then said, "Wait."

Waiting was something the missionaries had been doing a lot of lately. They really didn't want to do more of it with Matt's life on the line. But there was no choice. They worried that they had cried "Wolf!" too many times before in pleading for release for more minor illnesses. Would Matt now die in front of them because the gangsters did not believe he needed help?

As always, the afternoon was hot, even for people without a fever. Matt lay in the first room, where the captives had been held originally—right inside the back door they were not supposed to use. Seeing Matt's suffering, Sam moved the rock and the post and opened the door to let in more air. The others tried to position fans to blow on Matt.

Suddenly Ping came storming over to Sam. The rest of the guards came too, demanding that Sam close the door. Apparently the door had been barricaded on purpose; it was not to be opened.

"We're going to shoot you!" one of the guards fumed.

"Okay, shoot me." Sam just stood there. "We have to do something for Matt."

Ping was furious.

"Don't make a big fuss over trying to get more air in here," Matt said. So Sam closed the door and returned the barricades to their original positions.

Toward evening Lanmò came back and announced that someone was coming to get Matt and Rachel.

"Where are they taking us?" Rachel asked, calling on Sam to help interpret.

The big chief said they were going to the mission.

"What mission?"

There was no reply.

Rachel was sure they weren't planning to take them all the way to the Titanyen base, as that would be dangerous territory for the gang.

By the time the vehicle arrived, Matt reported that he was feeling better.

"Look, you're going to be sick," the others told him. "Even if you have to act that way."

Matt thought he could possibly walk by now, but the others rejected the idea. The men banded together and carried Matt out to the truck, loading him into the back seat of the four-door cab.

Following along, Rachel was stunned to see the lot full of vehicles and men with guns. Besides the truck, there was an ambulance driven by Pop-A-Wheelie Chief and about four other vehicles.

While Rachel stayed close to Matt and tried to figure out where they were going, the guards informed Sam and Wes that the rest of the group would be moving to a new location and that everyone should put on their shoes.

Melodi was in the house when Ping marched up onto the porch and started yelling, "Get your shoes on!" She started to throw a few things into her striped diaper bag.

"No, no!" Ping screamed. "Just get on your shoes! Right now! Go!"

Melodi shoved the diaper bag into Courtney's hands and picked up Laura.

The gang herded Ryan and Melodi and the children into a truck. Looking out the window, they could see Sam and Wes standing outside, facing the vehicles. Ryan's heart sank to his toes. From his angle, it looked as if their hands were tied behind their backs. Melodi was also scared for the two men.

"Open the door!" she said. "They can get in here!"

Sam and Wes did not get into the truck but climbed into the ambulance with Austin.

Pop-A-Wheelie Chief took off, nearly doing a wheelie with the ambulance. After a short drive, the vehicle with Matt and Rachel separated from the other vehicles.

Thump! Bump! Ryan and Melodi's family jostled along in the pickup as it careened from one pothole to another. As always, the bouncing questions were even worse than the physical discomfort.

Where are we going? Will Matt and Rachel be okay?

In the darkness, Melodi saw a shadowy building off to the left.

"You've got to be kidding me," Ryan muttered, staring at a second building. "We're right back where we started!"

Slowly everyone understood. The gang wanted Matt and Rachel to tell the outside world that the hostages had been moved to a different location.

They quickly settled back into the house, now just fifteen of them. It was nice to have a little more room, but everyone missed Matt's dry humor and Rachel's quiet presence.

Everyone wondered what was happening to Matt and Rachel. Were they really being taken to a safe place where Matt could get medical help?

Saturday Evening, Haitian Back Roads

In the four-door pickup, Rachel watched fearfully as the driver, hidden behind a facemask, took them through Haitian back roads with his headlights turned off. He had even spread a blanket over the dashboard so none of the interior lights could be seen. Both the man in the passenger seat and another man in the back seat carried automatic machine guns. The four or five men riding along in the bed of the truck were also heavily armed.

For over an hour, the truck wound this way and that through the Haitian bush. For a short time, the truck took a larger road before cutting back into the brush. Rachel could not see how this route could be taking them toward help.

The driver continued to drive by moonlight. Sometimes the gangsters would open the windows and stick out their guns. Once they passed through a gangster checkpoint but had no difficulty. If the route was meant to confuse Rachel and Matt, it worked well. Within a minute of leaving the gangster camp, Rachel had no idea where they were.

Finally they stopped and the two were ferried off into another vehicle.

They were overjoyed to hear three amazing words: "You're safe now."

9:40 p.m., Titanyen Base

Barry, his phone always at the ready, saw it light up. It was his contact from the embassy.

"We have Matt and Rachel here. They've been released due to health. Come as quickly as you can."

Barry bolted out the door, notifying Phil. They gathered Matt and Rachel's luggage that Grace had prepared, jumped into a vehicle, and headed for the embassy.

"We want them to be flown to Guantanamo Bay, Cuba, to a hospital there, but they would rather go to the CAM base," the embassy professional told Barry.

By the time Barry and Phil arrived at the embassy, Matt felt even better than he had earlier. But after discussing it, they decided he should be evaluated by medical professionals.

Before boarding the helicopter to Cuba, Matt updated Phil and Barry on the condition of the other hostages. Phil and Barry thanked God when they heard that no one had been abused and that everyone was still together. Even though the food was scant, the hostages were surviving. All of them wanted very much to get out, but they were still praising the Lord.

At the embassy, Matt stepped on a scale. He had lost thirty pounds since the kidnapping. The good news was that his sweet onion chicken teriyaki flat bread with sweet and sour sauce, a little bit of ranch and chipotle sauce, jalapenos, lettuce, tomato, and onion couldn't be far away.

9:45 p.m., Walhonding, Ohio

The same moon that guided the gangsters down the dark Haitian roads shone down on a rural dwelling in Walhonding, Ohio.

Throughout the days of waiting, Matt's mom had come to appreciate the moon, knowing that Matt and Rachel could see it too from their prison camp. Often, when seeing the moon shining over the fields outside her bedroom window, she would cry out to God.

Tonight, with her husband asleep on the Lazy Boy in the living room, Matt's mom went back to the bedroom. She looked out the window through the blinds at the moon shining over the fields. Her mind went to Haiti, and tears came to her eyes.

"God, how much longer can we take this? And how long can they take it?"

She moved to the bed and picked up her headlamp and the book she was reading. After reading for a bit, she began to feel sleepy. She had just turned off the lamp and put the book away when her husband came into the room and turned on the light.

Why, the nerve of you! she thought. Usually he had enough courtesy not to turn on the light when he came to bed.

"Someone from the Haitian embassy is on the phone," he said. "Matt and Rachel have been released!"

Grudges forgotten, Matt's mom leaped out of bed.

"Do you want to talk with Matt?" the caller asked. "We have him right here."

Did they?!

Matt's voice was soft and sounded weak. But there was no doubt about it—it was really Matt.

"Matt, are you okay?"

"Rachel and I are. But please pray for the rest of them."

Matt and Rachel were very concerned about their friends left behind.

Chester County, Pennsylvania

That Saturday night, Rachel's mom was talking to her son on her husband's phone. She heard the buzzing of another call coming through as they talked. When she ended the call, she handed the phone back to her husband. With one glance, her husband realized that an FBI agent working on the case had tried to call. He called the number back.

"Daddy, we're released."

It was Rachel!

Sunday, November 21; Day 37
Gangster Camp

Ryan took the prayer watch at 4 a.m. the morning after Matt and Rachel had left. A short time later, Lanmò San Jou's white Prado came flying in. Almost before the vehicle came to a stop, blows and screaming began. Someone was being beaten. Had some of the guards been found sleeping?

"What should we do?" the hostages asked each other.

But there was nothing to do. Through a crack in the wall, they could faintly see two men being beaten. The men screamed and moaned and begged for mercy as the horrible beating continued. Then the two were tied hand and foot and shoved into a small room at the end of the porch.

When morning came, the two men were brought out. Their faces were swollen and dirty and caked with dried blood. One had a broken tooth. One of the guards informed the hostages that the men were rival gangsters doing bad things like stealing money from churches. Apparently this was a crime in the eyes of the 400 Mawozo, but stealing seventeen missionaries was not.

The departure of Matt and Rachel combined with the early morning beating created an emotional upheaval. Some of the hostages were ecstatic because of Matt and Rachel's release, while others found the possibility of not being released by Thanksgiving very discouraging. Surely God would deliver them before the forty-first day!

Everyone wondered if Matt and Rachel had really gotten out to a safe place. Judging by all the armed men escorting them, they must have anticipated possible trouble. The reports of the guards varied. One said Matt and Rachel had been flown back to the United States, while another said they had been taken to the Dominican Republic. Yet another reported that they had returned to the CAM base.

Dale was one of the ecstatic ones. He was happy that at least two of the seventeen had gotten out alive. He felt confident that Matt and Rachel had reached safety where they could give updates to Barry and the families of all the hostages.

If there was no other cause for happiness, it was Kasondra's birthday. Turning fourteen required celebration. Even Froggy joined the festivities by bringing scrambled eggs and bread for breakfast, along with oily macaroni. Later he brought chicken and potatoes—not much but enough for everyone to taste—along with the normal rice and beans.

I ate the most delicious chicken bone of my life, Melodi wrote.

Sam was in a discouraged state of mind, but the two men who had been beaten concerned him. He felt he should try to reach out to these sufferers. In the afternoon he asked the guards if he could give them water.

"Yes, but not bottled water," Ping said. "They have to drink out of the bags." He also refused to allow Cheryl and Melodi to wash the men's battered faces.

Sam took bags of water to the men, who gratefully accepted his offer. Since they were tied hand and foot, and could not hold the bags of water on their own, Sam held the water bags to their mouths.

"You need to pray to Jesus," he told them. "Jesus can help you." But he didn't say much. The men introduced themselves as Peter and Grasia.

Later that night, Sam felt like God wanted him to go and share the Gospel with the two new prisoners.

Sam really had no interest in preaching that day. It was Day 37 of captivity, with no end in sight. He was totally discouraged.

"God, we've preached, we've prayed, we've sung songs, we've shared your love, and no one, almost no one, has responded to your call."

Sam had been preaching since they first arrived in the gangster camp, and there seemed to be few results. He felt about as excited to preach as Jonah did when he was called to go to Nineveh.

"God, if you want me to go, you're going to have to fill me," Sam finally said that night before he went to bed. He still felt that God wanted him to go to the prisoners and share God's love.

8 a.m., Berlin, Ohio

At long last, some good news!

Not only had Matt and Rachel been released, but the update they provided was encouraging. The hostages were all together, and although many of them had infected bug bites, no one was seriously ill. Also, the hostages were preaching the Gospel to their captors.

Still, Matt emphasized what he thought his friends in the gangster camp would say, "Do whatever you can to get us out of here."

Miami, Florida

In a hospital in Miami, Matt reflected on the success of his restaurant tour. In the gangster camp, when he had said he would stop at every restaurant on the way home from the airport, he had been joking to lighten the mood. At the same time, he really did want to do something of that sort. After all, he had lost thirty pounds.

Matt and Rachel's helicopter ride to Cuba had landed them at the hospital early Sunday morning. Matt had not eaten anything since his hard-boiled egg portion Saturday morning, and he was almost starving.

"Could we get something to eat?" he asked.

"Sure!" the hospital staff told him. "We can warm up some food from last night." When they brought up the dish, Matt stared in disbelief—it was rice and beans. Matt tasted it and found it almost flavorless. There were also some hard, chewy fish.

Matt couldn't believe it. His visions of feasting after being released dissipated like steam off a plate.

On the Coast Guard flight to Miami, Matt aired his grievances to the FBI agent accompanying them. He told her of his disappointment in the food. She promised that when they arrived in Miami he would be served something that didn't involve rice and beans.

When the plane hit the runway in Florida, Matt and Rachel looked out at the cloudless blue sky with a joy almost like disbelief. *Are we really free?* they wondered. FBI agents stood on the runway to welcome them. Right beside the runway, they saw a huge, beautiful rainbow.

How could that be? There wasn't a cloud in the sky. Matt and Rachel stared at the rainbow, praising God for His deliverance and for this sign of His faithfulness.

Matt would have loved going to a restaurant for a good meal, but instead, the doctors admitted him to a hospital for further evaluation. Trying to be helpful, one of the FBI team members offered to go to Wendy's and get Matt a bag of hot, delicious burgers and fries. Matt consented with a smile.

The agent bought the food and went up to Matt's room. Since Matt hadn't been transferred yet, the FBI official seated himself outside the door to wait, not realizing that the lag time between the ER and the room would be several hours. By the time the agent realized he would need to go find Matt, the bag of Wendy's food was cold.

The next day in the hospital, Matt got rice and beans again.

"It was kind of ironic," Matt remembered later. "I guess the Lord was teaching me that it's not all roses even if you're not in captivity."

Monday, November 22; Day 38

On Monday, the missionaries learned from the guards that the radio had announced the release of two of the kidnapped Americans. Everyone felt great happiness at hearing this confirmation of Matt and Rachel's safety. It didn't take a lot of imagination to picture Matt sinking into an easy chair, saying, "It's so good to be home, uh, home, uh, home!"

But it was hard to have him gone. Andre had no one to scold by saying, "Matt, Matt, Matt; that's enough of you!" And the habit of addressing each other with multiple names, such as "Wes, Wes, Wes" or "Sam, Sam, Sam" seemed a little less fun with Matt gone.

The guard they called Mr. Attitude also filled them in on some other news. "Six hundred U.S. troops are here in Haiti," he told them. "You will be leaving soon."

This time the missionaries were not convinced. "They can say whatever they want to say, and we can choose if we want to believe it," Kay said.

Later that day a white helicopter thumped over the mountains and briefly touched down. The hostages looked at each other. Perhaps the U.S. government had decided it was time for action. Everyone half-expected a midnight raid.

As they lay in bed in the darkness, Ryan told Melodi what they should do if shooting started. Since their bed was right beside two doors, he said that he would take Andre into one corner and Melodi should take Laura into the other corner close by.

Through the night, rain poured over the two block buildings and turned the dust of the courtyard to mud. Water stood in puddles, presenting Ping with the formidable challenge of keeping his sandals clean.

There was a raid that night, but not the kind they anticipated. As Melodi lay in bed, trying to sleep, she heard a guttural gnawing sound. Suddenly some rice and beans came crashing down onto the bed— followed by the rat!

That was the end of storing rice and beans up on the catwalk. After that, they tied the box of leftovers in a plastic bag and hung it on the electric wire that doubled as a clothesline.

Besides the rat raid, rain dripped in through the roof in places, forcing several people to inch away from the worst of the wetness. But there was not much room to move. It was not a very restful night.

To pass the time the next day, some of the single men dug canals with sticks to help the water drain off the road and out of the camp. Their feet sank into the mud, and they felt as gleeful as small children in puddles.

"Digging in the mud and water was the most fun I had in a long time," Dale remembered. "We were also doing something useful."

After the ditch digging was over, Sam and Wes moved on to spy work. Guard Rookie was listening to the radio, and they wanted to listen in. Wes casually walked around one side of the house, and Sam walked around the other to see if they could get close enough to hear the news. Rookie kept eluding them, but the two finally got close enough in one part of the yard. For all their efforts, they were rewarded by hearing one brief comment about tourism in Haiti. Because of all the recent kidnappings, tourism had been stopped.

In another corner of the camp, Froggy walked up to Kay and began chatting.

After they had talked a bit, Kay asked Froggy, "Where would you go if you died today?"

"I'm not going to die today."

"You never know. You could. Where would you go if you died?"

"I'm not going to die today."

"Somebody could shoot you," Kay suggested calmly.

"No," Froggy said. "Nobody's going to shoot me."

"You could go out here on the road and get killed."

"No, I'm not going to get killed. I'm a great driver. I'm really careful."

Kay again asked Froggy point-blank where he would go if he died, and again Froggy ignored the question.

Dale, nearby, leaned over to Kay, whose Creole was better than his own. "Ask him what that black thing is on his arm, that ring."

Kay asked Froggy about the black bracelet.

"That protects me," Froggy said.

"That doesn't protect you," Kay replied. "Only God can protect you."

Instead of answering the question about his destiny, Froggy then changed the subject. "You won't leave here until after a year," he told Kay and Dale.

That morning Wes had overheard one of the night guards scolding Ping. The night guards came as reinforcements, with extra big guns. "All white people know how to run guns," the night guard said. "You shouldn't leave your guns lying around."

Later that morning Wes walked past the couch. It was placed between the two buildings, not far from the power strip where the guards charged their phones at night. It had a sheet over it. When Wes lifted the sheet, his eyes widened. There was the big assault rifle, the one the guards took turns using. The magazine was in it, and there was no one around.

Wes considered returning the gun to one of the guards and saying, "Here, did you lose something?" But he restrained himself and replaced the sheet.

For some, the euphoria of Matt and Rachel's release was followed by gloom. As the time until Thanksgiving shortened, it has hard not to wonder if anyone remembered them. They were sure their families had not forgotten them. And they now had Matt and Rachel on the outside world to advocate for their release. But what would they be able to do? Anything?

Sam still did not feel like sharing the Gospel with the beaten men, but he willed himself to obey God's voice. Forcing himself to be civil, he read verses and stories from a *Flanbo* booklet to the prisoners.

Sam watched the faces of the two men and thought of the thieves crucified with Jesus. Just like the two thieves, one of these two men, Grasia, was proud and arrogant. But Peter, the other one, seemed ready to hear the message. He had a humble heart.

Peter had stolen money from churches and admitted to being involved in immorality.

At the end of the readings, Sam led the men in prayer. Peter then prayed, not audibly but under his breath.

When Peter said "Amen" at the end of his prayer, Sam looked up at him. "It was as if I could see the joy of the Lord on his face," Sam remembered later.

The next morning Sam went over to talk to Peter again. He looked happy. "Peter," Sam said, "do you believe that Jesus is the Son of God?"

"Yes, I do," Peter said. A radiant smile spread across his face.

"Have you repented of your sins?"

"Yes, I have," he said. "I'm sorry for my sins."

"Do you accept Jesus as your Lord and Savior?"

"Yes."

"Do you have Him in your heart right now?"

"Yes, yes!" Peter's smile was the most convincing proof of all. "I do have Jesus in my heart!"

Sam gave him a big bear hug. "Welcome to the kingdom!"

If Sam was a blessing to Peter, Peter in turn was a blessing to him and the rest of the missionaries. They found out that the guards were manipulating the two men with mind games.

"We are going to kill you," they told Peter. To Grasia, they said, "We won't kill you unless you let this other one run away."

Peter did not expect to live long, but his newfound joy was obvious to everyone. "I am not afraid to die," he said. "I am ready to meet Jesus."

Chapter twenty-one

KEEPING ON

Tuesday and Wednesday, November 23, 24; Days 39, 40

Gangster Camp

*N*ow that they were back at the original location, someone asked one of the guards about the second shack closer to the entrance. "Oh, that's the devil's house," he replied.

No one knew exactly what this meant.

The fire ants were out of control. Besides biting people, they crawled into the food, even chewing happily inside sealed bags of crackers with no visible holes. The containers of rice that were saved for the little boys were wrapped in a bag that was twisted twice, then placed in a bucket with soap on the rim and a tub over the top of the bucket. The rice was still full of ants in the morning. The missionaries just blew or brushed them off and ate the food anyway.

To get rid of them, Ping decided to clean the house with Clorox.

First he needed to go to town to get some, which presented a problem. Who would watch the prisoners, including Peter and Grasia, who were tied up under a tree?

Finally Ping thought of a great idea. He went over to the tree and got Peter and his companion and marched them back to the courtyard between the houses. He sat them on chairs facing the missionaries.

"Now," Ping said. "These guys are going to guard you. And don't run away. Because if you do, they'll shoot you!"

The missionaries looked at Peter, their new brother in Christ, and Peter looked back at the missionaries. Soon everyone was laughing.

As Ping went on his way, Sam looked at the ties around Peter's ankles. "Aren't those things too tight around your legs?" he asked.

"Watch this!" Peter said. He reached down and moved the knot, loosening it.

The two captured gangsters clearly were not kept in the camp by physical force. They were kept there by the psychological control of the gang. They could have escaped, but likely they would have been found and killed.

Many nights, the guards told Peter he would be killed. "Tonight the big chief is going to come, and then we'll kill you." The night would pass, with nothing happening, then the next day they would say it again. Sometimes they changed the story and told him, "We're not going to kill you after all." Despite this manipulation and mental torture, Peter remained strong.

The missionaries assumed they would eventually be released. But Peter's future, even if he wasn't killed, looked bleak. Would he be able to maintain his faith long term? The group prayed for him, and even hoped that perhaps he could join them if they got released.

One day while Wes sat on a chair taking his turn to pray, Sòlda dived under his chair. One of the guards had thrown a piece of coconut shell at him and hit him in the side.

A few days later Melodi asked Carrot Top about Sòlda.

"He's sick," the orange-haired guard replied. Soon after that, he reported that Sòlda had died.

Still trying to catch a lizard, Brandyn hit one with a coke bottle, causing it to shed its tail. Now there were two de-tailed lizards running around, one with a knob of a tail beginning to grow back and one with a newly removed tail. But still no one had caught a lizard.

Then one day Brandyn successfully landed a kettle lid over a lizard. Everyone cheered. Finally they had caught one of the little creatures. As Brandyn lifted the lid to take a peek, the lizard shot out from under the lid and skittered away to safety. Everyone booed. The victory over the lizards had been short-lived.

Andre's too-large underwear was a small problem, but one that continued to frustrate his mother. Melodi had asked Cheryl what could be done, and Cheryl tried to think of a way to pin the underwear so it would be the right size. But Andre was an active boy, and a pin would not stay.

One day Cheryl was standing at the edge of the bushes looking out over the fields that she had called the Red Sea. She gazed at the mountains and the clouds, drawing strength from the beauty of nature. She glanced at the ground close to her feet and saw something shiny. She reached down and picked it up, thinking it was a pin.

But she discovered it was a needle—with the thread still attached. Stunned, Cheryl ran to Melodi. "Look what I found! We can fix Andre's underwear!"

The ladies rejoiced over this miracle, and Melodi rushed off to sew up the underwear. God had indeed sent them one more miracle. Big or small, they praised God for them all.

One day Cheryl and Shelden were inside the house when they heard Froggy arriving in his vehicle. "Where's Shelden?" he called, his voice booming through the camp. Although the little boys no longer participated in fist bumps, the gangsters liked to talk to them.

Shelden headed for the door, but before he made it out to the porch, he was sick and vomiting. He vomited the rest of the day.

"I think my sickness was a curse from Froggy," Shelden told his mom that night.

Cheryl didn't know what to think. She just wished she could discuss it with Ray.

Even in the absence of any meaningful change or hope of deliverance, the missionaries kept on. It was all they could do.

One thing they continued to do was sing. They often sang "Little Black Sheep" for Andre and "I Have Decided to Follow Jesus" for Shelden. They sang "One More Miracle, Lord," for everyone. This song ascended to heaven so often that the gangsters must have almost had the English words memorized. All the missionaries liked the song, but they still struggled with the last verse.

Sometimes they felt almost too discouraged to sing. Someone would start a song, and the others would feebly join in. As the song progressed, the voices grew stronger and more hopeful, gaining strength from the music. Thankfully, God never allowed all the hostages to be discouraged on the same day.

Often someone would just lead out in a song, and the others would join in. Sam knew a song that fit perfectly with difficult times. So one day he started off with, "When sorrows like billows roll over my soul . . ." He stopped, realizing no one was joining in. "Does no one know that song?" No one did.

A few days later Sam started the same song. "When sorrows like billows roll over my soul . . ." He got about the same distance and then asked again if no one knew the song.

Finally it got to be a joke. No matter how many times Sam started singing "When sorrows like billows roll over my soul," the same number of people joined in. Zero.

Of all the things the group kept on doing, praying was the most consistent. The round-the-clock prayer chain continued, as well as the morning and evening prayers. They prayed for their families at home and for their mothers in particular. They prayed for their own health and for the salvation of the guards.

Most of the hostages enjoyed their turn on the prayer watch as a brief moment of solitude. They often wandered into a corner to pray or stood at the edge of the irrigation ditch gazing out over the fields and papaya trees toward the mountains—out there where normal life went on.

Most of all, the 1 p.m. prayers for deliverance went on. Fervently they prayed to be home by Thanksgiving.

Once when the group was praying and singing, Austin noticed Mr. Attitude's skinny frame sitting beside one of the buildings. It looked like he was wiping tears from his face. It gave Austin a new sense of compassion. Who really was this young man? Was he just an insecure boy who put on a loud, mean facade to cover his insecurities?

The hostages kept on talking about food, even without Matt to rattle off the toppings he would load onto his sweet onion chicken sub. They begged the guards to bring them more *pate,* and sure enough, Zigzag brought some.

Wes usually just stayed out of the afternoon food conversations. Today, however, he began naming all the foods he could think of.

"Strawberry pie!" he called out.

Dale and Ryan groaned at the thought of something so good.

"Roast beef!" Wes called out next. "Peanut butter pie!"

A moan rose from Dale and Ryan.

"Shut up!" Sam said.

"Trail mix!" Wes called out. "Fry pies!"

Another chorus of delight followed from Dale and Ryan, along with more protesting from Sam. Finally Sam got up and walked away, doing exactly what Wes usually did.

The group kept on discussing books. Perhaps Wes's sudden burst of food talk meant he was finding out what the main character in *Unbroken* had discovered. This book followed the story of two men adrift on the ocean on a raft for forty-six days. While starving, the main character and two others (before the one died) found that talking about food actually made them less hungry. The main character described his mother's cooking in great detail, recounting the steps she took in making spaghetti and pumpkin pie. They did this three times a day, in place of meals.

Austin's favorite part of *Unbroken* was when the main character became a Christian and found the strength to overcome his nightmares and post-traumatic stress, and to forgive those who had persecuted him.

The kidnapped missionaries in the book *In the Presence of My Enemies* had experienced many of the same emotions as the CAM missionaries. "Everything in our lives had been snatched away from us in one swift moment," the author wrote. "No one cared that Martin was an excellent pilot, or that I could make a great pizza. We were no longer defined by our ministry or careers; we were just two human beings . . . with no idea of what would happen next and no way to influence it."

This was true for the missionaries kidnapped in Haiti too, or at least it felt that way. It no longer mattered that Wes was a good mechanic, that Dale was a good electrician, that Austin knew how to build a house, or that Cheryl could make excellent Thai curry. Ryan's Home Improvement had been put to some use, of course, but without much appreciation on the part of the captors. Melodi, Wes, and Dale were glad they could write on the paper towels with the pen, but there was no way to share their words with the world.

But did they really have no way to influence what happened next? The missionaries kept discussing this. Did God want them to simply pray and wait? Or should they make plans to escape?

Dale, who had hoped no money would be paid to the gang, found his opinion wavering. The joy of Matt and Rachel's departure was followed by deep gloom. Oh, how he longed to go for a solitary walk back to the woods on his parents' hobby farm! Or to spend a night with his brothers in the cabin they had built! Dale loved quiet time. He loved to be alone out in nature. Here in the gangster camp there was always someone close by. And the mountains across the fields were too far away.

Sam, too, felt despair set in. He thought of last year this time when he had been driving through the Pocono Mountains and heard God call him to more service. What had that been for? "Lord," he prayed, "did you call me to Haiti just to get kidnapped? Just to sit here rotting in this gangster camp?"

Their opinions on ransom still varied from day to day and from person to person. Everyone wanted to leave, and with increasing desperation. It seemed less and less important how that release was obtained.

On the other hand, most of them still did not want the gang to receive money for wrongdoing. They feared that if ransom were paid, it would be detrimental to both CAM and other missions.

"If someone actually does give ransom," Sam said one day, "it still doesn't mean we will be released." Although Lanmò San Jou had demanded ransom, Santa Claus had told them from the beginning that the other gang leader was demanding that he be released from prison.

I just felt spiritually empty, Dale wrote, and just felt so hopeless. It felt like we're going to rot out here for a year. After all, that was what Froggy had said in his conversation with Kay. Most likely he was just trying to get their attention. But what if his words were true?

Thursday, November 25; Day 41
Thanksgiving Day

Thanksgiving morning dawned not as the hostages had hoped. When the sun rose, it shone over the brush at the edge of the gangster camp.

Thankfully, not everyone felt gloomy. But for many, it was a day of grief, of questions. Why had God not answered their prayers and freed them before this holiday?

Still, everyone tried to think of something for which to thank God. They went around the circle, with everyone sharing something he or she was grateful for. Then they made another round.

Wes said he was thankful for peanut butter. Rare as it was, it had appeared on several occasions. He also thanked God for the DLP, the dear little plane. It certainly hadn't delivered them, but it was a welcome diversion. The group had concluded that it was just a media plane or perhaps a training plane.

Kay thanked God that they had not been tied hand and foot like the other hostages, and that they had the freedom to pray and sing. She also thanked God for her heritage. She could have been born in a poverty-stricken Haitian village like so many of their friends. Or, like young Bigotry, she could have been raised as a gangster's assistant.

Cheryl thanked God that they would be leaving soon. She didn't know when, but she was confident that God would answer their prayers. Cherilyn thanked God for the chance to get to know everyone and for the sunrises and sunsets she enjoyed so much. Courtney was grateful for the chance to serve God. In comparison, the lives of the guards seemed hopeless and pointless.

Brandyn thanked God for *pate*. Kasondra thanked God that her mom had gotten kidnapped with them. Even though she didn't like to see her mom suffer, she knew how much harder it would be without her. Shelden thanked God for the orphanage. Perhaps in his young mind, the fun on the swings had been the last happy moment before the drudgery of living in a gangster camp.

Dale was grateful for the lessons he had learned through their suffering. "God is teaching me to not worry about the next day or the future." In the second round, Dale thanked God for the ability to laugh and share jokes. Though Matt was gone, taking his dry humor with him, they could still laugh despite an uncertain future.

Sam said he was grateful for salvation. He couldn't think of much else. His depression had not lifted. In the end, what mattered more than the confidence that he would spend eternity with the Lord?

Austin said he was grateful for the memories they shared. Whether books they had read or memories of family or friends or traveling, the conversations about times past helped people stay sane in the gangster camp. "It helped us keep our minds off the boredom," he said later. "Off the seemingly endless hours of not having a lot to do." Austin also thanked God for his "Smucker reflexes" when the sheet fell down while he was in the shower. Between the inherited reflexes and Brandyn's assistance, he had survived the event.

Melodi said she was thankful for water. Andre was thankful for mangoes. Ryan said he was thankful for family. He certainly referred to his small family there with him in the gangster camp. He also remembered his larger family, scattered far away. Were they together today? Were they thinking of him?

The days of riding in Grandpa's tractor with cousin Grant in Kansas were so far away. But just last year, a few days after Thanksgiving, Grant had been bursting with eagerness as he told Ryan and Melodi about his new girlfriend. He had persuaded Ryan to stay in Kansas just a few hours longer so they could deliver a shed together.

Grant had gotten married about seven months later, after Ryan and Melodi had moved to Haiti. They had missed the wedding, but Ryan was happy for this favorite cousin.

And though not mentioned specifically by anyone except Ryan, everyone was thankful for Laura. They all gained strength from this little one who did not fear the future or wonder why God had not answered their prayer. Dale said she was "the highlight of almost every day."

After the sharing time, Sam asked Westley if he could borrow his pen. He collected a nice length of the white paper towel and walked around behind the house to seek a little privacy. He sat down on a chair and again asked God some hard questions. "Did you call me here just to rot?"

And then, just as He had in the truck in the Pocono Mountains, God answered. The God of the universe, unlimited by geography or captivity, touched Sam's heart.

"Sam," he seemed to hear God say, "I didn't call you to go to Haiti to reach out to the Haitian people. I called you to Haiti because I wanted to change you. When you were back in the United States, you weren't even near your fullest potential for my kingdom."

Sam's heart felt suddenly light and free. Even though God had brought his weakness before him, He had accompanied the message with hope.

"Lord, that's right," Sam prayed. "There were times I had the opportunity to share the Gospel, and I didn't take it. Lord, if you take me out of here, I want to proclaim your faithfulness. I'm ready to die. If you want me to lay down my life, if more souls can be won through that, I'm ready to do it."

Then Sam began to write a letter to his family. As he wrote, he realized how much he had been struggling with bitterness toward the gangsters.

If someone had asked Sam a week earlier if he had forgiven the gangsters, he would have said, "Yes, of course." Now he realized that he still harbored resentment and asked God to take it from him.

In addition, he realized that he might never make it out of this gangster camp alive. He was the one who was blamed whenever there was trouble. If an attempted escape failed and the guards chose to kill someone, Sam was sure it would be him. Likely he would never see his family again. So he wrote the letter, hoping that if he died, perhaps one of the others could get the letter to them.

As he wrote the words on the paper towel, tears flowed down Sam's face.

Dear family,

Today is Thanksgiving Day. I woke up this morning with my thoughts and prayers directed towards you. Words cannot even begin to express the thankfulness that I feel for a Christian family like I have! . . . This is the 41st day that we find ourselves with the bandits who kidnapped us. I don't know if we will survive to tell the story, or if you will even have the opportunity to read this note.

There were times since we were kidnapped where I struggled with unforgiveness and ill-will towards our captors. I just want to let you know that by God's grace I have forgiven them, and hold nothing against them.

Here the tears flowed in buckets, but Sam kept going.

Most of them, if not all of them, have grown up in dysfunctional homes. They haven't had much opportunity to hear the Word of God being preached in purity and truth . . . I just hope and pray that they've been impacted by the words and the songs that were shared with them during the time we spent here. I long to see these men in heaven some day! Family, if I never see you on this earth again, then I will be waiting with joy and anticipation to see you all in heaven!

I love each one of you dearly,

Your son, brother, and friend in Christ,

Sam Stoltzfus

Sam folded the white paper towel letter and slipped it into his wallet. Even if he never made it home to Pennsylvania, perhaps his wallet would.

Although Thanksgiving was not a holiday in Haiti, Froggy happened to bring something different that day— roasted corn and bean sauce with dumplings. It was a delicious change.

Titanyen Base

Back at Titanyen, those on the base talked about what they should do for the holiday. It wasn't a holiday for the workers on the base. Besides, they really didn't feel like celebrating with a lot of food when the hostages likely were hungry.

In the end, Phil and Grace invited everyone to their place. They had a good time, complete with some special food.

Chapter twenty-two

"SIT DOWN OR I'LL SHOOT YOU!"

November 26–December 3; Days 42–49
Gangster Camp

The morning spaghetti and evening rice and beans continued to arrive like sunrise and sunset. Sometimes the missionaries dipped into the huge stock of banana puree. The puree came in boxes of glass jars and had almost become a joke. The ingredient list included water, sugar, citric acid, and bananas, and could hardly be described as wholesome food. However, everyone ate it, and Melodi fed it to Laura occasionally. But after so many jars, they became tired of it, just like the moldy cake and the stale Doritos.

Perhaps the poor nutrition also interfered with the healing of the infected bug bites. Cheryl had a great number of them, and they seemed to be growing worse. They were beginning to interfere with her walking.

It was hard for Cheryl to understand why God had answered so many other prayers but had not delivered them from their bondage or healed her wounds. One day she remembered how people had asked her before she and her family came to Haiti if it would be safe there. Cheryl had replied that if the Lord was taking them to Haiti, He could care for them there.

Now, in her suffering, Cheryl cried out to God, "Lord, I told people that if I came to Haiti you would take care of me."

In the silence that followed her prayer of complaint, Cheryl sensed God asking her, "Do you still believe that?"

Taken aback, Cheryl considered the question. *Yes,* she resolved, *I do still believe that.* With this affirmation, her courage and faith grew stronger.

Kay also had a few persistent sores. One felt like a metal rod scraping away at her bone from the inside. The pain was so great at times that she could barely walk. The wound sat right at the bottom of her skirt, where the fabric tended to rub if the wound was not wrapped. She would lie down and rest until she regained the courage to go on. Sometimes the wound seeped sticky fluid. This drainage ran down her leg and into her Crocs, making her foot stick to the sole.

The ladies took an old T-shirt and cut it into strips with a razor. They dressed their wounds with pieces of aloe vera and then wrapped them with the bandages.

When Froggy came upon Kay with her leg wrapped, he flew into a small frenzy, ripping at the bandage to pull it off. "You are not allowed to wrap these!" he bellowed.

Kay explained that the pain was too great if she didn't wrap it. Also, the dust of the gangster camp seemed to irritate the wound if it was unwrapped. At night the fire ants crawled into the wounds and bit into the raw flesh. Kay knew that Froggy honestly believed the sores should be left open to the air. In his mind, the wound would not heal and scab over if it were wrapped. Kay continued to wear the wrap at night when Froggy couldn't see it.

The ants continued to bite, but there was not much to do about them. Laura would wake at night, crying, whenever an ant bit her. In the morning, ant bites covered her baby skin.

Ryan's contact lenses had now been in his eyes for over six weeks. He was thankful that he could still see. Andre continued to struggle with stomach pain and fevers. When it was hot, he often found it difficult to sleep unless Ryan fanned him.

In addition to the small plane sometimes circling over them, the hostages now noticed a new, larger plane. The little plane had been christened the DLP, or dear little plane. This one became the BFG, the big friendly giant. But would it, like the other one, simply circle above them week after tedious week?

Then the last working pen ran out of ink.

"It felt like a real loss," Wes remembered. "We didn't have a whole lot and that was one of our most valuable things."

Melodi and Dale, who had also been keeping records, hoped

November 27, Middle East
"A believer imprisoned in the Soviet Union is quoted for saying, 'I had the physical sense of being prayed for. Even when I knew nothing and received no letters, I felt the warmth as if sitting near a fire. It was like hearing someone praying for me and thinking about me. This supported me so much. It is difficult to explain, but I felt and knew I was not forgotten. This was sufficient to make me resist the most difficult moments.'

"I pray this over your loved ones. May they sense the prayers we pray. May they sense that inner warmth of belonging. May they remember they are not forgotten."

that the loss of the pen meant that God was about to deliver them.

It seemed easiest to avoid discussing the prediction each person had made for their release. Day by day the prediction dates expired. Only Kay's doleful prediction of Christmas Eve was left.

Cheryl's sores grew worse and worse. Finally she could barely walk. The team continued to ask the gang to let her go to the hospital, and the leaders came and took pictures of both Kay and Cheryl's sores. Kay had several severe wounds, including one on her hand that had developed an eight-inch red streak. But Cheryl had almost fifty sores.

Cherilyn noticed that her mom was not eating much. She told her that she had to start eating more. How could she heal with no nutrition?

Pop-A-Wheelie Chief came to look at the sores and promised he would try to get Cheryl released. He said the decision wasn't his to make, but he would do his best. As he left, he mumbled, "These people are going to die on our hands."

One day the gang brought cream for the wounds. On closer inspection, the hostages discovered it was skin-lightening cream.

Wonder what CAM is doing? Wonder what our churches are doing? Wes wrote in his diary on Sunday, November 28. That night, he developed a raging fever. He felt better by morning but was still not well.

On Monday Dale shared that it was his mother's birthday. She would be 55 years old. How he wished he could call her.

I just can't stop daydreaming about home, Melodi wrote the day before the pen ran out of ink. **Clothes are falling apart. I have never been so consistently drained.**

The men's facial hair was redefining their appearance. Beards and mustaches grew thick, and hair fell over their ears.

When December hit, the group guessed again which day they would get out of captivity. But even after everyone had picked a new day, Kay's date was still the farthest away.

The hostages also discussed the sixtieth day of captivity. Someone thought the U.S. government might take action if nothing happened before then. However, Day 60, December 14, still seemed far away.

One day Kay approached Mr. Attitude. What Kay lacked in stature, she made up for in courage.

"Hey, we want some *pate*," she said. "I want to learn how to make them. I need someone to teach me how to make them."

Kay had lived in Haiti for years but had never had a lesson in making them. What better time than now, when there was nothing to do? As Mr. Attitude stared down his nose at her, she went on, "Do you have a cook who could show us how to make *pate?*"

Mr. Attitude's face suddenly lit up. "*We* are going to teach you how to make them," he said.

Sure enough, the next day the guards made a fire and heated up a pot of oil, then called for Kay.

Kay called for the others. "Come on out, whoever wants to watch."

They went out and stood around the fire. By this time Kay's sores hurt so badly that she wasn't sure she could stand and watch. But she did for a while, watching the pale dough drop into the sizzling oil and come out shiny and brown. The guards made some *pate* with salami, but then the meat was gone and they had to make the rest with nothing inside.

They seemed to think it was worth it to teach these Americans how to make this specialty food. Despite her painful feet, Kay enjoyed the lesson. She had never imagined receiving cooking lessons from armed gangsters. She only wished the lesson had happened while Rachel was there, because she had wanted to learn it too.

Saturday, December 4; Day 50

Lanmò San Jou arrived with news: "You're all leaving, today or tomorrow."

Pop-A-Wheelie Chief also congratulated the hostages, implying that a ransom was finally being paid.

The missionaries didn't want to get their hopes up too high, but even the guards were excited. Froggy brought them better food than normal, along with cold sodas, for the evening meal, as if he wanted their last memories of him to be pleasant.

Berlin, Ohio

As the days ticked by with no progress, the teams in Ohio and Titanyen continued to discuss their options. Had it been a mistake to get professional help to offer ransom money rather than having Barry work with the gang?

On the ground in Haiti, Phil and Barry wondered if the hostages would be free by now if they had remained firm about not paying any money. The government authorities did not think so. They had told Barry from the beginning that if CAM refused to pay, the hostages would be killed. But Barry, with his long history of fearlessly trusting God, felt that God was not limited to what had happened in the past.

Others suggested that CAM had messed up the situation by being too slow to pay ransom or to accept help from other negotiators.

Government officials were stumped by the long captivity. The emerging complication seemed to be that the gang was asking for more than just ransom money. Reportedly they wanted a gang leader released from prison, something outside of the control of any American organization.

Tommy reminded the group that action plans that fail always cause those involved to second-guess whether the right thing had been done. He was willing to accept that they may have made the wrong decision, but a different action plan could have resulted in the same defeat. There was no way to know what plan would have the best outcome.

Again, the agony of disagreement and the longing for resolution strained the team members.

But everyone was united about one thing: they wanted the hostages to come home.

The crisis team had received a suggestion that a three-day fast be proposed to break the powers of spiritual darkness in Haiti. They announced this fast for the coming Monday, Tuesday, and Wednesday, from December 6 through December 8. People were invited to participate in as much of the fast as they wanted, whether parts or all of the three days.

The crisis team also finalized plans to host the families of the hostages for a meeting. It would be a chance to help them process what was happening and find comfort in each other's stories.

Of course, everyone continued to hope that the missionaries would be set free before either of these dates arrived.

7:13 p.m., Titanyen Base

Everyone at the Titanyen base was invited to Phil's house for supper Saturday night. The meal was over, and people had gravitated to the easy chairs. Barry's phone was dying, with only 1 percent battery left, so Phil's daughter Olivia brought him a charger. Barry plugged it into the charger, and almost immediately the phone began to ring.

It was his contact at the American Embassy in Port-au-Prince. "The drop is being made," the caller said. "They've agreed to release everyone. So be ready."

Barry leaped out of his chair. The entire house went into a frenzy of anticipation and excitement. Could it be? After all these endless days and nights, had the time finally come? The great burden of the past weeks felt as if it were shifting, preparing to slide into the Caribbean Sea.

"We had better wait to get our hopes up," one of the women cautioned.

"We can't," Barry said. "I can't control my hopes."

The others couldn't control their hopes either. People praised the Lord as they talked and raced around. The men prepared the vehicles. The women talked about when they should make the coffee to have it fresh for the returning hostages.

Twenty minutes later the embassy called back. "It fell through."

Barry's heart sank to his toes as the caller continued. "But San Jou said we'll do it tomorrow night."

Barry sighed. "Do you believe him?"

"It's hard to say. You can't believe these guys. They're all cracked out. I can't tell you for sure."

As the excitement in the house plummeted, Barry tried to dissect the message. Why had it fallen through at the last minute? There was no way to know. Perhaps the gang leader had been spooked about something. Later it was reported that he needed to attend a voodoo ceremony to call on his god for protection.

Sunday, December 5; Day 51
Titanyen Base

After going to a church in Port-au-Prince to preach, Ray returned to the CAM base in the afternoon. Everyone waited as patiently as possible to see what would happen.

Ray had been a bit worried about Cheryl ever since Matt and Rachel had been released two weeks before. When Barry and Phil returned from talking to Matt and Rachel, they had said Cheryl was not doing well. They weren't very specific. "Cheryl says she loves you," they said. "But she has some sores on her feet and is not doing well." Ray didn't know what to think.

Up until this time, Ray had pictured his family as they had appeared when they left for the orphanage on October 16. But after hearing Matt and Rachel's report, he realized they may have suffered some wear and tear. But he prayed about this, trusting that God knew exactly how Cheryl was doing.

In the evening, Ray walked over to the top story of the single men's dorm to look out over the water. Phil and Grace and Olivia soon came to keep him company, bringing snacks with them.

Evening, Gangster Camp

As darkness approached, the hostages sat outside on the couches, chairs, and buckets between the two buildings. During the day, the furniture was placed against the devil's house because of the shade it cast, so even after the sun went down the seats were often close to this building.

All day the group had kept thinking about the promised release, trying not to get their hopes up too high.

Sure enough, as the day advanced, the guards said they weren't sure who would be released. Maybe just Cheryl because of her sores.

With her five children there, Cheryl wasn't sure if she wanted to go. Finally she decided she would be willing to leave on one condition—if six-year-old Shelden went with her. She would not leave without him.

Supper had not yet arrived. Kay sat on a bucket, with Cheryl on the couch beside her holding Shelden. Brandyn sat in the middle of the couch, and Melodi sat at the other end, holding Andre.

Suddenly the white Prado pulled in, along with a four-door pickup truck. The vehicles circled around the buildings until they were facing toward the exit again. Lanmò San Jou jumped out of the Prado and swaggered over to the group of missionaries. Without a word, he grabbed Kay by the arm and hauled her off the bucket.

The group watched in stunned amazement, breathing in the strong scent of cologne and staring at the headlights of the trucks as they lit up the gloom of dusk.

"Somebody go with her!" Melodi managed to shout.

Sam leaped up and caught up with Lanmò San Jou. "What are you doing with Kay?" he asked in Creole. "Please tell me what you're going to do with Kay!"

"We're taking her to the hospital."

And why didn't you tell us this would be happening? Sam wondered. But he didn't say that. He just thanked the gang leader.

As the guards showed Kay to the pickup, Lanmò San Jou walked back to the group and grabbed Cheryl's arm. This, at least, was less surprising since everyone had been expecting Cheryl to be taken to the hospital.

As Lanmò talked, Sam translated. "He wants to take you, but not Shelden."

"I'm not going without him," Cheryl said.

Because of her severe sores, Cheryl had difficulty standing, especially while holding Shelden. Brandyn leaped up too, supporting his mom. The guards, including Ping, yelled at Brandyn, trying to push him back down on the couch. Brandyn fought to stay upright, telling them he wanted to help his mom.

"Please let him stay with me," Cheryl said. She wanted Brandyn to walk with her and Shelden to the truck.

The guards got angrier and angrier at Brandyn. "Sit down or I'll shoot you!" Ping yelled.

"You can't take Mom without taking Shelden!" Brandyn yelled back.

Lanmò San Jou raised his hand to strike Brandyn, then backed off and ignored him. Finally Brandyn sat down.

One of the guards tried to rip Shelden out of Cheryl's arms as the other hostages watched, horrified.

"I'm not going without my baby!" Cheryl yelled, sitting back down on the couch, her arms tightly around her son. "I'm not going without my child!"

The hands of the guards wrapped around Shelden as they tried to pull Cheryl's arms off her son. Shelden began to scream.

Lanmò San Jou put his hands up in frustration and stepped back, letting his bodyguards and the other gangsters deal with the situation.

From the end of the couch, Andre watched as the guards tried to rip his friend from his mother's arms. So far, Andre had not been traumatized by the kidnapping. Although he wanted to go home, he was too young to understand what a hostage was. But now Melodi saw his eyes fill with horror.

Kasondra, sitting with the group, suddenly remembered that Cherilyn was in the house. She raced inside, screaming for her older sister. "They're taking Mom and Kay!" she yelled. "And they're not letting Shelden go!"

Outside, the guards yanked Cheryl back to her feet.

"I rebuke you in the name of Jesus!" Brandyn yelled.

The guards backed off, and everything calmed down.

"Okay, come," they said. "Okay, you can come with us." Escorted by guards on either side, Cheryl walked toward the truck with Shelden. Ping was among the guards, but the other guards were unfamiliar. They had arrived with the vehicles.

Brandyn collapsed on the couch and began to cry, saying, "Mom! Mom!"

Melodi put her arm around him. Dale came and sat on the other side, where Cheryl had been sitting. The whole group started praying aloud for Kay and Cheryl and Shelden and the rest of Cheryl's children who would not be going.

Chaos suddenly erupted again, and Shelden started screaming. Melodi tried to keep Andre from watching, but he wanted to see what was happening. Brandyn sprang up and raced toward the front of the house, but a guard grabbed him. His shirt ripped, buttons popping.

"Do you want to have only a dad?" the guard snapped in Creole. "Do you want me to shoot your mom? Make Shelden shut up or we're gonna shoot!"

Finally Froggy told the guard hanging onto Brandyn to let him go so he could join his mother.

Over beside the truck, parked close to the porch, Cheryl had been hugging her older children goodbye. She then put Shelden in the truck with Kay and prepared to get in herself, a painful process because of all the sores. Before she could get in, the guards opened the door on the other side and tried to yank Shelden across Kay's lap and out the open door.

Shelden and Cheryl both screamed. Shelden clamped onto the headrest. On the porch, Cherilyn, Courtney, and Kasondra started yelling, "No, no, you have to take both of them! He can't stay here. He's too little. You have to take both of them."

Several times one of the missionaries rebuked the guards in the name of Jesus, and each time they jerked back.

Back on the couch, Andre started whimpering, "I want to go into the house. I want to go into the house."

The door to the house was on the porch, close to all the action. "We'll just sit here and pray," Melodi told Andre.

Finally Cheryl pulled Shelden back out and headed for the porch. She seated herself on the railing with Shelden in her arms. Brandyn joined them, wrapping his arms around both of them. They saw Lanmò San Jou walk off to make a phone call.

In the truck, seated between two guards with guns, Kay evaluated her situation. She was afraid the gang wouldn't let Shelden go, and then Cheryl wouldn't go. *I won't go by myself,* she decided. She looked at the guards around her and tried to figure out the best way to escape.

Lanmò San Jou came back to the porch and again tried to tear Shelden out of Cheryl's arms. He then made another phone call and finally seemed to get permission for Shelden to leave.

The conflict had taken what seemed like a long, long time. In reality, it had lasted about half an hour. Before the white Prado pulled away, Sam approached Lanmò San Jou again.

"What about the rest of us?" he asked. "Are we going to be leaving anytime soon?"

"You will be leaving later tonight, in groups of twos and threes," he replied. Then he climbed into the Prado and pulled away.

They never saw him again.

Cheryl and Shelden and Kay crowded together in the middle of the back seat of the pickup, and then a guard got in on each side. At least one of them had a gun. After the doors were slammed shut, they were squeezed in tightly. As they left the clearing, Cheryl saw the rest of the missionaries sitting in the yard, praying.

"God bless you!" voices called out. "We're praying for you! Goodbye, Mom!"

Lanmò San Jou's white vehicle led the way out through a maze of gangsters. Once outside the camp, they continued through the barren Haitian countryside in the blackness of night. Finally, at the edge of Port-au-Prince, the vehicles stopped and the three hostages were transferred to an ambulance. A different driver took the ambulance into town.

"I still have four children back there," Cheryl told the driver. "But my husband is somewhere else in Haiti. Could you let him know?"

"Oh, where's your husband?" the driver asked.

When Cheryl told him that Ray was at Titanyen, the driver called ahead to the embassy and told them to call Ray and tell him that Cheryl would be arriving soon.

———

As the truck carrying Kay, Cheryl, and Shelden rolled through the darkness of the Haitian countryside, an exhausted calm sank over the group left behind. Cheryl's children kept talking about how glad they were that Kay was along, as she could speak Creole. If they got dropped off at a roadside clinic somewhere, she would be able to communicate with the people.

And besides, as Ryan pointed out, "Kay has nerves of steel."

The guards herded everyone into the house through the door on the porch. A heavy stone and a post still barricaded the back door of the house.

Finally inside the house, Andre tried to process his feelings after watching the gangsters attempting to rip Shelden away from his mother. "I need to shoot those bad men," he told his mom.

Melodi didn't know what to say. Like Andre, she was badly shaken by the drama of the evening. She tried to remind him in simple language that God would take care of the bad guards. She helped him pray for Shelden, Kay, and Cheryl and tried to comfort him.

Before they went to sleep, the whole group sang "Children of the Heavenly Father."

Like his son, Ryan replayed the evening's scene in his mind. He decided he had been wrong in some of his assumptions about the guards, most notably Ping.

As the head of the guards, Ping had seemed dedicated to their well-being. He didn't always know how to make things comfortable, but overall, Ryan had thought he truly cared for the missionaries.

Now he remembered Ping's yelling at Brandyn, "Sit down or I'll shoot you!" He remembered the guards ripping at Cheryl's arms as she clung to Shelden.

Worst of all, he thought of what Lanmò San Jou had told Sam. Instead of the original promise to release everyone, he had changed his mind. What a letdown. They would now release them by twos and threes, he had said.

Ryan's heart filled with dread as he considered the possibilities. *Melodi and I and our children are a family of four. Will they take Melodi out alone with the children into the dark night, with Andre screaming for me? Or will they maybe send one of the girls with Melodi and tear Andre away from her?*

Ryan felt that his eyes had been opened. Even the fatherly Ping did not really care about their comfort and safety. They were only property. If the gang leader asked the guards to lay down the law, Ping was willing to get ugly.

The events of the evening heightened Ryan's growing concern about the environment of the camp. Violent, graphic music blared from speakers. With Andre learning more and more Creole, he would soon start understanding it. At the very least, he would learn the tunes and rhythms of the songs.

Day after day, week after week, they had been forced to watch the violence, the prostitutes coming and going, and the buying and selling of drugs and cigarettes. How long could this go on?

There were also health concerns. For some things Ryan was thankful. After fifty days, he still had his contacts in his eyes, and they were still working. Melodi was getting thin but otherwise doing well, and Laura seemed fine except for the ant bites.

His biggest concern was Andre. He was often hot and feverish. And he seemed to be getting worse. Would he suddenly become too sick to recover? Did God really want them to sit here passively? Or was He calling them to take action?

The thought came to Ryan that the remaining hostages were now a group of ten young adults and teenagers who were healthy enough to carry the two small children and walk ten miles if they had to. With Cheryl's sores, that would not have been possible.

7:13 p.m., Titanyen Base

Julia Grant and Kay's sister-in-law Rachel were sending each other messages. Rachel told Julia that a good friend of Kay's, a young mother, had just passed away. Julia read the message with sorrow as she remembered Kay telling her about this woman's courage and strength as she faced her terminal illness. Rachel had finished her message by saying, "Well, that's enough about me. What's going on with you?"

Julia was just ready to type a reply when Barry's phone rang. It was the embassy. "Cheryl and two others have been released," the caller said. Barry and Julia assumed it was Cheryl and her two youngest children. Barry immediately called Ray.

Ray was still up in the third-story dorm when Barry called with the news. "We need to go to the embassy," he told Ray. "Meet me at the warehouse."

When Ray heard that Cheryl had been released, but not all the others, he was concerned. *What condition is she in? Why has she been released?*

"Can I go get my Bible?" Ray asked Phil. He went back to the house for his Bible.

By the time Ray returned with his Bible, Barry and Phil had decided to take two vehicles. Although the embassy had said only three hostages had been released, this made no sense. The ransom had been paid, and the professionals negotiating with the gang always negotiated for the whole group, not for only a few.

Lanmò San Jou had said that if he got the money, he would release the remaining fifteen missionaries. Now, as they headed for the embassy, Barry and Phil hoped he would be true to his word, and they would be able to fill their vehicles.

When they arrived, an officer escorted them through security. "Do you know who the other two people are who were released?" one of them asked the officer.

"No, I don't know their names," the officer said. "It's a lady and a child."

"Oh, it must be Melodi and the baby," Ray said.

"No," the officer said, "it's a boy about this height." He held his hand out about waist high, and instantly Ray knew it must be Shelden.

They arrived at the front door of the embassy and entered a seemingly endless maze of hallways, checkpoints, and doors. "I don't know how many doors there were," Ray remembered. "I wondered when I would finally see my wife."

They passed through a lobby packed with officials, went down another hall and through another door, and there was Kay, smiling cheerfully at them.

She's smiling, Ray thought. *That's a good sign.*

Barry took a picture of her to send to her family. She looked great.

Ray was pointed down yet another hallway to a door. "Your wife is inside here with the nurse," the official said.

When the nurse opened the door, Ray saw a small exam room with

Cheryl sitting on the table, smiling. When she looked up and saw Ray, her smile grew wider.

This is great! Ray thought, thinking of the verses he had chosen to comfort an emotionally distraught wife. *I won't need to do much comforting!*

As Ray headed into the room toward Cheryl, he met Shelden, who was sitting in a chair right inside the door.

"Dad!"

Ray stopped and picked up Shelden.

"I never heard Mom scream so loud, Dad!" he began. "It's not fair that the others had to stay at the camp."

"I know," Ray said. "But God wanted you to be here with Mom, and that's good. I'm so glad you're here."

Just then the nurse stepped out of the room and Ray, Cheryl, and Shelden had a joyous reunion.

Julia was so curious to know what was happening that she called Barry.

"I have Cheryl and Shelden and Kay Yoder with me!" Barry replied.

Julia thought of the warnings from professionals that released hostages would need counseling and support for their broken mental and emotional state. She was excited to see Kay and Cheryl, but what kind of fragile condition would they be in?

Julia and Grace quickly scrambled to put together some snacks. When the vehicles returned, they ran to meet them.

They saw Cheryl and Shelden happily reunited with Ray. And there was Kay, Julia's long-time friend, smiling and laughing and eager to greet them.

Tiverton, Ohio

In early December, the families of the hostages planned to gather at the Christian Aid Ministries base in Ohio. Kay's family made the trip from Michigan and stayed at her brother Reuben's house in Ohio.

On the weekend before the gathering, one of Kay's good friends passed away. Kay's family planned to attend the funeral.

On Sunday evening Kay's sister-in-law called Julia Grant at Titanyen. She told Julia how much she wished she could tell Kay that her friend had passed away.

"You might be able to tell her soon!" Julia said. "Something is happening!"

The news passed through Reuben's house like electricity. *Something is happening! But what?*

Soon the phone began to ring. "It's the FBI!" Kay's dad exclaimed. As the cheering and clamor rose around the family, Kay's dad bolted to the front porch so he could hear better. Soon he shared the news: "Kay has been released!"

It was some time before Kay herself called, but when she did, they talked for over an hour.

Chambersburg, Pennsylvania

Back in the States, Cheryl's other daughters had spent Sunday evening with their grandparents, Cheryl's mom and dad. When the girls left to go to their married sister's house for the night, Cheryl's mom and dad began to prepare for bed.

Suddenly Cheryl's mom heard the girls tearing back into the house. *What in the world is going on?* she thought. *Why are they coming back?*

She went out to see what was wrong, and was nearly bowled over by the wave of excited girls and good news. "They got released! Mom and Shelden!"

Chapter twenty-three

"WE NEED HELP"

December 6–12; Days 52–58

Gangster Camp

*A*t prayer time the next morning, Ryan shared his concerns with the group. "I don't want to see a scene like that again," he said. "Can we talk about escape? If we're still here three days before Christmas, would you be willing to consider running?"

The topic of escape had been so divisive recently that some didn't even want to talk about it. But this morning everyone seemed agreeable. Ryan felt new hope. Everyone was desperate. There seemed to be no end in sight—no hope of release except for people who got sick.

Sam had always wanted to escape, but the continual presence of smoke, profanity, rap music, and prostitutes increasingly wore on him. He felt that Satan was trying to get a foothold in his life.

Dale, too, had come to the point of frustration with the evil environment. In discussing escape, Dale had always been held back by the fear that if they ran, the guards would be shot. Would the missionaries be responsible for their deaths? Now, however, Dale thought of how often the guards had heard the Gospel preached to them and had rejected it. He felt assured that the responsibility rested on the guards, not on the missionaries.

Wes too wanted to escape, but he still felt strongly that they would have only one chance; they dare not mess up. Drawing from the books he had read, Wes proposed digging a tunnel. It wouldn't have to be real long, just from the floor of the house to behind the brush that surrounded the clearing. The only problem was that the guards entered the house occasionally, and there would be no way to hide piles of dirt. So likely they would have to start the tunnel from the brush and work in.

The tunnel idea prompted lively discussion and some scorn. What would they use to dig with? And who would dig?

Finding digging tools was a problem, but the pieces of rebar they had found appeared promising. As for who would dig, the single men seemed the logical answer. Unfortunately, Sam was out of the question. Whenever the guards wanted anything, they would start hollering, "Sam! Samuel!" They would notice immediately if he was gone.

But how would they get up through the concrete floor of the house?

This was definitely a problem, but Wes noted that the concrete was poor and could probably be broken. If they could dig the tunnel accurately and end up under the house, they could cut out a piece of cement and escape through the floor. Opponents, however, had a valid point: cutting this hole would create too much beating and banging.

And finally, how long would digging the tunnel take?

Wes did the calculations, based on the available hours for working and the amount of dirt he thought the workers could move. If things went well, it would take about a month, landing them well past Christmas. Of course, if they had started when Wes first thought of the tunnel, it would be almost done by now . . .

Another problem with the tunnel idea was that the gangster camp seemed to demotivate everyone. No one felt like working.

Ryan then brought up the idea of just slipping out the back door, the one barricaded with a heavy rock and a post. Of course, this plan required walking through the yard at a time when the area was reinforced with night guards. Generally, the guards congregated more heavily on the porch side of the house, but they passed the back door when they went to the outhouse. And the power strip where they charged their phones and speakers was right beside the back door.

During the last few weeks, Melodi's sense that they needed to escape had also continued to strengthen. After watching Cheryl and Shelden being ripped apart, that feeling was now stronger than ever. Like Ryan, Melodi had seen the true colors of the gangsters coming out. They were driven by greed, not by concern for their captives.

We should be thinking about how to escape, Melodi thought. *Not in some hazy, theoretical way, but in a practical way.* Whether Wes's tunnel idea fell into a "hazy, theoretical" discussion or a "practical" discussion was not quite clear to anyone.

As Melodi shared her feelings with Ryan, they agreed that if they wanted to get out, they would probably have to escape. The gang leaders kept saying they would be released, but then nothing happened. Also, neither of them liked the idea of being ransomed or rescued by force.

One morning as Ryan lay in bed, he thought of making signs to communicate with the planes that kept circling above them. One day it would be the DLP, the dear little plane, and the next day it would be the BFG, the big friendly giant. Could it be that God wanted them to ask for help?

When everyone got up that morning, they assisted Ryan with his idea. Someone collected some large pieces of cardboard lying around and brought them into the house. Using charcoal from the fire, they wrote messages on the cardboard in huge letters. One sign said *SOS,* and the other said *We Need HELP.*

The trickier part of the plan was carrying it out behind the backs of the guards.

They decided to use "heads" and "tails" as code words. Some of the group would go to a place where the guards could not see them and wave the signs at the plane. Others would act as sentries at the corners of the buildings. If a guard approached, they would say "tails." If everything was fine, they would say "heads."

The next day as they were waving their signs, they thought the plane throttled back in response to them. To keep from being detected by the guards, the sign-waving didn't last long. The planes, however, continued to circle, sometimes for up to six hours a day.

On the third day they changed their strategy and took the signs to the north side of the house, where the morning sun would hit them. This time the pilot cut his circle and flew right over them, quite low. The missionaries were sure they had been noticed, and probably photographed. Even if nothing came of it, they found comfort in the presence of the planes.

There was little other comfort in the gangster camp. Lanmò San Jou had not reappeared with promises of release. And the guards, who had been so happy over the last weekend, had grown quiet again.

Andre continued to suffer from his illness. Several times he had accidents due to diarrhea. At least twice when Andre failed to make it to the outhouse, Cherilyn swooped in to assist Melodi. As Melodi helped Andre clean up, Cherilyn removed the "vile garments," as Melodi later called them, and scrubbed them clean without one word of disgust.

One day the guards decided to clean the house with Clorox again. They removed everything from the house and washed the whole building. Wes was glad there was no hole in the floor, although of course that was why he had planned to start the tunnel from the outside.

To keep good airflow through the house, the guards opened the back door, pushing aside the rock and the post. When they were finished, they closed the door but didn't barricade it.

That night, after the guards herded the group into the house, Courtney and Kasondra discussed the unbarred door. Was it possible that God was giving them a hint that it was the night to escape? They decided they would not share their thoughts with the group yet.

"God," they prayed, "if you want us to leave tonight, let the door still be open at 8:00." It was around 7:30 when they made this decision.

The girls resumed talking with the people around them, and Kasondra lay back down on her bed. She and Courtney usually slept closest to the barricaded door.

At 8:00, the watch beeped and Kasondra sat up. "It's 8:00!" she whispered to Courtney.

At the same moment, they heard a *thunk* as the post and rock slammed back into position against the door, barring them inside.

Almost a week had passed since Cheryl and Kay's departure, and food was running low. They weren't even getting moldy cake and stale Doritos anymore. Someone suggested that Melodi ask for more food.

The group had learned that if Sam or Ryan asked for food they often received only a tongue-lashing, but if Melodi or fourteen-year-old Kasondra asked, the results were much better. So Melodi went to Froggy and politely asked for more food.

He laughed. "You want more food?"

"Yes, the children are hungry."

Froggy pulled out his phone, said something into it, then stuck it into Melodi's face. "Tell him what you want."

"Can you bring a few groceries, please?"

The person on the other end laughed and asked what she wanted. So Melodi named everything she could think of. Bread and juice. Peanut butter. Coconuts. Peanut butter. Avocados and mangoes and bananas.

Definitely peanut butter.

Not only did Wes and Dale and some of the others really like peanut butter, but it kept well and did not grow moldy. In an almost meatless diet, the protein in peanut butter helped satisfy their food cravings.

Sure enough, Pop-A-Wheelie Chief came that weekend with snacks. There were three loaves of slightly moldy bread, juice, two jars of peanut butter, and a can of Pringles.

The group decided that the Pringles should be saved until the moldy bread was gone. They put the Pringles and other items they wanted to save in a pillowcase and knotted it shut. Then they looped Ryan's belt through the knot and hung the floating pantry from the catwalk above Ryan and Melodi's bed.

Courtney, the divvying-out expert, got the job of spreading twelve slices of bread with peanut butter and handing one to each person. They did this after the 1 p.m. prayer time. The snacks were a morale booster even if they showed that the gang had no plans to release them anytime soon.

Pop-A-Wheelie Chief also brought a fluffy, furry carpet, as if he was looking out for their comfort during the long winter ahead. **I wish they wouldn't keep trying to make us so very comfortable,** Melodi wrote with a pen that Eeyore now let them use.

Peter and Grasia were still being held captive. Sam tried to encourage Peter every day. Peter had no idea what it meant to follow Christ, but he was eager to learn. Knowing that his own life in the gangster camp was held by a thread, Sam wrote Peter a letter. He included the address of a Haitian Christian Peter could turn to if he ever got his freedom. Sam also included his own number so Peter could reach him even if he was back home in the United States.

Peter received the letter with gratitude. But that night it fell out of his pocket and Grasia destroyed it.

With Andre's sickness growing worse, the situation in the gangster camp weighed heavily on Ryan's heart.

One night at bedtime, Ryan tried to remember the verses from the book of James about asking God for things without wavering. Melodi and the others tried to help him with the passage. Melodi thought sure she could remember the verses, as she had taught them to her students.

"But let him ask in faith, nothing wavering," Ryan quoted. "For he that wavereth is like a wave of the sea driven with the wind and tossed. For let not that man think that he shall receive any thing of the Lord. A double minded man is unstable in all his ways."

They could get most of it, but they thought they were missing something. At any rate, the verses said that people should ask in faith without doubting, so they decided to pray that God would take them home that night. They would believe that God would rescue them that very night. Ryan left his shoes on, and they all went to bed, hoping and believing that God would deliver them in the middle of the night.

The next day Melodi mulled over the passage. She pondered their prayer for deliverance and the fact that it had not been answered. Suddenly the first part of the passage flashed into her memory. It was the verse right before the verses they had been able to remember. "If any of you lack wisdom, let him ask of God, that giveth to all men liberally, and upbraideth not; and it shall be given him."

She found Ryan right away and quoted the verse. Yes, he remembered it now too. They realized they had not been praying for wisdom. "God," they prayed, "give us wisdom. Help us know what to do."

Titanyen Base

The night after her release, Kay felt very low. Oh, it was good to be back in her own apartment on the base. It was good to be able to talk on the phone to her family again. It was good to drink tea and to eat other foods besides rice and beans.

But as the evening progressed, Kay's thoughts pivoted to the little house in the gangster camp. *Probably the rice and beans are arriving about now,* she thought. *And soon the guards will lock them up for the night.*

Grace had invited everyone for supper. Kay didn't know if she had the strength to sit at a table and eat good food while her friends suffered. But she forced her steps over to Phil's house.

When she arrived, Ray said Cheryl was struggling too. As they talked, Kay and Cheryl comforted each other. They were so glad to be free, but they wished they could help share the suffering of the others.

Barry and Phil and the rest of the team thanked God for the safe return of Kay, Cheryl, and Shelden. But as the hours passed, and the promised full release did not take place, they concluded that the gang had reneged on their end of the deal.

Reportedly, Lanmò San Jou now said the gang would not release any more hostages until the other gang leader was released from prison. If he released the other hostages, he said, he could be killed himself.

Barry and Phil knew there was nothing to do about the leader in prison. The United States government *could* not release him, and the Haitian government *would* not.

Although the third-party negotiator working on the case could not give many specific details, he remained hopeful that the other hostages would soon be released. But as the days passed, it was easy to wonder if there was any way forward. If Lanmò San Jou didn't have the authority to release the hostages, who did?

It was becoming clear that this kidnapping was different from the ones the gang had carried out previously. This time they had white Americans. They had women and children and a baby. They had leverage. And they knew it.

The gang leader's empty promises made the situation even worse.

There were few options left. Would the government resort to a tactical response? Government officials had said this could result in the death of several hostages and some of the kidnappers. So far they had been reluctant to do this unless there was imminent loss of life.

Phil would have to go back to Ohio soon; he had other children living at home. With a heavy heart, he scheduled a flight for his wife and daughter for Thursday, December 16. He told Barry he would stay for the next weekend, but eventually he too would have to go back.

Laurel Creek Lodge, Ohio

As the family meeting took place at Laurel Creek Lodge in Ohio, the families shared the emotions and struggles they were facing. They found comfort in talking with others who understood what it was like to have a loved one held hostage.

During prayer time the last evening of the meeting, Austin's parents shared what Cheryl had told them. She had a message for the mothers: the single men had told her to tell their mothers they were praying for them.

"We really went into puddles then," Dale's mom remembered. She had wondered how Dale was doing as a prisoner with nothing to do. She knew he liked to be active, and she also knew how much he liked his time alone.

Austin's mom knew that her second son usually had a lot of energy and good cheer. She thought he would be positive in the face of difficulty and stress. She hoped so. But she also knew he could have some really dark times. She had felt certain that his trip to Haiti would be a life-changing experience. But she had never expected this.

Sam's mom remembered him as a little boy, often at the nucleus of a conflict with his brothers, unafraid to speak his mind. She had no doubt that he was sharing the Gospel with boldness. But was it getting him into trouble?

Wes's mom had at first found it almost impossible to accept that her quiet, steady son was in the hands of evil men. She knew he had a huge imagination and loved to plan and strategize. How had he been dealing with confinement and captivity?

But one thing the mothers had not thought of was that their sons were praying specifically for them. It not only warmed their hearts, but it also gave them hope that everything was still all right in the inner world of their sons.

Chapter twenty-four

THE CONFLICT

Monday, December 13; Day 59
Gangster Camp

*D*ay 59 was like many of the days before—marked by boredom, too-familiar food, and Andre's sickness.

Andre screamed on and off for over three hours, often crying out, "It hurts!" He was raging hot and often tensed his body. Melodi began to doubt if he would ever get well. Several people prayed out loud for him. By morning he finally slept, but he was still feverish. Austin took his pulse. He counted 140 beats per minute. Melodi noticed a pulsating lump in his neck. She and Ryan prayed that they would know what to do if the guards said he could be released but refused to take the entire family.

It had now been over a week since Kay, Cheryl, and Shelden had left—and since Lanmò San Jou had promised them they would soon leave.

Ohio

"Approximately thirty-four years ago, twenty men from Orangewalk, Belize, were going by tractor and wagon through the jungle into the fields to work. A guerrilla band captured them, but two escaped and ran back to the colony.

"The captives became discouraged and started to doubt if they would ever be delivered. One of the men prayed, 'Lord, if it is your will that we be delivered, please show us a monkey.'

"Almost immediately, all the men saw two monkeys. Seeing monkeys in that area was rare, though not impossible.

"It was that day or the next that the men were delivered.

"I am praying that the hostages in Haiti would see a monkey—or a rainbow, or whatever they need—to strengthen their faith in the Lord."

Sam continued talking to Peter, encouraging him and teaching him what it meant to be a Christian. On the outskirts, Ping listened to Sam, laughing. None of the guards liked Sam's fearless preaching, and Ping had begun mocking him for presenting the Bible as truth.

Sam decided it was time to preach to Ping. In his powerful preacher voice, Sam called on Ping to repent of his sins. He pointed out sin in Ping's life.

Ping quit laughing and got angry. He began to yell back at Sam. Ryan, sitting on the couch, hollered "Amen!" several times to support Sam's points.

That evening the group met for their devotional time at the usual spot beside the devil's house. They had a wonderful time praying and singing. They prayed for deliverance. They prayed for strength. They prayed for Peter.

As they sat outside looking at the sky, God blessed them with a beautiful double rainbow. How wonderful it was to know that the God who had sent a rainbow to Noah so long ago was still watching over them.

The rainbow provided hope in an increasingly desperate situation. They had not heard from Lanmò San Jou, and Andre was still sick and running a fever.

"Maybe if you would pay some money, you could go home for Christmas," Mr. Attitude told them in his loud voice. He seemed to indicate that a ransom payment would benefit both parties. The hostages could leave, and he would have a merry Christmas.

So maybe no ransom had been paid. The hostages didn't know what to think. Or, worse yet, had a ransom been paid but the gang had changed their minds? Had they decided to demand more money, or the release of the gang leader from prison? It would be no surprise if they broke an agreement.

Later that evening it began to rain, turning the dusty compound into thick, sticky mud. After heading inside and being locked in for the night, the hostages talked.

"Let's have a Pringles party!" Ryan suggested. The lone can of Pringles hung from the catwalk above. Someone got it down and popped off the lid.

The guards had received a new supply of drugs and alcohol and seemed to be especially loopy. With the rain falling, they had retreated to the porch to stay dry and were not walking around the building.

"Here's our opportunity!" Sam said. "All we need to do is place our trust in God and try to make an escape. Sure, we're going to look like pigs by the time we get back to the CAM base, and our feet will probably be bleeding. But once we have a good hot shower and sit there in our chairs, we're going to say it was well worth it. Here's our opportunity! They aren't doing their laps!"

As the Pringles can circulated, opinions bounced around the front room of the house, where most of the hostages had gathered. Andre and Laura had fallen asleep on the mattress and Cherilyn was in the back room, close to the barricaded door, but everyone else was in the discussion.

Ryan suggested that the group present a sign to God about whether they should escape. They had been discussing the idea for so long; was it not time to let God decide?

"If the moon is covered and it's dark at 1:00," Ryan suggested, "let's try to go. If the moon is shining, let's stay here."

The moon itself was neutral, neither loved nor hated in the case of an escape. A dark moon would provide cover to the missionaries, but a bright moon would help them find their way.

With the recent rain, there were still clouds in the sky. But there were also hints that it might clear, so the hostages had no way of knowing which way it would go.

Sam was on board with Ryan, of course. Wes also found it exciting, though he confessed that his knees turned to jelly just thinking about it. Dale had made peace with his responsibility for the guards and was ready to go. In the doorway to the back room, Brandyn sat close to his sisters Courtney and Kasondra. Austin stood in the doorway behind them.

But, as was normal, not everyone agreed. Brandyn and Austin suggested adding more signs. What about saying if the moon is dark *and* the generator is running? This would provide a noise cover. And what about adding that the guards needed to be quiet?

"Okay," Ryan said.

The discussion went on for a long time as they tried to decide what they could lay before the Lord. Finally they decided to go around the circle and have each person share whether he or she was on board with laying a sign before God. Ryan and Sam encouraged everyone to talk. They didn't want anyone to feel pressured into agreeing.

Wes said he supported letting God decide in this way. Sam and Dale did too, and of course Ryan did because it was his idea. Melodi said she would do whatever Ryan did. Courtney and Kasondra also agreed. Brandyn thought for a long time before saying no. Austin also thought for a long time, then he said he would be on board if no one tried to fudge the signs. For example, if the guards had the radio on, did that qualify as being quiet? But if the signs were predetermined, he would support it. Cherilyn, who wasn't part of the discussion, was informed of the question but needed more time.

Then someone brought up the question of whether it was even right to ask for a sign. In the Bible, hadn't Gideon been reproved by the Lord for asking for a sign? Of course, they had no Bible to verify the actual wording of the account, but this started a whole new discussion that now felt hopelessly fragmented.

Ryan and Sam finally decided that further talk would not be helpful, as not everyone was on the same page. Ryan knew that for a matter of life and death like this, they needed to be unified.

"Let's drop it for tonight," Sam said. "Let's just go to bed and sleep on it."

Ryan agreed completely. They were not united.

As most of them headed for bed, Austin and a few of the others decided to stay up to pray.

Tuesday, December 14; Day 60

Early the next morning, not long after everyone got up, the words began to fly.

"Well, we missed our opportunity," Austin heard someone say.

Those who had been in favor of escaping had clearly stated that no pressure would be applied to get the others to agree. But Austin felt that comments like the one he had just heard would make those opposed feel responsible for the continued captivity of the group.

"Hey," Austin said. "Around 12:30, most of the signs looked favorable. But then at 1:00 the guards got up and got noisy, the moon was bright, and the generator was not running. We were not supposed to go."

"Well," Melodi said, "I'm not surprised. We weren't going to go. We weren't unified."

At morning prayer time, Brandyn shared a vision he had had a few nights before after he had finished his prayer watch. After falling asleep, he had begun to dream, but it didn't feel like a dream. It was a very orderly sequence of events, more like a vision.

In the vision, Brandyn was high in the air like a drone, looking down on the gangster camp. He saw the bus, the white Prado, and the gangsters all around. All the missionaries were in the bus. The top of the bus opened, and God's hand reached down and picked the missionaries out one by one. God's hand also cut Peter's chains, allowing him to run free, down a path to the home of a pastor who would be able to protect him.

In the dream, Ping was praying in a corner, saying he needed to leave the gangster camp, and Lanmò San Jou was sent to jail. His gangsters said they didn't want to be gangsters anymore; they wanted to live good lives. In the meantime, the giant hand took the missionaries back to the CAM base at Titanyen. In the vision, the devil's house was converted into a church. Brandyn saw Lanmò San Jou and Pop-A-Wheelie Chief and all the other gangsters leaving church. Ping was the pastor and had just preached the sermon.

Brandyn had told Melodi the vision earlier. She didn't belittle the vision but had told him it would be wonderful if something like that happened.

However, at the morning devotional time, someone said that Brandyn's vision did not seem relevant to their immediate situation. This hurt Brandyn, who had considered the vision a bright spot in his recent days.

Then Austin shared why he had been up at 1 a.m. He and some of the others who had not been in favor of escaping had stayed up late to pray about whether or not they should leave if the signs were all present at 1 a.m.

At this point Sam came up for air. "Austin, I can't believe you!" he said. "You would barely say how you felt, and then you went and prayed and put the signs before God when we had decided we're not going to do it because we weren't all agreed!"

Some of the others were also surprised, if less vocal. They wondered what those who were praying would have done if the signs had all been positive at 1 a.m. Everyone else had been asleep, since they had decided for the sake of unity not to run.

Opinions flew back and forth. Everyone felt either hurt or frustrated or both. Austin and the others who had stayed up late the night before went back into the house to pray. This time they asked God to speak to someone about the topic of escape. It didn't have to be one of them, but, *Please, God, speak to someone!*

For the rest of the day, no one brought up the topic of escape. It was the sixtieth day, the day they had looked forward to with such hope.

Ryan mulled over the situation. He still felt very burdened about the need to escape. He was the oldest person in the hostage group now, even though he hadn't hit thirty yet. He was the only married man and felt some responsibility not just for his family but for the whole group. Now, instead of being free, they were having church problems. Freedom seemed as far away as the mountains beyond the papaya trees. But despite the stalemate, the feeling of urgency to leave had not left Ryan.

In the course of the day, the group noticed something of interest. The huge rainstorm had ruined the wiring for the power strip by the barricaded door where the gangsters liked to charge their phones and speakers at night. To keep such a thing from happening in the future, the gangsters had rewired it, with a great deal of effort, under the shelter of the front porch.

As usual, Froggy came by with the food. But this time he pestered Melodi with a question: "When do you think you're going to leave?"

"Oh, I don't know," Melodi said. "I'm ready to go right now!"

"Oh, no, no, no. You're gonna be here a year yet."

No one really believed him, but it was a depressing thought.

Chapter twenty-five

ONE MORE MIRACLE

Wednesday, December 15; Day 61

Gangster Camp

On Wednesday morning the group had devotions with the stiff courtesy of estranged friends who are not able to talk about the issues that really matter. No one mentioned their disagreement except Sam, who apologized for speaking so hotly the morning before. Even the song "One More Miracle, Lord" seemed stiff and overused.

When Froggy brought breakfast, Wes asked him if he had brought oil for the generator, which had not been running. No generator meant no fans at night. This made things very difficult for Ryan and Melodi whenever Andre needed to be fanned because he was so hot.

Froggy said he would get some. But in addition to his forgetfulness, Froggy seemed to be less and less eager to spend money on them, so they had no idea if he would follow through.

Wes decided to slip into the bushes and try to stomp a trail in the tangled brush. The way things were going, it wasn't likely they would need it anytime soon. But perhaps sometime Lanmò San Jou would make good on his word and release the girls and the families. If that happened and only the single fellows were left, an escape would suddenly look more realistic.

Wes went to the outhouse, and from there took a dive into the bushes. He had arranged a time to come back and a sentry who could meet him with "heads" or "tails."

Without discussing it with each other, Ryan and Melodi both prayed a similar prayer. They asked God that if He did not want them to escape, He would show it in Wes's countenance—he would come out of the bushes looking discouraged.

Wes was gone for almost two hours. At the appointed time, someone gave him the "heads" signal, and he slipped through the brush back into the clearing. He walked across the yard with a big grin on his face. He saw Ryan watching him.

"What you got on your face there?" Ryan asked.

"That mountain is not that far away!" Wes said. "I was practically under the mango tree! If we can get to that trail without the guards seeing us, we would have all night to run."

Ryan looked at Dale, who was nearby. "Dale, is God nudging you?"

Dale jumped at the surprise question. "I don't know. Is He nudging you?"

Ryan wanted to say "Yes!" but instead replied, "I think I better go pray about it."

Ryan began to pace and pray, circling the house. On the porch, Cherilyn was using a plastic fork to comb Melodi's hair. Andre sat on Melodi's lap, hot and sick.

Melodi had thought about talking to Cherilyn about the escape conflict. Maybe if they talked one-on-one, they could come to understand each other better. However, no words had yet come to mind. There seemed to be no good way to broach the serious subject. So she defaulted to more benign topics: family gatherings and memories.

As Ryan passed the porch, he heard Melodi telling Cherilyn the story of his cousin Grant. Warmth filled Ryan's heart as he thought of the cousin he had played with on the Kansas farm. Ryan loved to go to Grant's house because he had such nice toys. And Grant loved to go to Ryan's house to experience the delightful hubbub of a big family.

Even after Ryan's family moved to Wisconsin, they still returned for visits. When Ryan's family pulled in for a visit, Grant would come rushing out of the house and give Ryan and his brother a big hug.

This was the story Melodi was telling Cherilyn, and every time Ryan made a loop around the house he heard a little piece of it. Of course, he didn't need to hear Melodi tell it; he knew it well.

Ryan's grandmother had three mentally handicapped children who required total care. This meant that Ryan's grandparents had spent years and years caring for these special-needs children. At a developmental level of two- to three-month-old infants, the special-needs children awakened multiple times each night.

Ryan's grandparents washed load after load of cloth diapers. They sacrificed vacations, events, and sleep. They gave up things that other people didn't even think to count as blessings.

Ryan's grandparents finally found they needed help. After much wrestling and many tears, they placed their two oldest handicapped daughters in a state hospital for people with special needs. They visited the girls frequently, taking their other children with them.

Time passed. The other children reached adult age and gradually moved away from home. Ryan's grandparents continued to care for their third handicapped child at home, born after the older girls had moved into the state hospital.

One day a vehicle drove in the lane. Several administrators from the state hospital climbed out. They informed Ryan's grandparents that they had found a growth in their daughter's abdomen and had done some testing.

The scans revealed not a tumor but a baby. The hospital had informed the authorities of the crime done by one of their male employees, and the culprit was now facing prison time.

In the meantime, the professionals explained, they would do everything in their power to help with the situation. They would take care of the abortion. They had brought the paperwork with them. All they needed was the signature of a guardian.

Ryan's grandparents had no illusions about the situation. The doctors said the child would likely be born with severe disabilities.

What a blow! If anyone knew what it meant to raise a special-needs child, they did. If anyone had memories of sleepless nights and missed opportunities, they did. If anyone knew what it meant to be so tired you were not sure you could go on, they did.

And yet they refused to sign the paper. Abortion was wrong. It was murder. It was not an option. They sent the administrators away without the needed signature.

Grant was born early, but he was a fighter. Ryan's uncle and aunt from Kansas, who had been wishing for more children, had agreed to adopt the little boy. They were aware of the doctor's warnings that the child might not be normal, but they were ready to accept him regardless of the circumstances.

As the months passed, Grant's adoptive parents realized that their fears for his health and development were unfounded.

"Thank you, God!" Ryan prayed now as he kept circling the house. "Thank you for grandparents who were willing to do the right thing even when it was hard!"

Then, just like a flashlight switching on in a dark night, God's voice lit up Ryan's thoughts, chasing away his last doubts about escaping.

"And this," he sensed God say, "is what I want you to do."

Ryan quit praying. He had his answer. He knew he needed to take his family away from the gangster camp. He went to the porch and picked up his sick son. He took him into the house. With tears streaming down his face, he fanned his son. As Andre fell asleep, Ryan continued weeping. Melodi came in when her hair was finished. She saw the tears on Ryan's face, but she also saw his big smile.

"I think I've got my answer," Ryan said.

Ryan told her everything. How he had been walking and praying. How he had heard snatches of the story Melodi was telling Cherilyn. How he had spontaneously thanked God, and how the answer had flashed back at him.

Ryan had received permission from God to escape with his family. No, it was more than permission—it was a request that must be followed.

By now Melodi was weeping too, harder than she had cried at any point since the kidnapping. But they were both excited. After days and weeks of not being sure what to do, they felt that God was clearly working.

"It feels like we're almost home," Melodi said.

It was almost time for the 1 p.m. prayer time for deliverance. Andre had fallen asleep, but he would wake up again if no one fanned him. Ryan made his way out to join the rest of the group, while Melodi peered through the cracks in the house and tried to listen while fanning Andre.

Instead of starting into prayer like normal, Ryan said he had something he would like to share.

He then told them everything. He told of his cousin Grant and his grandparents and how he had been reminded of the story as Melodi was telling it to Cherilyn. As he talked, he wept. He told them that just after thanking God for his grandparents, he had heard God telling him to take his family out of this place. As Ryan spoke, he could not stop crying. He was so overwhelmed that God had spoken. He also mentioned that he and Melodi had both prayed about Wes's reaction after spending time in the bushes.

Ryan said he understood perfectly what God was asking; he would not require any more signs from God. "I don't think the generator will be running," he said. "And the moon will probably be bright. The guards will probably be awake. But we are going to step out in faith. Any of you are more than welcome to join us."

Ryan told the group he didn't really believe the guards would shoot anyone who stayed behind. Whether to go would be everyone's personal choice. Again Ryan asked them to share where they stood on the matter. He hoped his story had not divided the group even worse.

Again they went around the circle to report whether they would join Ryan and his family in the escape effort. In the house, Melodi strained every fiber of her being to hear.

There were only twelve people left now, and four of them were Ryan's family. That left eight people to report. Everyone knew what some of them would say.

Sam. Yes, definitely. He had felt for a long time that God wanted the group to simply take a step of faith and leave the results up to Him.

Dale. Yes. As he spoke, he looked up and noticed Melodi peering through the door. He hoped she could hear.

Wes. Yes.

Courtney. Yes.

Kasondra. Yes.

Brandyn. Yes.

The next person in line was Austin. No one knew what he would say.

"This morning when Wes came out of the bushes and we were talking about it, that was the first time I felt peace about it," Austin said. "I am ready to go!"

Cherilyn again asked for more time, until after prayer. So the group prayed as they normally did, with everyone taking a turn.

Finally the prayer was over, and everyone looked at Cherilyn. She nodded her head. She was ready to go.

The entire group transformed. They were together! They were unified! Sam later said that they had experienced almost every human emotion during their captivity. But December 15 was the first time they experienced unbridled joy and excitement. For the first time since their kidnapping, they had real things to do. They had plans to make. They had a purpose.

God had sent them one more miracle.

"If it doesn't work out tonight, we will wait for another night," Ryan said. "But let's make plans and work together."

Working together on this topic was new territory. Everyone talked and shared ideas. They were a little scared, but they were excited.

They discussed what they would take along, and what would fit in the diaper bag. It was their only bag. They would take their wallets and their diaries and the necessary things for the children. Matt's medications and the old worn clothes would be left behind. When they had talked earlier about escaping, Melodi had torn up a green sheet to make a baby carrier for Laura. She now tucked this into the diaper bag.

Next they discussed how to exit the back door, which was barricaded with a heavy rock and a post leaning against it. The door had a gap at the lower end. A piece of lathe covered this gap, but it was now fastened with only one nail and could be swung to the side. They decided they could use a stick to push the rock out of the way. They could also use this stick to move the post just enough to start opening the door. Once the door was open far enough for someone to reach through, that person could grab the post and lift it away—as quietly as possible.

Once out the back door, they would have a short walk to the outhouse where Wes had started his trail. Not until they were in the brush behind the outhouse would they be out of sight. Until then, they faced the danger of being seen.

The guards had often sat by the back door to charge their electronics, but since the rainstorm they no longer did this. However, the guards still occasionally patrolled the area. And there was no way to predict when a guard would make his way to the outhouse.

To encourage the guards to stay away from the back door, the hostages moved the couches and chairs to the other side of the house. They also positioned the drums of bathing water beside the shower in such a way to provide some cover. They hoped for rain, which would encourage the guards to stay on the porch.

Wes found a stick they could use to push the cement rock away and put it inside the house. He also widened a few cracks in the block walls of the house to allow for more surveillance on what was happening outside.

But they all knew the bottom line: there was no way to guarantee that they would not be seen. The generator, which normally provided a steady background noise, had been out of oil for several nights. They would have to trust God with the details.

One other important detail had to be attended to. The peanut butter and other snacks that Pop-A-Wheelie Chief had brought the night before should be eaten. It could not be said of Wes or Dale that they had left good peanut butter go to waste.

When Froggy brought supper that night, Wes started toward him to remind him about the oil for the generator. On his way, he had a thought that stopped him in his tracks. Tonight was God's night to work. He had already asked Froggy for oil once, with no success. He decided he would commit the generator problem to God and let Him figure it out. He turned around and walked back.

"Did you ask Froggy for oil?" someone asked.

Wes said he had not. He had committed it to God.

After supper, Andre's rice and beans for breakfast were hung on the clothesline.

The sunset that night was beautiful. The sky was on fire with a glorious panorama of color. The hostages stood facing the sunset and sang "Is That the Lights of Home?"

The hostages sang with joy. Sam knew they had come to a fork in the road. He was ready to go to either his heavenly home or his earthly home. It didn't really matter which one.

Wednesday Night, Titanyen Base

Back at Titanyen, Cheryl and Ray hosted the rest of the team for a meal of Thai curry.

It was a bittersweet night. Grace and Olivia planned to leave for the airport the next morning at 10:00. Phil couldn't stay much longer either, although he had agreed to wait until the weekend.

There had been a flurry of discussion at the base that day, watching what appeared to be a private airplane flying repeatedly over the base. What could it be doing?

A few people couldn't help getting excited. Kay and Cheryl, whose thoughts constantly went to their friends in the gangster camp, discussed the plane. Could the group have escaped, and no one knew it yet except the FBI? Perhaps they were using a plane to see if the hostages were approaching CAM.

They might have escaped this morning and be lying low in the bushes somewhere, Kay thought. When it began to rain, she remembered that the prisoners had often talked about leaving during a rain.

"You know, if they haven't left yet, maybe they will now," Kay told Cheryl. Both ladies knew that Day 60 had passed and their comrades would be getting desperate.

At the base, they were also feeling desperate. They were exhausted with waiting, waiting, waiting. They had prayed that God would move in some way before Grace and Olivia left. But now that deadline was only hours away, and nothing had changed.

Chapter twenty-six

"SAMUEL, WE HAVE A PROBLEM!"

7 p.m. December 15; Day 61
Gangster Camp

Right after sunset, rain began to fall, but it didn't last long. The hostages had been hoping for a good soaker that would put the guards on the porch for the night. This shower was brief, but it did prompt the guards to move the couches onto the porch to keep them dry. When the rain started, the missionaries filed into the house through the porch door.

Carefully they went over their plans. They decided not to make any efforts to open the door before 1 a.m., as the guards still occasionally came crashing in to check on them in the middle of the night. They would open the door multiple times almost every night, but normally not after 1 a.m.

Once the door was successfully opened, Wes would slip out to assess their surroundings. If everything looked good, he would come back and say, "All clear."

If there were delays, they could wait a little, but not too long. They decided 3 a.m. was the latest they could leave and still have enough nighttime hours left for the long hike.

The group chose the order they would use. Wes would go first, because he had made the trail through the brush. Melodi would follow him, carrying Laura. Ryan would come next, carrying Andre. The faster the children could get out, the better. As much as possible, they would alternate men with the girls and women to keep the line steady.

Wes. Melodi and Laura. Ryan and Andre. Courtney. Brandyn. Kasondra. Austin. Cherilyn. Sam. Dale.

Ryan and Melodi would get the children up before they opened the door. This way if they cried a little, it would be nothing unusual.

While Wes had the responsibility of leading the way, Dale and Sam had a big job too. Being the last ones, they needed to shut and barricade the door. Sam would move the rock back into place, and Dale would put the post back against the door.

They planned to stack the two mattresses on top of each other to create more solid ground. Everyone was to be ready to go when the "all clear" signal came. They made a brief attempt at creating dummies with extra bedding, but they knew it would not trick the guards for long.

Wes gave instructions about the path he had stomped through the brush. He told the group to take it easy. Stay low, go slow. There was still a twelve-inch carpet of vines on the ground, so everyone was instructed to lift their feet high to avoid tripping. But at the same time, everyone should try to duck to stay below the tops of the brush.

With the plans made, everyone made at least a cursory attempt to go to bed.

Suddenly they heard the booming voice they knew so well. No vehicle had come in, but Froggy was here. Evidently he had walked into camp, something he did occasionally. They heard him talking outside, and then he yanked open the front door of the house.

"Samuel, we have a problem!"

Ryan, fanning Andre with a foam food box, felt his heart sink. Had the guards somehow uncovered the plot to escape?

Sam asked what the problem was.

"We don't have any oil for the generator."

Ryan's eyes widened. He continued to fan Andre.

"Yeah," Sam said, mustering as much sadness into his voice as he could. "It hasn't run for two nights. It would be kind of nice to have some. The children are really hot."

Froggy seemed troubled by this, even though Wes had reminded him about it at breakfast time with no results.

"When the fans don't run, I don't get any sleep," Ryan told him as he kept fanning Andre. "Because I have to run the fan."

After considering the situation and promising Andre he would bring bananas for breakfast, Froggy pulled his phone from his pocket and called his superior about the oil. He did not usually bother Lanmò San Jou with these details; instead, he called Pop-A-Wheelie Chief.

Half an hour later, the hostages heard the sound of an approaching motorbike. The oil had arrived. Soon after, they heard the generator sputter to life. The two fans came on with a welcome whirring noise.

The missionaries praised the Lord, thrilled to see that God was working on their behalf.

"Lord," Ryan prayed, amazed, "you want us to have a generator! I thought you were going to work without it."

In the back room close to the barricaded door, Cherilyn said something to Kasondra and could tell she had offended her. This didn't seem normal, so Cherilyn lay down beside her younger sister.

"Are you scared?"

"Yeah."

"It's going to be okay," Cherilyn said. "Do you want me to walk behind you?"

"Yeah, sure."

Cherilyn prayed with Kasondra, who soon fell asleep as usual. Cherilyn talked to Austin, who had been planning to walk behind Kasondra, and they agreed to switch.

Everyone tried to get some sleep, although of course the prayer chain was still going.

As they tried to sleep, both Melodi and Sam heard a ruckus outside on the front porch. Apparently a couple of the guards had been sleeping.

"Get up and do your work!" Ping yelled. He had always been a vigilant chief of the guards, scolding people who were not doing their job. Tonight was no exception. "You're supposed to be guarding this house. Don't be lying here sleeping!"

Sam watched as one guard walked down the lane and other guards shone their flashlights into the darkness. They were definitely not sleeping.

Sam also listened to the sound of the generator. Was it

about to run out of gas? He heard the engine ebbing and flowing, sometimes almost dying, but then gathering strength to cough on. Sam had no idea whether it was low on gas or not, but he knew there was a gas shortage and the price of fuel had risen. *Just watch that engine run out of gas,* he thought.

"Lord, please keep it running," he prayed.

Kasondra drifted off to sleep and fell into a dream. She saw a ring of angels surrounding the prison house. She saw a little girl angel standing beside the trail the missionaries were planning to take. In her dream, when the line of hostages walked out the door, the little girl angel came up to Kasondra and grabbed her hand and walked with her into the bushes. As they walked, they chatted, and the girl angel told Kasondra that her name was Caroline Maria. In surprise, Kasondra realized she knew that name. Yes, it was the name of her sister who had miscarried at twenty-three weeks. When Kasondra woke from the dream, her fears were gone. She was not scared after that.

Austin had the prayer watch around midnight. Most of the house was quiet. Outside, however, the guards were wide awake, talking and playing music, probably still on a high from their last batch of drugs.

Then it was 1 a.m.

12 a.m., Titanyen Base

That night Kay struggled to sleep. At midnight she sat in her living room, crying out to God. She often struggled to get to sleep if she went to bed, remembering her brothers and sisters in captivity in the tiny, stuffy house, herded inside at an early hour.

What was that? A whistle? Kay rose to her feet and moved to the door. *Could the other hostages be standing outside the gate, whistling to get someone's attention to let them in through the gate?*

She had struggled to sleep almost every night since her release. But she had never before felt so strongly that the group might even now be out in the Haitian countryside.

She went outside, peering into the darkness. At last, deciding the whistling must have been a bird, she turned back to her apartment to try once more to sleep.

"O God!" she cried. "If they are out there, please bring them safely home!"

Chapter twenty-seven

"I FEEL GOD"

Thursday, December 16; Day 62
1 a.m., Gangster Camp

*I*t was time to put the plans into action. The people who were awake nudged those who were still asleep.

By pulling off a small piece of lathe above the front door, Austin and Wes had made a surveillance hole earlier in the day. Dale got down on his hands and knees close to the front door, and Wes climbed onto his shoulders to peer out the little hole.

What Wes saw was not especially encouraging. It was almost full moon and the moonlight was about as bright as it ever was. The guards seemed restless. Their music was playing, and the missionaries could hear them talking. They were drinking, and occasionally they jumped up to walk around.

The night guard reinforcements were there with the big guns. Three of them had moved out into the yard, from where they could see behind the house. They probably couldn't see the outhouse from there, but it was close.

However, the group had put the events of the night into the hands of God, and they decided to proceed. The generator was still running, coughing out its lungs in the backyard. It was 1:30 by the time the children were up and awake and everyone was in line in the back room of the house, surrounded by the verses Cherilyn had written on the walls. "The angel of the Lord encampeth round about them that fear him."

Using the stick, Dale and Wes pushed and prodded the rock until it rolled away from the door. It finally flopped over, hitting the ground with a thump. Ryan felt the vibration in the ground. Everyone tensed, expecting a guard to come and check on the noise. No one did, but a little later Mr. Attitude passed by as he headed to the outhouse. Wes ran around to the peek hole above the front door to see if anyone had noticed the rock thumping down. As he stood there looking out, Mr. Attitude came walking back.

"Mwen santi Bondye." Mr. Attitude's voice sounded even less stable than normal as he talked to himself.

Did I hear right? For a moment Wes thought he had misunderstood. But the words had been so clear: *"Mwen santi Bondye"* (I feel God). Wes sensed the guard's agitation and discomfort. *What is he seeing or sensing that makes him so restless?*

Mr. Attitude walked on.

Back at the door, Brandyn pulled the piece of lathe away from the gap in the door. No one had thought about removing the nail earlier. Now the nail came out with a screech. The hostages looked at each other. The thumping rock had not brought anyone over. Would this?

Courtney slid over to the door on her hands and knees and looked out. Her eyes widened as she saw the moonlight shining down on Ping, staring at the door.

"Ping is right outside!" she hissed. "He's staring at the door!"

Everyone froze, scarcely breathing. They expected Ping to burst into the house at any moment and start yelling. Instead, he just stood outside the door. For maybe a minute, while the hostages stood like a line of wax figures, he stared at the door. Then he walked away.

Instantly everyone made a dive for their mattresses, kicking off their shoes. They expected Ping to come boiling in the front door. Once again they kept perfectly still.

But Ping didn't come.

"Shall we try yet tonight?" someone asked Ryan.

"Let's definitely keep our eyes open," Ryan said. He didn't feel it was up to him. He would let the younger men make the decision. Both he and Melodi fell asleep.

Sam lay awake, thinking. Perhaps tonight was not the right night.

Dale resigned himself to eating spaghetti for breakfast once again. He dozed off.

Finally, about forty-five minutes later, Sam went to confer with Austin. "Should we try it yet tonight? What do you think?"

"You know what," Austin said. "I think the Lord blinded Ping's eyes! Let's go!"

Sam couldn't believe his ears. Austin, the cautious one, was now encouraging him to have faith. What a wonderful moment!

"You know what," Sam said. "Let's do go!"

Wes and Brandyn began to work on removing the post leaning against the door. Brandyn stuck the stick up through the gap and pushed on the post. Wes leaned against the door to keep tension on the post to keep it from sliding. When the door was open wide enough, Wes reached out and grabbed the post. It was too heavy to lift with one hand, but as soon as he could squeeze out the door, he grabbed it with both hands and set it against the side of the house.

The next thing Ryan knew, someone was waking him.

"The door's open!" they whispered. Ryan shook himself fully awake. He hadn't put on his shoes or picked up Andre. Melodi was still sleeping. Quickly he woke her up and they gathered their footwear and the children.

In the meantime, Wes had slipped around the corner of the house and into the shower. From behind the tarp, he looked around the yard. He saw the three guards facing the house, but he was hopeful that the water barrels would provide cover. Of course, around the corner, five or six more armed men sat on the porch. After their recent scolding by Ping, it was doubtful any of them were sleeping.

Wes hurried back to the house.

"The coast is clear! Let's go."

The missionaries filed out. Melodi was behind Wes in a second, carrying Laura wrapped in a pink swaddle. Ryan followed her with Andre, and the rest came behind in single file, out into the bright, bright moonlight. Whether the group forgot Wes's instructions, or whether he forgot them himself, "take it slow" did not happen.

As they entered the bushes, Wes glanced at his watch. It was 2:50 a.m., just ten minutes to spare from their cut-off time. He led the way into the bushes, but kept a close eye on the line behind him. With his hands, he motioned, *Stay low.* He pointed toward the yard, mouthing, *Guards right there!* By the light of the bright moon, it was easy for the others to see Wes.

As Ryan, carrying Andre, dived into the brush after Melodi, the three-year-old began to whimper for his mom.

"Quiet!" Ryan whispered.

Andre stopped whimpering.

Dale was the last in line. Carefully they shut the door. Sam replaced the rock, and Dale took the post from the side of the house and moved it back into place. He turned to go, then noticed that the post was slightly crooked. He turned back, righted it, and then turned again.

By this time, Sam was diving into the bushes. Dale caught up in a moment's time.

The people in front looked back soon after getting into the brush and were shocked to see Sam and Dale already falling in behind them.

In less than a minute from the time they left the house, the group was standing in the shade of the mango tree. Behind them, there was no yelling, no gunshots.

"Did you barricade the door?" someone whispered to Sam and Dale.

"Yes," Sam replied.

As Dale noticed the speed of the group, he allowed himself to smile. Despite instructions, no one was taking it slow.

"I expected to be scared to death," Ryan remembered, "but I felt so strongly that the Lord was in this, and I just felt peace. My heart rate was high, I'm sure. But it was fun!"

But there was no time to stop and exult. They had a six-foot-wide irrigation ditch to cross. Some of the men leaped to the other side, but

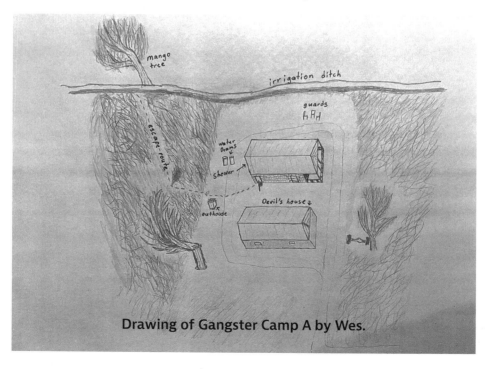

Drawing of Gangster Camp A by Wes.

it was too wide for the girls.

"Come on, come on! Let's go, let's go!" one of the young men said. Sam stepped into the ditch to help the girls across. Ryan handed Andre across to one of the men on the other side. Then he took Laura from Melodi. He took a big step across, but found himself straddling the ditch and holding Laura.

"It was not a very organized ordeal," Dale wrote later.

"Someone help Ryan!" Brandyn said.

Dale grabbed Ryan's arm and hauled him and Laura across with a mighty heave.

Finally everyone was on the right side, muddy or not.

The limestone quarry on the side of Goat Mountain stood out like a second moon, beckoning them to come. The group found their positions in line again, and headed off down the footpath.

"Just say if I'm going too fast," Wes whispered to Melodi. "I'll go as fast as you can keep up, but just say if it's too much. You can pass Laura back to the others. There are lots of people to carry her."

They knew they needed to head northwest to get to the highway. Once there, they planned to borrow someone's phone and call Barry.

About 150 feet down the path, their mud-covered feet passed a bridge over the irrigation ditch. They concluded that the bridge was God's sense of humor.

"Mom, look at the moon!" Andre said. "It's beautiful!"

The moon was big and bright. It seemed to be hanging in the sky just for the line of ten people walking west between the flat fields.

From his position at the back of the line, Dale could see the whole line spread out down the footpath. It was night, but the moonlight reflected on everything light-colored, especially the white veils of the women, which bobbed with the rhythm of hurried footsteps. Everyone's adrenaline was high and the heart rates were up.

The only thing that could dampen their joy was when their thoughts strayed back to Peter, still locked in the small room beside the porch. If only he could be in the line with them!

"I so long to see Peter again!" Sam remembered later. "I hope I can see him in heaven sometime if not before!"

For about two hours, they made excellent time. The path would go west and then angle back to the north. Ryan and Melodi switched places early on so Ryan and Wes could consult about directions.

Ryan and Melodi also passed both Laura and Andre down the line so others could share the burden of walking with extra weight. Melodi moved with Andre, walking behind whoever carried him. He was still scared, but as long as he could see Melodi, he was fine.

"Are we going home?" he asked once while Dale was carrying him.

"Yes," Melodi said. "We're going home!"

"Okay!"

Melodi waved at him, and he waved back over Dale's shoulder.

"Do you like being passed back and forth?" Dale asked.

"Yes!"

For a while, Cherilyn tied Laura on with the cloth baby carrier Melodi

---

2:45 a.m., Accident, Maryland
Ryan's former teacher heard his alarm go off and staggered out of bed. It was time for his fifteen-minute prayer slot. He threw on some clothes to wake himself up and walked out to the living room to pray for the kidnapped missionaries. He knelt on the carpet.

But instead of prayer ideas, he heard a song in his head, one he had not heard for months. One line was something about watching what God can do.

He tried once again to focus on praying. But he couldn't really think of anything to pray for. And that song kept playing in his head. "Watch what God can do."

Puzzled, he went back to bed.

had made. Water bags also changed hands as throats grew parched.

Several times they passed houses or small villages.

In one village they hesitated, afraid to go on through. They decided to keep going and just stay close to the bushes on one side. As they marched, Ryan suddenly said, "Whoa! There's a donkey lying right there looking at us!"

"We tried to make sure he was comfortable," Ryan remembered, "and he didn't say anything."

But in that entire two-hour time span, they met no people. And they heard only one dog bark. In a country full of roaming dogs, this was astonishing to everyone. Anytime there was a question about which way to go, the group stopped and prayed, and then re-formed their line. Every time the path turned a corner in the right direction, they said, "Thank you, Lord!"

Bernville, Pennsylvania

An Anabaptist author awoke early on the morning of December 16. None of the hostages were related to her, but she had prayed for them every day since they had been kidnapped, often several times a day.

This morning, as the twelve escapees walked across the Haitian countryside, the author fell asleep again and had a dream. In her dream, all the hostages were free.

"We have to stop acting guilty," Ryan said. They decided if they met anyone, they would just say "Good morning" and hope and pray the person would find it perfectly normal to meet twelve white Americans dashing through the Haitian countryside at 4 a.m.

At about 5:00, the group realized they were approaching a body of water. As they drew closer, a huge flock of birds lifted off the water with a splashing and whirring of wings.

The escapees looked both ways and could see no end to the

water. They decided to head west beside the body of water. Eventually this should take them out to the road.

They didn't know that they had run up against Trou Caiman, a shallow body of water named after the American crocodile. Although the crocodiles had been hunted until none were left, the lake was known for its flocks of orange-pink flamingos with black-tipped wings. It was surrounded by saltbush flats.

The missionaries walked over this hard, cracked land, smelling the fishiness and saltiness of the water. After a short time, they came to the western edge of the lake and were able to turn north again. The path was surrounded by thorns and cactus plants twice as high as a man, but they plunged ahead anyway.

Suddenly the path through the thorns quit. The moon had gone down, and they could no longer see the limestone quarry. There was nothing to do but keep on, straight into the thorns. They could still see the sky if they looked up, and sometimes they could pick out the Little Dipper and the North Star, which told them they were headed in the right direction.

Wes forged ahead, breaking off branches to enable the others to pass. There had been no cacti in Tennessee, but his years of experience in the woods helped him. The going was painful. Every few steps they stopped to pull out thorns. Some of the thorns were like fishhooks and resisted being pulled out. Andre cried out occasionally when they bit into his flesh. Brandyn took off his socks and gave them to Andre, who was barefooted.

"We ended up in the worst briar patch I have ever seen," Dale said later. "The only comfort we had was that no gangster in his right mind was going to look for us in that briar patch."

With the moonlight gone, it was now so dark that each person had to stay within reach of the person ahead or risk losing the group. This was especially true of Wes and Dale, who wore dark shirts. Several times the group stopped to count themselves, as they had planned to do. Wes said *one,* Melodi said *two* and *three* (for Laura), and on down the line. One time there was just enough of a pause after *eleven* to cause everyone's heart rate to rise before Sam said *twelve.*

At one point, the cactus plants and thorns encased them so thoroughly that they could not see the stars. They stopped and prayed, then plowed on.

After about an hour of this misery, Dale took Wes's place. Between the two of them they forged a path directly into the walls of cacti. Ryan had no idea how they did it.

Finally they broke out of the thorn patch. The eastern sky was brightening. They saw a side road ahead. A herd of cows rushed down the road as if they were being turned out to pasture. The group hesitated, expecting to see the cow herder, but no one followed the cows.

They knew a road could be dangerous. But by this time, they were so ready for an easy path that they decided to take it. They took off down the road, moving fast. Melodi, carrying Laura, suddenly tripped and fell hard. Laura began to scream. Everyone stopped, afraid that one or both of them had been badly hurt.

"Are you okay? Are you okay?" Ryan asked.

"Yes, I'm fine. I'm okay." Blood oozed from Melodi's scraped knees, and she felt some pain, but she was able to walk.

But Laura was still screaming.

Dale had run up the road to scout and now came running back. "There's a trail going off from the road up ahead. Can you make it up there?"

The whole group ducked off the main road onto the trail suggested by Dale.

"We can't go this way!" someone said. "It's probably leading straight to someone's house!"

But staying on the road with a howling baby hardly felt like a secure option either.

"Maybe it's time to turn ourselves in," Ryan said. Laura was still screaming, and Ryan wasn't convinced that Melodi was fine after the bad fall.

Minutes after hustling onto the trail, they heard two vehicles passing on the road behind them. They were thankful they had not come past when the whole group was clearly visible on the road.

Melodi soothed Laura as they kept walking. Eventually the frantic crying turned to snuffling and Laura relaxed.

"Cherilyn, could you carry Laura again?" Ryan asked.

Cherilyn came forward immediately and knotted the ragged green carrier around her shoulders, supporting Laura against her chest.

The trail soon turned to a cow path. They were in the mountains now, climbing. The sky turned pinker and brighter. At exactly 7:14 a.m., the sun came over the horizon. The hostages turned and looked back over the valley through which they had come. They could see the sun shining on the mist rising off the lake.

They decided it was time for most of the group to hunker down while Sam and Wes, who were the most fluent in Creole, went to look for a phone. They took the Haitian money from the diaper bag and made sure they knew Barry's phone number.

7 a.m. CST, Monterey, Tennessee (8 a.m. in Haiti)

In the bakery on the farm where Wes grew up, his mother and sister Carol started their morning routine around 4 a.m. On the morning of December 16, they began as usual with Carol making bread.

But Carol was not happy. She went through the motions of mixing the various doughs for sourdough bread, wheat bread, white bread, and jalapeno cheese bread, but she was clearly depressed.

Her mother could see that something was wrong. However, she had told her children that as they struggled with Wes's captivity, they would sometimes need to process things without other people prying.

"We are going to have times when this is going to be really hard on us," she had told them. "And at those times we must give each other space."

So her mother said nothing. Carol was a self-controlled person and could speak when she wanted to.

Shortly after sunrise, Carol began to talk. "I always wanted to dream that Wes is free," she said. She knew other people had dreamed about the hostages, and she wished for the same experience.

Then she confessed that she had dreamed about Wes, and in the dream he was free. It had been wonderful.

"But then I woke up and found out it's not true."

Chapter twenty-eight

"THE LORD DELIVERED US"

7 a.m. Thursday, December 16
In the Countryside

*W*hile the others sat down behind a knoll, Sam and Wes prayed and then set off. They had seen a woodcutter in the distance and decided to go talk to him. He was cutting wood to make charcoal, one of the largest industries in Haiti.

Ryan watched Sam and Wes until they disappeared from view. The group realized that back in the gangster camp, it would be clear by now that they had escaped. Melodi prayed that the guards would run for the hills to a new and better life.

As Sam and Wes headed toward the woodcutter, they encountered a farmer in a yellow shirt. They knew he had seen them, so they decided to talk to him. Wes, however, felt his heart sink as they got closer. Around both wrists, the man wore black bracelets.

"*Bonjou,*[1] how are you?" Sam kept his voice casual and friendly. They had determined to stay vague, so Sam told him, "We ran into a little bit of a problem. Our phone batteries died." Sam didn't think this was an untruth, as they assumed their phones were dead. "Would you happen to have a phone where we can make a phone call?"

The farmer patted his pockets, and Wes could see they were flat. The man said he didn't have a phone. Sam asked if he knew where they could find one.

"Yeah," the farmer said. "Up there by the road you can get a phone. Just knock on any of the house doors. Someone will help you out."

"Could you show us which house? We have a little money. We can give you a tip."

"Sure." The farmer led them to the top of a hill. From there, he pointed to a house with a brightly painted door. He assured them that the occupants of the house would let him use a phone.

"Do good people live there?" Sam asked.

"Yes," he replied.

Sam gave him a tip, and the man went on. Sam and Wes headed for the house with the painted door.

Success seemed so close, yet so fragile. What if the farmer had pointed them to the house of a gang member? What if they were walking into a trap?

When they got closer to the house, they saw that the front door was up a steep bank. They decided to walk around the house.

Cautiously Sam and Wes crept around the house. This was the moment. Would they look around the corner and see a gangster with dreadlocks and an arm full of black bracelets? Sam peeked around

---

[1] "Good morning."

KIDNAPPED *in Haiti*

the corner, ready to bolt.

There sat two men with trumpets and sheet music, as if they were practicing for church. Sam's fears all but evaporated.

The trumpeters were full of questions, but Wes and Sam tried to be as vague as possible. The men wanted to know if their vehicle had broken down on the highway. Wes and Sam explained that they were out walking and needed to borrow a phone.

The main spokesman explained that he would let them borrow his, but he was out of minutes.

"Do any of your neighbors have a phone we could use?" Sam asked, trying to keep his voice from sounding desperate.

"No, I don't think so," the man replied.

"Well, we have a little bit of money. We can give you some money, and you can go buy minutes. We'll just make a couple of phone calls and then you can use whatever is left for yourself."

"Oh, but it's way down there," the man protested. "Down in town."

"Well, we really need to talk on the phone."

"Okay, okay. Yeah, sure."

Sam and Wes gave him 500 gourdes, about US$5. He jumped on his bicycle and pedaled away. Sam and Wes waited nervously. Would he come back?

About fifteen minutes later, the man reappeared, coming up the hill on his bike, panting and sweating. He had put 250 gourdes of minutes on his phone. He handed over the phone. They dialed Barry's number. Someone picked up.

"Hello? Hello?"

"Hello?" Sam and Wes said.

"Put it on speakerphone!" the man said. "Or he can't hear you." Neither Sam nor Wes wanted to talk on speakerphone, but there was nothing else to do.

They put it on speakerphone and tried again.

"Barry, this is Wes!"

"Hello?"

Wes felt himself choking up, so Sam jumped in.

"Yeah, Barry, this is Wes and Sam. The Lord delivered us!"

"Uh . . . uh . . . uh . . . What did you say?"

7:40 a.m., Titanyen Base

Barry woke up the morning of the sixteenth feeling completely drained. Phil's wife and daughter were leaving in a few hours. They had prayed for God to work before they left, but nothing had happened. Soon Phil would leave too.

Barry had a morning habit of kissing his family goodbye when he left for work.

Today he was too discouraged. "I'm leaving for work," he said as he headed out the door.

Over at Phil and Grace's house, Phil was preparing to head to the office too. Grace and Olivia were packed for their flight and would need to head for the airport at ten.

Phil had set his mind to reality. It would be another endless day of waiting. Waiting for the release. Or for more news. Or a call from the gang demanding more money. Waiting to see what God had in store.

Barry had encouraged the team by saying that God often waits until our own resources are gone before He acts. But now, even Barry was discouraged.

In her apartment, Kay awakened with a question on her mind, remembering the nighttime feeling that the hostages were outside somewhere. *Are they here yet?* As she came to full consciousness, disappointment set in. They must not have come, or she would know.

She walked out to her little kitchen to make some tea. She would take the tea and step outside to have her devotional time surrounded by the beauty of nature.

———————

As he headed for the warehouse, Barry's phone began to ring. He was annoyed. *Here come the phone calls again. Everybody wants to know if there's any news. And as always, there's nothing.*

I'm not answering, he told himself.

But he did.

"Hello? Hello?"

He heard nothing. Whoever was calling probably had bad service. Maybe he should hang up.

But then he thought he heard a familiar voice. It sounded like he was saying, "This is Wes."

"Hello?" Barry asked, almost in shock. *Could it really be Wes?*

Next he heard Sam's voice, "Yeah, Barry, this is Wes and Sam. The Lord delivered us!"

Barry was too stunned to function properly and could do nothing but mumble at first. He reminded himself that he was the director of the base and needed to pull himself together.

"Are you all delivered? Or is it just you?"

"We're all together. We're all here. The Lord delivered us last night."

"I'm coming right now. Where are you at?"

"Goat Mountain."

"Can you please drop me a pin?"

Sam explained that they were using someone else's phone. He described again where they were, and Barry thought he could find it.

When he got off the phone, Barry knew he should call Phil, but he was too wound up.

At the breakfast table, no more than five minutes had passed since Barry had left without giving the normal hugs and kisses. Julia and the children kept eating their breakfast. They too were disheartened to see Barry so discouraged.

"We were all just kind of at the end of our rope," Julia said later.

Suddenly the front door burst open, crashing back against the small table behind it, and Barry's arm reached in to grab his truck keys.

"They've escaped! I'm going to pick them up." With no further explanation, he disappeared out the door.

Julia leaped to her feet and dashed after him. "What's going on? How do you know? Who called you?"

"Wes just called me. I have to go find them. They're on Goat Mountain somewhere."

Grace opened the front door of their house, ready to go outside. She found herself face to face with Barry, preparing to knock. "Where's Phil?"

Grace stared at him. The tone of his voice told her that something had happened. Phil appeared quickly behind her.

"They've escaped!" The intensity on Barry's face left no doubt about his words. He was dumbfounded but ecstatic.

Neither Barry nor Phil nor Grace ever found sufficient words to describe the wave of adrenaline that hit them that morning. In a matter of minutes, they went from the drought of despair to the over-flowing joy of relief, hope, and action.

"Do Ray and Cheryl know?" Grace asked. "Am I allowed to tell them?"

"Yes," said Barry. Phil jumped into his vehicle, which was parked as always right outside the house and ready to go at a moment's notice. He followed Barry's vehicle as they lost no time heading down the road.

Grace and Olivia jumped into the Gator nearby and drove furiously to Ray and Cheryl's house.

Ray and Cheryl had finished breakfast that morning and were getting ready for the day. Ray planned to head to the office soon for the men's morning devotional time.

Suddenly they heard someone pounding on the door.

"That's not a good-morning knock," Ray said. "Somebody has a message." He raced to the front door.

It was Grace.

"They're free! They're free!" she shouted.

"They're free?" Ray repeated, staring at Grace. After two months, the words sounded like a phrase from a foreign language, requiring further explanation.

"They all escaped! They called Barry. And he and Phil are on their way to pick them up!"

Grace and Cheryl whooped and hollered. Ray, a calm man, was not quite as expressive, but he too was overwhelmed with rejoicing. Grace asked Ray if he could message the

> **7:30 a.m., Williamstown, New Jersey**
>
> "Hey, I had a dream this morning," the produce manager of a farmers' market told his boss when he arrived at work.
>
> "Well, what was your dream?"
>
> "I dreamed that the hostages are free."
>
> "Oh, good!"
>
> Later that morning, another worker burst through the door, phone in hand. "The hostages in Haiti are free!" he announced.
>
> For the produce manager, it seemed he was hearing the news for the second time.

Ohio office and cancel the tickets for her and Olivia.

Cheryl knew where she needed to go next.

Kay was standing in her kitchen by the sink, her mind still twisting and turning like the steam coming off her tea. Suddenly Cheryl burst through the back door.

"They've escaped!"

8:08 a.m., Berlin, Ohio

Bobby Miller opened his email to find a forwarded message from Phil Mast on the ground in Haiti.

"Pray hard," it said.

Obviously, something was happening, and Phil didn't have time to say more. But what could be wrong? Phil's wife and daughter were planning to fly home later in the morning. Maybe something was happening with their tickets.

Bobby spent some time in prayer in his office. Soon it was time for the 9 a.m. prayer time for the kidnapping situation. At the copier in the hallway, Phil Troyer met him with a message: "Better stay here. We need to meet."

Tommy Wagler was in-house that day to interview the executive staff. He had also received the "Pray hard" message. He and the people he was with stopped what they were doing and bowed their heads for a special time of prayer. Then they proceeded with the interviews.

Just before 9:00, Phil Troyer stuck his head in the door with news: "Word is that the rest of the hostages escaped."

The daily schedule abandoned, everyone moved to the conference room.

At the Side of the Road

Back at the house with the brightly painted door, Wes and Sam decided to split up. Sam would walk toward a small police checkpoint about two-tenths of a mile away, while Wes would go back to the others behind the knoll and let them know that Barry and Phil were coming.

Sam called Barry back and said he planned to touch base with the police.

"Sam, be careful what you say," Barry said. "Be very vague."

As Sam walked toward the checkpoint, he felt as if every eye in Haiti were on him. People in vehicles passing by on the road stared at the white man with unkempt facial hair walking beside the road. A man on a motorcycle, looking suspiciously like a gangster, came to a complete stop to stare at Sam.

Get me out of here, Sam thought.

Arriving at the checkpoint, Sam started talking to one of the three police officers. Sam asked if he could wait there for someone to pick

Bridgewater, Virginia

Weeks before the escape, a woman near the mountains in Virginia was awakened from sleep in the early morning hours by a farmer's skid loader. She was shocked that this noise had awakened her, because normally she slept deeply. She did not wake up when the dog barked and often did not even hear her husband's alarm clock.

I guess I had too much coffee to drink yesterday, she decided.

But the next morning she heard the skid loader again. And the next morning. Finally she realized that God was asking her to pray for the hostages in Haiti and everyone involved. She always prayed a simple prayer before falling back to sleep.

This happened every morning until December 17, when the sound of the skid loader failed to rouse her. The day of the escape was the last day the skid loader awakened her.

him up. Meanwhile, unknown to Sam, the farmer with the yellow shirt had found the rest of the missionaries and talked to them. He now arrived and began telling the policemen about the white people hiding behind the knoll.

"Hey, what's going on?" the one officer asked Sam.

Sam tried to beat around the bush.

"Are you in trouble?" the policeman asked. "You're trembling."

"Yeah, yeah, we're in trouble."

"Just relax. You're with the police. We're going to help you. Where do you live?"

"I'm from the United States."

"No, no, where do you live in Haiti?"

"Titanyen."

"Okay. Are you from the group of seventeen missionaries that got kidnapped two months ago?"

"Yeah."

"Hey!" the policeman yelled to another officer. "Call down to the base for reinforcements." He then turned back to Sam and continued asking questions.

"So, did the gang release you?"

"No, actually we escaped. The Lord took us out of there."

"Oh, oh, oh, okay," the officer said. "So you just left the house and got out of there?" With a look of amazement on his face, he turned to the officer on the phone. "Tell them to send reinforcements right now. They've escaped!"

***

The larger group of missionaries were making their way down to the highway just as Barry and Phil pulled up close to the police checkpoint to pick up Sam.

Barry saw the line of missionaries coming toward him, spread out down the side of the road in the shadow of the brown mountains. They were no longer in their order, but Wes was still in front, wearing the same blue shirt and tan pants he had been wearing two months before. Dale carried Andre, and Courtney carried Laura. Melodi's knees hurt worse now than they had after the fall, and she hung on to Ryan's arm for support.

As Barry's vehicle rolled to a stop, traffic zipping past him, he exclaimed, "Hallelujah! The day has come!"

"Good to see you, Barry!" one of the men shouted.

"Good to see you too!" Barry said, breaking down as he gave a few quick hugs. "The Lord is good!"

They quickly jumped into the vehicles. The officers wanted Barry to wait for an escort, but Barry said, "No thank you," and headed back out into the heavy traffic.

In the vans, the missionaries, no longer hostages, talked and talked. Dale sat in the front seat beside Barry. About fifteen minutes into the drive, Barry said something about Dale's dad, then added, "Do you want to call him? I have his number."

"What?!" Dale couldn't believe his ears. "Yeah, of course!"

Melodi went next, placing a call to her parents.

Sam rode in Phil's vehicle. His thoughts turned to his family, and the families of the other former hostages.

"So I take it our families are okay?" Sam asked.

"Yeah, yeah. They're all okay."

Sam broke down and wept.

Titanyen Base

Back at the base, Julia and Cheryl and Kay knelt down in Barry's living room and prayed that Barry could bring the group back safely. They also prayed for the guards who had been watching the house that night, remembering what Ping had said would happen.

After they got up, Cheryl said, "We'd better pack!"

They got up and started packing, knowing the escaped hostages would likely not be staying there. Julia stacked schoolbooks and collected clothes.

Suddenly the little boys came running in.

"They're here! They're here!"

Ray stood at the gate, waiting. He had battled a burning desire to call Phil or Barry to see where they were. But he decided he had been waiting on the Lord for two months, and he could continue waiting.

Then Ray's waiting was over. He saw the vans approaching.

A Haitian employee with a huge smile and tears streaming down his face opened the gate.

Calm man or not, Ray waved his arms and began running toward the vehicles. He saw Courtney in the first van and the rest of his children in the second van. Ray leaped onto the running board of one of the vehicles, praising the Lord. He began to yodel, a skill he had learned in Kenya.

All across the compound, people came running. Julia and her children headed up the hill toward the vehicles. She saw Shelden running ahead of her toward his big sisters. She saw Ray with his daughters and son for the first time in two months.

It was a foretaste of heaven. Julia, like the others, found no words to describe what it was like. Everyone, white and black, was delirious with joy. People cried and laughed and praised the Lord.

Everyone formed a circle and Ray led in prayer, arms raised to heaven, thanking God for protecting the group as they escaped through the night. "Thank you for what they've learned, God!" Ray added.

"Amen!" many of the former hostages agreed.

The cooks Cherilyn had helped in the cook shack before the

kidnapping came rushing up to greet them with huge hugs. One of them informed the hostages that she had dreamed that morning that they had escaped.

Laughing and talking, the escapees shared stories about walking through the night, and how they had passed Laura from person to person.

The former hostages soon fanned out to their apartments to make phone calls. The Noecker household messaged with cousins from Michigan. Someone asked Brandyn how they had escaped.

"With God, there's always a back door," Brandyn said.

8:40 a.m., Moorefield, Ontario

Dale's parents battled discouragement. Their hearts ached for their fifth child, but there seemed to be no way out. So far nothing had worked, and yet they knew God could work. They had prayed and fasted, and they knew others had too. But today the discouragement was severe.

Dale's dad stayed home from work. He felt exhausted, and even though it was still morning, he decided to take a nap.

A few minutes later his phone began to ring. Seeing a Haitian number, he answered.

The connection was so bad that he couldn't identify the speaker. But it sounded like a man's voice, saying, "The Lord delivered us! We escaped."

He still wasn't sure who he was talking to and thought of asking one of the proof-of-life questions. The government officials had asked each family to prepare questions that only one person could answer.

Then Dale's dad heard something unmistakable—Dale's laugh, the short laugh he occasionally tacked onto the end of his sentences. That was sufficient proof, and he knew he was talking to his son.

5:45 a.m. PST, Grande Ronde Valley, Oregon (8:45 a.m. in Haiti)

It was nearing Christmas. Melodi's mom had lit a candle, but there didn't seem to be much joy in the house. How could they celebrate with Ryan and Melodi and Andre and Laura still in captivity?

However, she made an effort to thank God for the answered prayers they had heard from the released hostages.

Early Thursday morning she was combing her hair when her husband's phone started to ring. He had gone out to milk the cow, so she went to get it. She was surprised to see a Haitian number.

"Hello," she answered.

"Hello, Mom! This is Melodi!"

"Melodi! Is it really you? Are you all right? What about the children?"

"Yes, we're all out! All of us! Everyone is fine."

A bit later Melodi called her sister Angie.

"Melodi! You're out!" Angie exclaimed.

"Angie! What did you have?"

Finally Melodi got to hear about the little boy named Cody Ryan, now two months old.

6 a.m. PST, Madras, Oregon (9 a.m. in Haiti)

Austin's parents were in bed when they heard a call coming in. They had been keeping their phones on their nightstands just in case.

They looked at the number. It was from Ohio.

After Matt and Rachel's release, something similar had happened. A call had come through in the night, announcing a family call in ten minutes.

"Must be another family call," Austin's mom said. "I wonder what happened." She listened as her husband answered the phone. She could not hear the person on the other end.

"Austin, is that you? Let me put it on speakerphone so Mom can hear you."

"I cannot even describe how it felt," Austin's mom recalled later.

9 a.m., New Concord, Ohio

Open suitcases were scattered around Matt and Rachel's house when Matt woke up. It was their first night back from Miami.

He got up and saw a text message from a coworker at the cabinet shop: "Is it true what I'm hearing about the hostages?"

Matt had no idea, so he decided to call Barry.

"Hello!"

Matt realized in shock that the voice belonged to Wes.

"Wes, Wes, Wes!"

"Matt, Matt, Matt!"

The service was so bad that the call ended without any further conversation. But Matt's heart was filled with indescribable joy.

Wes had answered Barry's phone. Something really had happened.

As in a daze, Matt and Rachel sat in their house for the longest time. It seemed like it could not be true. They had waited so long for this moment.

Soon they began making plans to fly back to Miami.

8:20 a.m. CST, Monterey, Tennessee (9:20 a.m. in Haiti)

In the bakery, Wes's mom noticed a Haitian number when her phone started ringing. She answered, stepping out the door for better service, but heard no reply.

"Can you hear me?"

She still couldn't hear anything intelligible. She heard a man's voice say "Hello," but it didn't sound like a familiar voice.

Finally she hung up and returned to her work in the bakery. About four minutes later she saw an Ohio number calling her phone.

Something is wrong. Or something is happening.

She grabbed the phone and stepped outside again, hoping the

connection would be better this time.

Back in the bakery, Carol was removing loaves of bread from pans and placing them on racks to cool.

Suddenly her mom burst back in through the door, still talking on the phone. Carol turned away from the loaves of bread to face her. "Wes?" her mom was saying. "Are you okay? Where are you?"

Carol stared at her mother. Had the stress of the last two months finally caught up with her? Or had something really happened? Her mother, now standing by the sink, hung up the phone.

"Praise the Lord! Praise the Lord! They're free!" she exclaimed.

Carol's normally calm face reflected a torrent of emotions. *I dreamed it and thought it wasn't true. Now Mom is saying it's true.*

What a moment!

9:30 a.m., Lancaster, Pennsylvania

Sam's mom took her father to a doctor's appointment. While he saw the doctor, she visited a small Mennonite shoe store to pass the time until his appointment was over. As she chatted with the owner of the store and prepared to leave, she noticed a call coming through on her phone. It was from Haiti.

Her pulse quickening, she answered, "Hello?"

"Mom!"

Sam's mom had no doubt. It really was her son!

8:30 a.m. CST, Ladysmith, Wisconsin (9:30 a.m. Haiti time)

The weather was not pretty in Wisconsin. Freezing rain had been falling, and now it was slowly turning to snow. Ryan's mom had just run to town for lettuce and tomatoes, as she was in charge of the hot dish at the sewing circle that day. Bad weather or not, events in Wisconsin usually went on. As she pulled up to her house, Ryan's younger sister burst out the door.

"They're out!" she screamed.

Ryan's mom stared at her. "The cows?"

"No! Ryan and Melodi and the children!"

Ryan had called during her trip to the store. His younger brother had answered the call, even though he didn't recognize the number.

"Josh! This is Ryan!"

The stunned younger brother had approached this unlikely call in a logical manner. "Are you my brother Ryan married to Melodi Martin?"

Ryan had his own proof-of-life question ready: "Are you my little brother Joshua Daniel Korver born May 19?"

Chapter twenty-nine

GOING HOME

Thursday, December 16

The first hot shower in two months was a wonderful experience. Austin's attack on his overgrown facial hair was not quite so pleasurable; he ruined the beard trimmer. The four single men found they had lost about 100 pounds collectively since being abducted.

Grace and Cheryl gathered what food they could find. There was homemade mango ice cream left over from the previous night, and someone had made energy balls. The Haitian cooks prepared the rice and beans they had planned for that day. Andre's friend, the lady who had always saved coconut water for Melodi and the children, even managed to slip them some.

Medical professionals soon arrived to look over the hostages.

"I probably shouldn't tell you this," Ryan told the nurse, "but these contacts have been in my eyes for sixty-three days."

"Oh! They look good!" she said.

The nurse dealt with a number of minor issues. Andre was suffering from a bad case of parasites. Melodi had scrapes from her fall and still experienced pain when she walked. And Wes had to have several cactus thorns removed from his knee. But overall, everyone was okay.

When the FBI agents arrived, they floated around the base with looks of amazement on their faces. During the earlier releases, they had been in the loop. But this was not a release, and they seemed as surprised as anyone.

The missionaries wondered how long they could stay at the base. Most of them looked forward to a night or two in their familiar beds.

It was not to be. "They're coming to get them," the officials soon told Barry.

It was decided that the group of hostages, along with Ray, would fly to Miami on a Coast Guard plane. By taking this flight, they would be able to avoid the airports with their security and baggage lines and COVID-19 checks. They would also miss customs, creating a strange situation on their passports. They all had an entrance stamp into Haiti, but they would have no exit stamp.

A motorcade of about a dozen vehicles took them to the airport. There were three vehicles filled with the missionaries, several vehicles from the embassy, an armored Suburban, and a number of police vehicles.

The Coast Guard plane was not especially luxurious. The crew rolled rows of seats into the plane and locked them onto the floor. Earplugs were handed to each person. But the missionaries were well taken care of, and everyone got a turn going up to the cockpit.

In Miami, the FBI whisked the group away to their hotel. "What would you like to eat?" they asked. "We'll get you anything you want." Someone suggested pizza, pop, and chips, and that was what was ordered.

About a dozen FBI agents introduced themselves, then passed out room keys and opened the pizza boxes to serve them.

Someone from the FBI applauded the group for working together so well.

"We spend millions of dollars training our people how to work together as a unit, and even how to handle hostage situations and potential escape scenarios," the person said. "But this group of untrained Christian missionaries did it perfectly."

They talked about the cohesiveness of the group, and the fact that they stayed together over the two months. The agents weren't sure there had ever been an escape by so many hostages at one time.

Remembering their major confrontation on Tuesday morning, just days before, the hostages couldn't help but smile. Despite their struggles, God had brought them through. By His own power, He had created the unity and cohesiveness that had caught the attention of government officials.

Melodi was not surprised that so many resources were spent on training people how to get along. How could people possibly handle close confinement and boredom if they didn't have God? Even though the missionaries all believed and wanted to obey what the Bible teaches about getting along, it had still taken a miracle to bring them together.

Everyone should have been exhausted that night, but instead, almost everyone was wired and stayed up late. For Melodi, Miami was a blur of aching feet and concerned people as she tried to find her things and get the children bathed and clean for the first time in two months.

It was almost too great a change in too short a time to be able to process everything. Less than twenty-four hours before, they had been locked inside two stuffy rooms in a gangster camp. Now each family had their own motel room, each with its own restroom and warm shower.

Atwater, Ohio

For weeks, Tommy Wagler's first thought every morning as he woke up was *Pray for the hostages.* On the morning of December 17, he thought the same thing. Then he remembered that there were no hostages anymore.

Wow! I can begin to praise again! Tommy thought. Of course, he and the board had praised God throughout the ordeal, but mainly they had always felt an urgent need to pray.

Final Thoughts

The day after the escape, the hostages met in the hotel conference room in Miami to sing as they had done for so many days. Matt and Rachel joined them in a happy reunion. Family members and some CAM staff would arrive soon. Barry and Phil and their families would fly in later that day.

"Finally," Sam said. "Now I can sing a song other than 'When sorrows like billows roll over my soul.'"

What a great thing to laugh at jokes now without the heavy burden of endless captivity to temper the joy!

But Sam had something else on his mind. Something to share at a family Christmas gathering. The letter he had written to his family! Thankfully, it was going home *with* him, not instead of him.

Before parting ways and leaving for home, the missionaries sang their theme song one more time. "And I thank you for one more miracle, Lord!"

God's Mysterious Ways

Barry and Phil and their families flew to Miami the next day on a commercial flight. On the flight, they talked to a pilot who told them that he had been the one buzzing the compound on Wednesday. His organization was planning to build an airstrip, and he had been trying to see if it would work.

He hadn't been searching for escaping missionaries, but somehow God had used that plane to speak to Kay, to prepare her heart for the return of her friends.

Perhaps God used a great number of unexpected things and people to perform His work throughout the kidnapping. Did God maybe leave in just a little confusion, a little mystery in the story, so He alone could claim the glory?

"I had a feeling," Barry reflected later, "that God planned this whole thing. Maybe I did some things wrong. Maybe other people did some things wrong. But God has something for us in this. It encourages me to know that God can work despite our failures, and God can wait until we run out of resources."

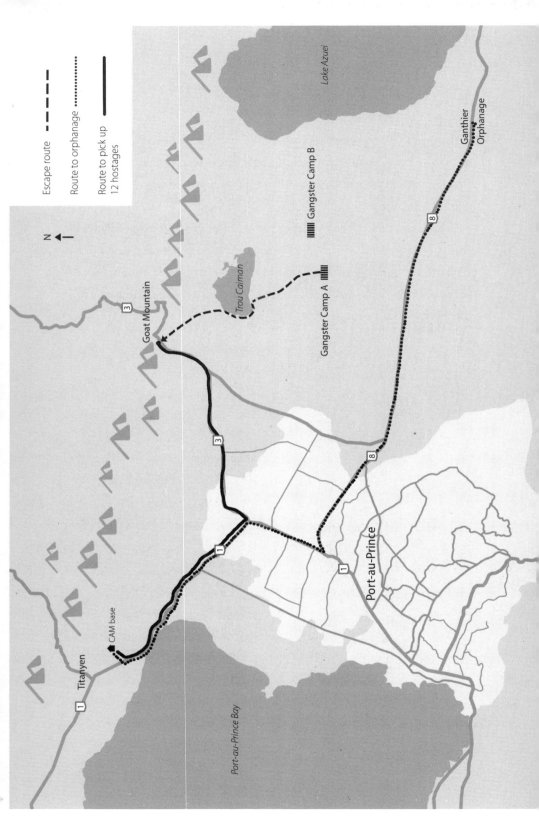

EPILOGUE

Seventy-two days after their deliverance, the seventeen former hostages sat in a circle once more. There was no need to seek the shade, as no one needs shade in Michigan in February. Snow blanketed the grounds of the log conference center where they met, with metal sap buckets hanging from the sugar maples on either side of the drive. Inside, the log construction gave the center a rustic feel. Not rustic like a gangster camp, but rustic like a warm fire on a snowy night.

Around the circle of chairs, the families of the missionaries mingled with the families of Barry Grant and James Yoder and other CAM associates. The ten mothers, along with the ten fathers, were there. Phil and Grace's daughter Olivia was there too, but her parents were still flying in from a funeral. Also there was Ryan's cousin Grant, along with his new wife.

The former hostages took turns sharing some lessons they had learned during their captivity.

Matt started by recalling how many ideas they had presented to God. "I felt like God missed so many good opportunities to show Himself strong. Sometimes we think we know how God should do something, and we're not really open. Maybe God has something else."

He said the major thing for him was to learn to simply trust that God knows what He is doing and to have a soft heart to His leading.

Wes was next. "I guess one thing I learned is, 'Don't get kidnapped!' But God used this situation. We all felt like God was really working in our lives. When you have hardly anything left, the most important things get really important. And the things you really valued a lot all of a sudden just sort of lose their value."

"I agree," Brandyn said, passing on the microphone.

"Oh, come on, Brandyn," Sam said. "You weren't this shy in the gangster camp."

But that was different. There was no need for a microphone in the gangster camp. Now the crowd required amplification so everyone could hear.

Kasondra shared that prayer was one of the biggest blessings of her time in captivity. "Praise God for how He brought us out."

"I learned not to take so many things for granted," Courtney said. "Especially our Bibles."

Kay shared that she had been blessed to see how God did so many miracles. "He completes His work," she said. "I learned to put my trust in Him more."

Cherilyn said she had been looking forward to this reunion since the day the group dispersed. She remembered the goodness of God in the gangster camp. "We watched God heal without medicine or any of the things that we think are necessary to our health. He showed me that

He cared about me. God cared enough to have me get kidnapped, just so He can teach me that He does have a plan and a purpose."

Austin shared that he learned that God's timing is perfect. He learned to simply remember and trust. "His ways are perfect," Austin said. "And His timing is perfect. Another thing I learned was just the power of surrendering to God."

Shelden said he was grateful for food—when he had it. "Because it wasn't always there."

Cheryl was next, with memories of struggles both in the camp and after she was released. She remembered the importance of surrender. "I guess I thought about it a lot because I was separated from Ray. I just had to surrender that to God and know that He had a purpose in our separation."

Ray, beside Cheryl, shared too. He discovered that faith and trust is a choice, not a state of mind. Every time someone asked him how he was doing, it reminded him that he could always make the choice to trust God.

"I learned," Ryan said, "that the people around you, your family, or whoever you have in a time like that, is all that really matters. It was a blessing to interact closely with people. When you're sleeping cheek to jowl, you learn to know people a lot better than you would otherwise."

Ryan also talked about the gangsters. "Whatever their motives were as gang members, they are humans. They are people created in God's image just like we are. I couldn't help but pity them. They are probably still there doing the same meaningless job of guarding people. And trying to get a high or trying to get intoxicated or trying to find happiness in some empty way."

Melodi said she wouldn't trade the experience of being a hostage for a million dollars, even though she does not want to do it again. "God seemed very, very real there," she said. "There's nothing like being in there where you can't do anything. We prayed and prayed. And prayed.

And prayed and prayed."

Then her memories moved to the miracle of their unity and the long trek to the highway. "Walking out, just knowing that you're in the middle of a miracle. At least that's the way I felt. It was so fun! I just felt so strongly like God was right there with us. And I hope I never forget that feeling."

Sam recalled how the faith chapter, Hebrews 11, came alive to him like never before. He also recalled the miracle of unity. "It feels like we've been through the thick and thin of everything. We walked through it together. Difficult times or times of not seeing it eye to eye with each other. But God brought us through that. We can sit here and love each other and be united and go forward."

"For two months," Dale said, "every day, two times a day, we'd gather. And it's hard to describe the feelings that we went through. And the feeling of sitting together with you all now."

Dale recalled the early days after everything was taken away. "We were scared; we didn't know what was going to happen next. But yet we had each other, we had prayer, we had our faith. We had no distractions, like our phones and our jobs. We had none of that. I felt a lot freer than I ever really had before. I never spent so much time in prayer in my entire life. That was just incredible."

Rachel completed the circle, remembering how she used to pray every day to get released. She would wonder and hope, *Is this the day?*

"Am I looking forward to heaven?" Rachel asked. "And living like it is my last day? Am I telling someone else about Jesus? Or am I talking about that person over there? I just want to leave that challenge with you all too, to live today like it is your last."

After everyone finished sharing, the Noeckers passed out "Kidnapping Survival Kits," packed in dish basins, to their former fellow hostages. Inside each one was a small Bible, a roll of toilet paper, and a package of baby wipes.

"For when the toilet paper runs out," Sam observed sagely.

There was also a journal, a bag of Doritos, a pen, and a soft tooth-brush with a tube of toothpaste.

And there was peanut butter. Peanut butter so smooth it didn't need to be mixed with pancake syrup.

Dale's basin had something more—his maroon pajama pants with an elastic band. Dale wore them for days and days in the gangster camp. It was only fitting that he should have them back.

But most of the souvenirs from the gangster camp were not tangible. They were the lessons learned and the memories made—an experience that will never be forgotten.

ADDENDUM

Conflicting Stories

*I*n the December 20 press conference hosted by Christian Aid Ministries, it was not clearly stated that ransom had been paid. Although CAM had intended to make this clear, it did not come across that way to listeners.

Because of this, some people accused CAM of hiding the fact that ransom had been paid. In addition, some reports claimed that the hostages did not escape but were released in direct response to the ransom money paid earlier, before the release of Kay, Cheryl, and Shelden.

The Haitian news media reported that the hostages had been released by the gang. Later, more reports filtered out through this "Haitian grapevine" that the gang leader had told the guards to stay away from the hostages after 9 p.m. that night.

But is this logical? After sixty-two days, is it reasonable to assume that Lanmò San Jou initiated a release on the very night that God laid it on the hearts of the hostages to flee? If he did, this seems almost more miraculous than if God had merely arranged that the guards not see the missionaries leave.

However, there are significant problems with this claim, including the fact that Lanmò San Jou was not there.

Even if the gang leader had been present, he likely would have amended his story so it would not conflict so much with the missionaries' story. If he did tell the guards to stay away after 9 p.m., he must have failed to inform his chief guard, who yelled at the other guards to stay awake. Neither did his second-in-command seem to know anything about it, as he approved a late evening run for oil for a generator that would not have been needed if a release was imminent. Froggy also seems to have been in the dark, as he promised to bring one of the children bananas the next morning.

And how did Lanmò San Jou expect the hostages to find out about their release? Was he hoping they would realize, in a windowless shack, that no guards were watching? Did he think that suddenly, in the middle of the night, they would decide to leave and walk through the darkness through unfamiliar gang territory? The idea seems ridiculous.

Did Lanmò San Jou send the rainstorm that moved the power strip to the porch? Did he light up the dreams of people hundreds of miles away with the realization that the hostages had escaped that night?

We also know that if the hostages did escape without his knowledge, Lanmò San Jou would have every incentive to put out a false narrative.

Even if these discrepancies were not present, why would we believe the words of a gang leader with a reputation for dishonesty rather than the matching stories of the missionaries?

The "Haitian grapevine" reported that the guards arranged for someone to meet the hostages. But how would they have known exactly where the group went, even if they had seen them leave.

An article in the *Yonkers Times* of New York quoted an anonymous source with "direct and detailed knowledge" about the incident.

> While many believe that the hostages escaped, they were allowed to leave by leaving a door partially open and the guard left, leaving them free to leave [*sic*]. And any Haitian who may have seen them on their long walk to freedom were [*sic*] instructed to leave them alone, and only to get involved and help them if asked. The guards were right there and saw everything and let them walk away.[1]

Some parts of this account are laughable. How could they have instructed all the Haitians in the area to leave them alone? It would scarcely be more ludicrous if the source had added, "The gang leader also silenced all the dogs that may have seen or smelled them." The phrase "leaving a door partially open and the guard left" sounds like it was taken from the stories of the hostages and reframed to suit the perspective of the informer. The article also contained errors in spelling and grammar at the time of access.

On January 5, 2022, an Associated Press article quoted the *Yonkers Times*, but then continued, "The ex-hostages have continued to say, in detailed and consistent accounts, that they escaped during a narrow window of opportunity under fear of being recaptured or shot."

The *Yonkers Times* later published another article defending its story by pointing out that the Associated Press had quoted them. They ended the article with a quote from a reader who stated it was "a little disappointing that the escape story was a fabrication."

---

[1] <http://yonkerstimes.com/new-details-emerge-about-christian-hostages-released-from-haiti-they-were-freed-and-a-ransom-was-paid/>, accessed on February 16, 2022.

So what actually happened when Ping walked to the back door and looked at the door and the misplaced rock?

Did he investigate the rock and walk away because the gang leader had told him to stay away from the house? If so, why did he bother looking at the door? And why was it even barricaded? The explanation that the door was deliberately left open does not fit with Ping scolding the guards and telling them to be more diligent. There is simply no evidence that Lanmò San Jou instructed the guards to release the prisoners. All the evidence points the other way.

The hostages believe that God blinded Ping's eyes, causing the rock to appear in its normal position. Ping stared for a long time, so what was he doing? We don't know. Perhaps with the generator throbbing behind him, he was listening for more clues about the noise he had heard. The most reasonable explanation for Ping's actions may be that God blinded his eyes.

Those who choose to believe that God did NOT blind Ping's eyes are left with an even stranger situation and an even more complicated miracle.

If God did not blind Ping's eyes, then he saw that the rock had been tampered with—and he knew what was happening. This would mean that Ping, a meticulous guard who for the last sixty-one days had insisted on having things done right, suddenly had a change of heart. Instead of rushing in and screaming, he decided to let them escape.

Ping always hated to have his authority questioned, as evidenced by his anger when Sam opened the door to give Matt more air. When given orders by the chief gangsters, Ping could be brutal, as when he threatened to kill Brandyn if he didn't sit down.

If Ping did allow the missionaries to escape, it seems clear that he had no instructions to do so from Lanmò San Jou. If that's the case, then something happened within his heart. Did he see the ring of angels that Kasondra saw in her dream? Did he "feel God" like Mr. Attitude?

If the hostages someday hear that when God worked out their escape, He also worked in Ping's heart to act on their behalf, would this negate God's deliverance? If they were to find out that parts of Kasondra's dream of angels around the house or Brandyn's vision of Ping preaching a sermon had come true, would they be disappointed in the way God had delivered them? No, it would only give them more reason to praise God for His unsearchable power and His ways that are far above the imagination of humanity.

In the meantime, perhaps God has left us these unanswered questions so that no one, other than God Himself, can take glory for this deliverance. Many people prayed, fasted, donated resources, and even risked their lives for the sake of the hostages. The hostages themselves planned, plotted, prayed, and risked their lives—but it was God who delivered them.

The fact that this deliverance contains some mystery only makes it more a work of God's greatness, not less.

ABOUT THE AUTHOR

Katrina lives in Elkhart, Indiana, with her husband Marnell and daughter Anina. She is the author of eight other books published by Christian Aid Ministries. These works include *Blue Christmas* (about her short-term volunteer work in northern Haiti in 2010), *Captain Garrison,* and *From the White House to the Amish.* Katrina is currently writing and self-publishing a middle grade Christian adventure series.

To keep in touch, subscribe to Katrina's email list at katrinahooverlee.com, or write to Katrina Lee, P.O. Box 2155, Elkhart, Indiana 46515. You may also write to her in care of Christian Aid Ministries, P.O. Box 360, Berlin, Ohio 44610.

ABOUT CHRISTIAN AID MINISTRIES

*C*hristian Aid Ministries was founded in 1981 as a nonprofit, tax-exempt 501(c)(3) organization. Its primary purpose is to provide a trustworthy and efficient channel for Amish, Mennonite, and other conservative Anabaptist groups and individuals to minister to physical and spiritual needs around the world. This is in response to the command to ". . . do good unto all men, especially unto them who are of the household of faith" (Galatians 6:10).

CAM supporters provide millions of pounds of food, clothing, Bibles, medicines, and other aid each year. Supporters' funds also help victims of disasters in the U.S. and abroad, put up Gospel billboards in the U.S., and provide Biblical teaching and self-help resources. CAM's main purposes for providing aid are to help and encourage God's people and bring the Gospel to a lost and dying world.

THE WAY TO GOD AND PEACE

*W*e live in a world contaminated by sin. Sin is anything that goes against God's holy standards. When we do not follow the guidelines that God our Creator gave us, we are guilty of sin. Sin separates us from God, the source of life.

Since the time when the first man and woman, Adam and Eve, sinned in the Garden of Eden, sin has been universal. The Bible says that we all have "sinned and come short of the glory of God" (Romans 3:23). It also says that the natural consequence for that sin is eternal death, or punishment in an eternal hell: "Then when lust hath conceived, it bringeth forth sin: and sin, when it is finished, bringeth forth death" (James 1:15).

But we do not have to suffer eternal death in hell. God provided forgiveness for our sins through the death of His only Son, Jesus Christ. Because Jesus was perfect and without sin, He could die in our place. "For God so loved the world that he gave his only begotten Son, that whosoever believeth in him should not perish, but have everlasting life" (John 3:16).

A sacrifice is something given to benefit someone else. It costs the giver greatly. Jesus was God's sacrifice. Jesus' death takes away the penalty of sin for all those who accept this sacrifice and truly repent of their sins. To repent of sins means to be truly sorry for and turn away from the things we have done that have violated God's standards (Acts 2:38; 3:19).

Jesus died, but He did not remain dead. After three days, God's Spirit miraculously raised Him to life again. God's Spirit does something similar in us. When we receive Jesus as our sacrifice and repent of our sins, our hearts are changed. We become spiritually alive! We develop new desires and attitudes (2 Corinthians 5:17). We begin to make choices that please God (1 John 3:9). If we do fail and commit sins, we can ask God for forgiveness. "If we confess our sins, he is faithful and just to forgive us our sins, and to cleanse us from all unrighteousness" (1 John 1:9).

Once our hearts have been changed, we want to continue growing spiritually. We will be happy to let Jesus be the Master of our lives and will want to become more like Him. To do this, we must meditate on God's Word and commune with God in prayer. We will testify to others of this change by being baptized and sharing the good news of God's victory over sin and death. Fellowship with a faithful group of believers will strengthen our walk with God (1 John 1:7).